The Serge–Trotsky Papers

The Serge–Trotsky Papers

Edited and Introduced by

D.J. Cotterill

Pluto Press

LONDON • BOULDER, COLORADO

First published 1994 by Pluto Press
345 Archway Road, London N6 5AA
and 5500 Central Avenue,
Boulder, CO 80301, USA

British Library Cataloguing in Publication Data
A catalogue record for this book is available from the British Library

ISBN 07453 0515 6 (hbk)

Library of Congress Cataloging in Publication Data
Serge, Victor, 1890–1947
    The Serge Trotsky papers / edited and introduced by D.J.
Cotterill.
    275p. 22cm.
    Letters have been translated from French.
    Includes bibliographical references and index.
    ISBN 0-7453-0515-6
    1. Soviet Union–Politics and government–1917-1936. 2. Soviet
Union–Politics and government–1936-1953. 3. Serge, Victor,
1890-1947–Correspondence. 4. Trotsky, Leon, 1879-1940–
–Correspondence. I. Trotsky, Leon, 1879-1940. II. Cotterill, D.
J. (David John), 1953-   . III. Title.
DK267.S453 1994
947. 084'1'0922–dc20   93-51068
                                                                CIP

Designed and produced for Pluto Press by
Chase Production Services, Chipping Norton, OX7 5QR
Typeset from editor's disks by
Stanford Desktop Publishing Services, Milton Keynes
Printed in the EC by
TJ Press, Padstow

Contents

Dedication

This book was originally devised in the late 1970s as part of a collaboration between Peter Sedgwick and Richard Greeman to get as many of Serge's titles into print as possible. The Serge–Trotsky correspondence thus became part of Peter's contribution to this endeavour. Sadly, however, Peter died during his preparation for the work and the project then lay dormant for several years until revived by the Serge centenary, when I became its editor. Whilst, for obvious reasons, this book is substantially different from any of Peter's projected versions, it draws extensively on the work Peter did, using his translations of Serge's material whenever possible, especially in the notes to the correspondence, which have been included with very few changes and are a work of great scholarship.

To my great regret I neither met nor corresponded with Peter Sedgwick and therefore turned to his friend Dr David Widgery to write an appreciation of Peter's contribution to intellectual life, Serge studies and indeed to this volume. As many readers will know, David himself died in late 1992 during the final preparations for this work and before he could complete his appreciation of Peter.

Maria Enzenberger, who translated for Peter the Russian language Serge–Trotsky letters included here, sadly also died before this volume could be published.

The achievements of Peter Sedgwick, David Widgery and Maria Enzenberger in their respective fields and in life need no further comment from me – they are there for all to see. This volume is therefore humbly dedicated to their memory.

Preface

It is common for writers to accumulate debts of obligation to others during the period of work on their volume, as no book is entirely the sole work of one person, however lonely the writing of it is. Happily this work is no exception to the rule, and this editor would like to thank all equally for their help and advice in its preparation. First, I should like to thank the Serge estate and Vlady Kibalchich for permission to use Serge's material. I should also like to thank Mrs M. Sedgwick for permission to use the translations made by her late husband, Peter Sedgwick. I am grateful, too, to Roger van Zwanenberg at Pluto Press for taking up this project along with other Serge publications, and for his belief generally in the quality of Serge's work. Similarly I wish to thank the staff at Pluto for their patience during the seemingly endless gestation period of this project – I do hope they can forgive me.

No work on Victor Serge, however large or small, can ignore the contribution of Richard Greeman, whose work over the years has borne the mark of true scholarship, in his writings on Serge and in his translations of Serge's novels. They are a genuine source of inspiration for others as well as myself and I have shamelessly plundered them here in the hope of a better understanding. A special thanks should go to my co-contributors – to Philip Spencer for his insightful introductions to Chapter 1 on Serge's early Bolshevism and to Chapter 5 on Serge's character as an Oppositionist, and also to Susan Weissman for her knowledgeable introduction to Chapter 4, taking us through the intricacies of Serge's relations with the Fourth International. Thanks are due too to George Paizis and Ian Birchall for help with translations from French into English – their individual contributions are credited within the references. I should further like to thank Ian Birchall for his kindness and patience in answering my many enquiries, for reading the drafts of the book in preparation and his many suggestions. Needless to say all the above are absolved completely of responsibility for any of the book's faults, which are all mine.

I would also like to take the opportunity to thank all the members of the Serge Centenary Group, especially Bill Marshall for so much help on Serge in the past, John Eden, Bryony Dixon and Richard Parry and all who made the celebration of Victor Serge's centenary such a rewarding experience. Finally I would like to thank my wife and partner Gill Furlong, without whom so little could be achieved, not just for her help on the notes and bibliography, but also for her unfailing support.

Acknowledgements

In Chapter 1, the following extracts were first published in *La Vie ouvrière*: 'Petrograd' (from 'La Ville en danger'), 'The Tragic Face of Revolution', and 'The Problems of Dictatorship'. The letter to Michel Kneller, a copy of which is in the Musée Sociale, Paris, is published here for the first time.

In Chapter 3, two pieces are taken from *La Révolution prolétarienne*: 'Crimes in Russia, Intrigues in Spain' and 'A Goodbye to Andreu Nin', and one from *Les Humbles* ('Notes on the Spanish Drama'). Two originally appeared in Spanish in *La Batalla* – 'Una Carta del Gran Revolucionario Ruso Victor Serge', and the letter to the Executive Committee of the POUM. Three extracts by Leon Trotsky are from *The Spanish Revolution (1931–9)*.

In Chapter 4, *The New International* originally published five of the documents: 'The Hue and Cry over Kronstadt', 'Once More: Kronstadt', 'More on the Suppression of Kronstadt', 'Reply to Trotsky' (from 'A Letter and Some Notes'), and 'The Masses Have Nothing to Do with It!'(from 'The Moralists and Sycophants against Marxism'). The letter to Wendelin Thomas and the piece entitled 'Intellectual ex-Radicals and World Reaction' first appeared in *Socialist Appeal*; 'Fiction and Fact. Kronstadt' and 'Ideas and Facts; Kronstadt 1921 – Against the Sectarian Spirit – Bolshevism and Anarchism' were originally published in *La Révolution prolétarienne*; 'Victor Serge and the Fourth International' is taken from *Writings of Leon Trotsky 1938–1939* and 'My Break with Trotsky' from the *Carnets*. The 'Letter to Angelica Balabanova' in the Serge Archive in Mexico is here published for the first time. 'Marxism in Our Time' appeared in *Partisan Review*.

Also from *Partisan Review* is the piece 'In Memory: LD Trotsky' in Chapter 5. The 'Obituary. Leon Sedov' was first published in *La Révolution prolétarienne*. The previously unpublished 'On Trotskyism' is in the Serge Archive, Mexico. The extracts entitled 'The Old Man – The Fourth International' and 'The Life of the Oppositionists' come from *From Lenin to Stalin* and *Destiny of a Revolution* respectively. Finally, entries for 1944 are extracted from the *Carnets*.

Glossary of Organisations

BOC Bloque Obrero y Campesino (Workers and Peasants Bloc). Spanish left centrist organisation based in Catalonia. Forerunner of the POUM. Previously known as the Catalan Federation.

CGT Confédération Générale du Travail (General Confederation of Labour). The major trade union formation in France.

CGTU Confédération Générale du Travail Unitaire (Unitary General Confederation of Labour). Formerly the left wing of the CGT, dominated by the Communist Party; became a separate organisation in 1921 and was reunited with the CGT in 1936.

CHEKA Special Commission of the Soviet Union for counter-revolutionary activity.

CNT Confederación Nacional del Trabajo (National Confederation of Labour). The anarcho-syndicalist trade union federation in Spain.

CPSU Communist Party of the Soviet Union.

FAI Federación Anarquista Ibérica (Iberian Anarchist Federation). Political wing of the CNT.

GPU The Soviet security police, absorbed into the NKVD in 1939.

IS The International Secretariat of the Fourth International.

KPD Kommunistische Partei Deutschland (German Communist Party).

NKVD Narodnyi Komissariat Vnutrennykh Del (People's Commissariat of Internal Affairs).

OVRA Italian Secret Service.

PCE Partido Comunista de España. The Communist Party of Spain.

PCF Parti Communiste Français (French Communist Party).

POB Parti Ouvrier Belge (Belgian Workers Party). The main social democratic party in Belgium.

POI Parti Ouvrier Internationaliste (International Workers Party). The French Section of the Trotskyist movement, formed by a merger between two groups in June 1936.

POUM Partido Obrero de Unificacion Marxista (Workers Party of Marxist Unity). Formed in 1935 by a fusion of the Workers and Peasants Bloc (BOC) with the former members of the Spanish Left Opposition led by Andrès Nin.

PSOP Parti Socialiste Ouvrier et Paysan (Workers and Peasants Socialist Party). French centrist party formed by the 'revolutionary left' under Marceau Pivert of the Socialist Party in June 1938.

PSR Parti Socialiste Révolutionnaire (Socialist Revolutionary Party). The Belgian Section of the Fourth International.

PSUC Partido Socialista Unificado de Cataluna (Unified Socialist Party of Catalonia).

RILU Red International of Labour Unions.

RP *La Révolution Prolétarienne*. 'The Proletarian Revolution', revolutionary-syndicalist newspaper founded in 1925.

RSAP Socialist Workers Party of Holland.

SAP Sozialistischer Arbeiter Partei (German Socialist Workers Party). Formed from a split in German Social Democracy in 1931. Joined with the International Left Opposition in 1993 in calling for a new International but moved rapidly to the right, endorsing a People's Front in Germany.

SFIO Section Française Internationale (French section of the Workers [Second] International). The official name of the French Socialist Party. In 1920 a majority of the SFIO left to form the French Communist Party; the reformist minority retained the name.

SPD German Socialist Party.

UGT Union General de Trabajadores (General Union of Workers). Spanish reformist trade union.

Chronology

1890 Serge's birth (30 December). His real name is Victor Lvovich Kibalchich.

1917 Russian Revolution. Trotsky is a major participant.
Serge is released from prison in France. He goes to Barcelona, then leaves to join the Russian army. He is detained in France as a Bolshevik suspect.

1919 Serge arrives in Petrograd. He works for the Comintern under Zinoviev.

1920–22 Serge participates in Comintern Congresses. He edits various journals.

1921 Kronstadt uprising.

1923–26 Serge serves the Comintern as a secret agent and editor of *Imprekor* in Berlin and Vienna. He returns to Soviet Union to take part in the last stand of the Left Opposition.

1928–38 Serge is engaged predominantly in writing but is forced to send his manuscripts to France. He produces *Year One of the Russian Revolution* (1930), *Men in Prison* (1930), *Birth of Our Power* (1931) and *Conquered City* (1932).

1933 Serge is arrested and deported to Orenburg, where he is joined by young son Vlady.

1935 Congress for the Defence of Culture in Paris. Paris intellectuals campaign in support of Serge.

1936 Serge is released from Orenburg but deprived of Soviet citizenship. His manuscripts are confiscated and he is expelled from USSR. He settles first in Brussels, then Paris. His return to Europe is accompanied by a slander campaign in the Communist Press.
February: election of Popular Front government in Spain.
May: election of Popular Front government in France.
July: Spanish Civil War breaks out.
December: Trotsky exiled to Mexico.

1937 *From Lenin to Stalin* and *Destiny of a Revolution* appear. Serge is elected a councillor to the Spanish POUM. He campaigns against the Moscow trials.

1940 Serge leaves Paris just as the Nazis advance on Marseilles. He tries to obtain a visa. Finally, he finds refuge in Mexico.

Trotsky's death (20 August).
1940–47 Serge lives in isolation and poverty. He writes *The Case of Comrade Tulayev* and *Memoirs of a Revolutionary*.
1947 Serge's death (17 November).

Introduction

This book concerns itself with the central political relationship of Serge's life and the one which dominated his mature years, that with Leon Trotsky. From the time of Serge's arrival in Russia at the height of the civil war in 1919, throughout the tumultuous early years of the Soviet Union, the opposition struggles of the 1920s, exile and beyond, both men's fates became inextricably linked. The core of this book is an examination of how this relationship functioned during one of this century's most crisis-filled epochs that saw the rise of Fascism and Stalinism, with its concomitant political repression, civil war and the most profound crisis to face Socialism until the present day. Thus the dialogues and debates between the two men presented here do much to throw light on the forces that shaped the postwar world and provide us with a window on the alternatives that existed and how the two men articulated their ideas, even during the darkest of days.

If, for most readers, the luminous presence of Leon Trotsky, one of the twentieth century's greatest political thinkers and revolutionaries, needs little introduction, the relatively more obscure figure of Victor Serge may need some background. For despite writing 20 books of history, politics, fiction and even poetry to set alongside a lifetime's journalism in both Europe and the Soviet Union, he remains still only partially revealed, and despite often being quoted in the pages of academic studies of the Soviet Union and of Stalinism and Trotskyism, he is often ill-represented by those who choose to use his work. (Anyone interested should take a look at the example of Deutscher's treatment of Serge in the third volume of his biography of Trotsky, *The Prophet Outcast*).

Serge had been born in Belgium in 1890 to a Russian father and a Polish mother, escaping respectively the arm of the Tsar's secret police and a stifling bourgeois marriage. Serge's early life was one of poverty and struggle and he was quickly drawn to the violent individualist strand of anarchism, editing its newspaper *L'Anarchie*. This connection was to earn Serge his first prison sentence when he became embroiled with the case of the Bonnot Gang – a group of armed bank robbers, whom Serge defended in the pages of his journal. On his release in 1917 he moved to Barcelona, and began his long physical and political journey that took him from Europe to Russia and back, and eventually to a final exile in Mexico, where he died in 1947. Politically, whilst retaining a loyalty to the principles of anarchist freedom, Serge adopted Marxism as his major frame of reference, under the influence of the events in Russia in 1917. This he maintained throughout his life despite the defeat of its ideals in Russia with the rise of Stalin, the struggle against which became, as with Trotsky, the main focus of his life and work.

The first chapter of the book outlines Serge's early adherence to Bolshevism and the figure of Leon Trotsky. The core of the work then deals with the relations between the two men in the wake of the defeat of the Trotskyist and Joint Opposition in Russia, concentrating on the period of intense activity during the 1930s. This is achieved by examining their private correspondence, as in Chapter 2, and by looking at the effects of the Spanish Civil War and Trotsky's attempts at forming a new International as a counter-balance to the Second (Socialist International) and Third (Communist International). A final assessment is made of Serge within the Trotskyist movement and as an 'Oppositionist' in Chapter 5.

In his introduction to Chapter 1, Philip Spencer traces the passage of Victor Serge from his political roots in anarchism to his 'particular' acceptance of Marxism. In doing so Spencer shows us how Serge was struck by the revolution's early libertarian aspects, adopting what he described, in Marcel Liebman's phrase, a form of 'libertarian Leninism' that for the rest of Serge's life formed the basis of his political thought, however tarnished the original ideals of the revolution had become. The documents in this chapter reveal to us Serge's early awareness and appreciation of the figure and personality of Leon Trotsky, with sections from 'La Ville en danger' about the civil war siege of Petrograd. In the letter to Comrade Michel we glean Serge's disillusionment with the trajectory of the revolution, which also reveals to us the extent to which he maintained a deep commitment to his former comrades, the anarchists. With the inclusion of extracts from 'The Tragic Face of Revolution' and 'The Problems of the Dictatorship', his early writings on the revolution, a useful contrast can be gained with later writings on similar themes in Chapter 4.

Chapter 2 concentrates on the cycle of correspondence exchanged between the two men following Serge's release from the Soviet Union in 1936, up until their final communication in 1939, amid acrimony and estrangement, a full year before the death of Leon Trotsky. In the introduction to the correspondence I describe the circumstances behind Serge's release and the anxiety of both men to resume an intimate contact after so many years of hardship. The introduction then goes on to follow the intricacies of their epistolary relations set against the background of the rise of Fascism, the consolidation of Stalin's position in Russia and the emergence of Popular Front governments in both France and Spain. It continues by showing how their later relationship was clouded by disagreements on the Spanish Revolution and the Fourth International, the formation of which Trotsky believed was his most important task outside the Soviet Union, and over which Serge had many reservations.

In Chapter 3, 'Serge, Trotsky and the Spanish Revolution' we see how Serge's dissensions from Trotsky's line on the Popular Front, already evident in the correspondence, began to create the preconditions for their eventual rift. We see how their conflicting assessments of various individuals, who at one time or another were close to both men, were a by-product of their altogether different organisational outlooks. We also see how these tensions, principally over Nin and the POUM, erupted into larger disagreements on the nature of Bolshevik history and the organisation of a new revolutionary vanguard – a process which is examined by Suzi Weissman in Chapter 4.

In her introduction to this chapter, 'Kronstadt and the Fourth International', Weissman provides us with a study of these controversies, principally over the Kronstadt revolt of 1921 following the crushing of the revolutionary wing of the Spanish Republican movement in 1937. Its context became the issue of Bolshevik history and provided Serge with a basis for a change in political direction which, if not a deviation from Marxism as such, was certainly a move away from the 'Bolshevik-Leninism' of Leon Trotsky. Weissman shows us how the agents of the GPU at the heart of the Trotskyist movement may well have exploited these controversies further with the issue of the publicity surrounding Serge's translation of Trotsky's *Their Morals and Ours*, to make it appear that Serge was slandering Trotsky's work and sabotaging the Fourth International. She further demonstrates that if these moves were not entirely successful, they did prevent a free exchange of ideas between the two men that could have provided the basis for a renewed understanding. For as we can see from the documents in Chapter 4, throughout the Kronstadt controversy and indeed in his essay 'Marxism in Our Time' Serge was as committed to International Socialism as Trotsky himself. Whatever their disagreements, Serge always retained the healthiest respect for Trotsky the man and thinker, if not for some of those who had attached themselves to him in later years.

In Chapter 5, 'Victor Serge and the Left Opposition' an assessment is made of Serge's contribution to the Oppositionist struggle against Stalin. In his introduction, Philip Spencer places Serge at the centre of Trotsky's struggle against Stalin both in Russia and later in the West; and shows that, despite whatever dissensions and disagreements they were later to have, Serge's Marxism was thoroughly 'Trotskyist' in character and would remain so. The documents in the chapter attest to that assertion and include 'The Old Man – The Fourth International', extracted from Serge's *From Lenin to Stalin*. Reactions to this book formed the centre of Communist slander against Serge in the 1930s, which prompted Trotsky's stout defence of Serge's contribution to the revolution. Also included is a previously unpublished piece by Serge called simply 'On Trotskyism'; an obituary of Trotsky's son Leon Sedov which contains much about Serge's deep commitment to their mutual cause; and a powerful evocation of the 'Old Man' himself in his obituary of Leon Trotsky, 'In Memory', written for *Partisan Review*, which lacks nothing of Serge's deep honesty in its assessment of Trotsky's life. The chapter concludes with some short entries from Serge's *Carnets* from the year 1944, when he too was living out his final exile in Mexico City, where Trotsky had met his death at the hand of Stalin's assassin.

What will be clear to the reader at the end of this book is that Victor Serge was no passive receptor of or mere servitor to the thoughts and actions of Leon Trotsky, but was himself passionately engaged in the pursuit of ideas and ideals and was an honest though critical friend to Trotsky. But if the polemic between the two contained here has the ring of tragedy, is it our tragedy also? For Serge himself, in transit once again to a final exile amidst a world torn apart by war, concluded his *Memoirs* thus:

> The future seems to me to be full of possibilities greater than we have glimpsed throughout the past. May the passion, the experience and even the faults of my fighting generation have some small power to illuminate the way forward!

D.J. Cotterill
London, November 1993

1   Victor Serge and Bolshevism

Introduction by Philip Spencer

For Victor Serge, as for many of his contemporaries, the Russian Revolution marked a turning point in his political life. It forced upon him a major shift in his political allegiances, a break with previous affiliations and the adoption of a new political theory and practice, revolutionary Marxism, to which he had hitherto been deeply hostile. This new commitment was not lightly undertaken nor was it in its essentials ever to be abandoned. It was the result of a number of experiences and choices which were common to many on the left in those years but which were faced, and articulated, by Serge in his own unique way. Cumulatively, these choices led him to adopt a particular form of Bolshevism with a distinctive political accent: what might be called, following Marcel Liebman, a 'libertarian Leninism', whose inspiration lay in the dynamic of the Russian Revolution of 1917 and the particular role that Serge perceived the Bolshevik Party to play within it.[1] This new political creed was never to be abandoned by Serge, despite the enormous pressures brought to bear upon him both personally and politically in subsequent years. It gave him a coherent frame of reference within which to work and think and write in the decades that followed. In all the major phases of his political life henceforth there was to be a consistency of vision and unity of purpose which sustained him through the darkest hours.

Prewar Anarchism

The path taken by Serge in arriving at this position was not an easy one. As with many others on the left before the First World War, Serge's loyalties were structured by the seemingly fundamental divide between anarchism on the one hand and Socialists (in whose ranks the Bolsheviks figured only as a fairly small if vocally radical section) on the other. This division had its roots in the classic dispute between Marx and Bakhunin at the time of the First International of 1864, over the role of politics

1

and the state in revolution. In the era of the Second International, formed in 1889, these divisions had hardened considerably.[2] Anarchists were contemptuous of the whole world of Socialist politics, with its bureaucratically organised labour movements and mass political parties increasingly preoccupied with parliamentary politics and legalised trade unionism. Within anarchist circles, Serge was mostly associated with the individualistic wing, where contempt for what was seen as the reformist collusion of the organised left led some to acts of individual revolt and protest. It was his loyalty to these associates that landed him his first jail sentence in France for refusing to cooperate with the state's prosecution of the infamous Bonnot Gang, a terrorist anarchist group of uncertain politics and provenance.[3]

War

Serge thus found himself in prison when the First World War broke out. There he had time and space (he was originally in solitary confinement) to meditate on the limitations of these primitive rebellions against society. Much as he admired 'the exacting idealism of uncomplicated men [who,] conscious of their frustration, battled like madmen', he could not help but reflect pessimistically on the vicious cycle of protest and repression within which they had been locked:

> In those times, the world was an integrated structure, so stable in its appearance that no possibility of substantial change was visible within it [...] Above the heads of the masses, wealth accumulated, insolent and proud. The consequences of this situation arose inexorably: crime, class struggles and their trail of bloody strikes, and the frenzied battles of One against All.

But none of these struggles held out much hope of success. In the end, even anarchism as an ideology of change and resistance had collapsed in the bourgeois jungle.[4]

The war shattered the stability of capitalist Europe and, for all its savage destructiveness, opened up new possibilities:

> This storm interpreted the world for us. For me, it heralded another purifying tempest [...] Revolutionaries knew quite well that this autocratic Europe, with its hangmen, its pogroms, its finery, its famines, its Siberian jails and ancient iniquity, could never survive the war.[5]

The impact of the war was felt everywhere, not least on the left. Old lines of division had to be radically redrawn, less on the basis of doctrinal difference (such as had pitted anarchists like Serge against Socialists of all stripes) than on the basis of response to the war. In the belligerent countries the majority, whether anarchist or Socialist, followed their leaders initially in supporting the war, in putting loyalty to (capitalist) nation far above loyalty to class, even to the point of gaily marching off to the front line to slaughter fellow workers.[6] Only a minority, again either anarchist or Socialist, stood firm to their prewar principles and opposed the war. All across Europe tiny groups gathered, hesitantly at first, to voice opposition to the war – in France, the Vie Ouvrière group around Alfred Rosmer and Pierre Monatte; in Germany, Rosa Luxemburg (jailed for her pains), Karl Liebknecht and a handful of followers. Only in far-off Russia did a significant majority on the left, the Bolsheviks, emerge to take the clearest and most radical position, denouncing the war as an inter-imperialist rivalry and supporters of the war as chauvinist traitors to the working class. Lenin's call for a radical realignment on the left, for a new international movement based on revolutionary opposition to the war, was to lead to a dramatic recomposition on the left, in which the prewar divisions between anarchists and Socialists were to play little or no role.[7]

In the isolation of prison, Serge may have known little or nothing of this or any other opposition, nor sensed yet its deeper logic. Independently, however, he had come to a similar judgement. 'The prospect of victory by either side appalled us [...] The two coalitions had practically the same social organisation: republics based on high finance [...] the same liberties equally stifled by exploitation.'[8] The question of how to smash the exploitative social system that created this nightmare now posed itself more urgently than ever.

Spain

Released from jail and expelled from belligerent France, Serge made his way to Spain, where revolution was already in the air, in circumstances not unlike those which, on the other side of the continent, were ultimately to propel the Bolsheviks to power in Russia. Finding work as a linotypist in Barcelona, Serge gravitated, still loosely within an anarchist frame of reference, to the most radical organisation on the Spanish left, the revolutionary syndicalist organisation, the CNT. Here, news of the first of the Russian Revolutions of 1917, the February rising which swept away the Tsar, was greeted with enthusiasm:

Reading the dispatches from Russia, we were transfigured: for the images they conveyed were simple, concrete. A minute clarity was shed over things: the world was no longer impelled along by helpless lunacy [...] The Spaniards [...] instinctively understood the Petrograd days, since their imagination transposed those events to Madrid and Barcelona.[9]

Imagination was followed by action: the Barcelona uprisings of that year were, to Serge, clear indications that everywhere what he called 'the same, intensely alive electric current, [was] crossing from the trenches to the factories, the same violent hopes [were] coming to birth'.[10] Even the defeat of the Barcélona uprisings did not diminish Serge's hopes.[11] But increasingly those hopes were vested elsewhere, in Russia – the land of his parents and, more vitally now, the prospective site of a successful revolution, although it transpired that this was to be one led by a political party, the Bolsheviks, which issued in the extreme form from the very Socialist tradition Serge had long opposed.

Serge determined to go to Russia to experience the revolution at first hand, not just as an observer but as a full participant; to put himself, as he said with commendable frankness to the Russian embassy in Barcelona, at the service of the revolution. For Serge, the gravitational pull of the revolution was irresistible. 'We felt', he wrote later:

as if we were leaving the void and entering the kingdom of the will [...] A land awaited us where life was beginning anew, where conscious will, intelligence and an inexorable love of mankind were in action. Behind us, all Europe was ablaze, having choked almost to death in the fog of its own massacres. Barcelona's flame smouldered on. Germany was in the thick of revolution, Austro-Hungary was splitting into free nations. Italy was spread with red flags [...] This was only the beginning.[12]

The Russian Revolution and Bolshevism

On the long tortuous journey to Russia, beset by obstacles both physical and political, Serge's political ideas clarified, increasingly focused by the significance of developments in the country itself. By now, of course, the Bolshevik revolution had taken place. Serge's response was unequivocal. For him the revolution was inevitable; it could not, as he put it 'stop halfway. The avalanche would carry on rolling right to the end [...] the peasants seize the land, and the workers the factories'.[13] This was of course precisely the Bolshevik programme of 1917: land, peace, bread and all power to the soviets! Despite the chaos and devastation that Serge fully recognised and never hid from himself or others,[14] the basic choice confronting him seemed clear: either to throw in his lot with the Bolsheviks as the party that had led the revolution to victory; or to adopt, passively at best, the camp of counter-revolution. Serge had no doubts. As a revolutionary, whatever his early anarchist criticisms of the Marxist view, he was radically inspired by the achievements of the Russian masses and their Bolshevik leaders. In the revolution Serge saw the realisation of his deepest beliefs and hopes. For the first time, the masses had risen up not simply in destructive defiance but to smash the very structures of oppression which had claimed them, setting up instead a radically new type of organisation, the 'Commune-State' as Serge was henceforth always to refer to it.

Libertarian Leninism

The use of this term (drawn directly from Lenin's *State and Revolution*, itself written in the middle of 1917) to describe the Russian Revolution signifies something of the ideological distance Serge had now travelled. His adherence to the Bolshevik party was more than conjunctural. In his enthusiasm for the revolution, Serge put all hesitations behind him and became a revolutionary Marxist, a Leninist in both theory and practice. At the same time, there was a deep continuity with his most basic political identifications. For there was no real defection here on Serge's part, no forswearing of his deepest commitments. Rather, Serge recognised in Bolshevism a means of realising those commitments most effectively, of translating dream and idea into reality. On this henceforth he was to be emphatic. It was the role of the Bolsheviks in leading the revolution, the Bolsheviks as the vanguard party of the revolution which commanded his adherence.

The revolution itself was for Serge a fundamentally libertarian phenomenon, radically democratic in both form and content at every level – focused by the destruction of the repressive apparatus of army and police, workers' control of the factories, and above all soviets as direct, revokable forms of government. The Bolshevik dispersal of the Constituent Assembly as an inferior bourgeois political form in favour of a new soviet form of government and representation, an act which has outraged liberal democrats for decades, met with Serge's clear approval. Following Lenin, Serge saw the soviets as an altogether more representative and more accountable form of democracy. Representation through universal suffrage was seen as inferior, insensitive to shifts in opinion, incapable of registering the revolutionary dynamic of workers wanting to take power directly into their own hands. The radicalisation of the masses in 1917 and their corresponding shift towards the Bolsheviks themselves had taken place at the level of mandated, revokable delegates in the soviet.[15]

The Vanguard Party

In the heat of revolution the Bolshevik Party which drove this radical political process forward appeared in a new light to Serge the ex-anarchist. Strategically he was in full agreement with a Marxist party which, embracing the programme of permanent revolution, cast aside the narrow shackles of orthodox Marxism with its historical schema dictating to workers what was and was not permissible in this period. But it was the evidence of how the Bolshevik Party translated this strategy into action which made the most impact on him. This had both a negative and a positive side. On the one hand, Serge was forced to witness the practical failure of the anarchism whose ideological weakness he had already acknowledged in prison.[16] On the other, the Bolsheviks had filled this vacuum magnificently, had in fact acted as he had always believed that anarchists should have done; 'taken up', as he put it, 'the responsibilities that the anarchists were incapable of assuming'.[17]

But it was more than a question of simple replacement. Serge followed the logic of the argument through to its conclusions. He now recognised and argued the need for a party in a way that would have been impossible for him before the war. In the 1922 article written for the French revolutionary-syndicalist journal *La Vie ouvrière*, Serge traced this logic quite specifically, arguing that readers of that political persuasion (which until recently had been his too) should recognise as he had done that the 'very logic of the facts' dictated the need for a party like the Bolsheviks. Here Serge articulated the classically Leninist themes of uneven levels of consciousness among the masses and the consequent need for a vanguard to combat the regressive tug of reactionary ideas. But, characteristically, he identified the leadership qualities of such a party in principle, and the Bolsheviks as a model in practice, in a particular way.

For Serge, the vanguard character of the party had to be proven – earned, if you will – in practice. This for him had been the signal achievement of the Bolsheviks in the revolution itself. The Bolsheviks came to power because they gained respect, because their solutions, their programme, their strategy made sense, pointed a way forwards.[18] But this leadership was not a simple, mechanical one-way process. In Serge's view, there was a profound interplay between the party and the masses in 1917 in which each learned from and shaped the other. The masses 'also create', as he put it; they were not inert or pliable or passive. Much of Serge's writing about the Russian working class in revolution lays great stress on its creativity, its capacity to invent solutions for problems, its moral qualities developed in the heat of struggle. The party's role was to turn these qualities to best advantage, to give clearer shape to the masses' 'confused aspirations shot through with flashes of intelligence'.[19]

Organisation

The Bolshevik Party was able to play this role, according to Serge, not only because it had a programme which made sense of these aspirations and pointed a way forward, but because of the way in which it was organised, because of the kind of political party it had become. Here again Serge felt impelled to draw radical conclusions from the evidence of anarchist practice:

> The anarchists were rendered incapable of any practical initiative through their divisions [...] their lack of organisation and discipline. Whatever they enjoyed in the way of real capacities and energies were wasted in small chaotic struggles [...] They were an amorphous group without definite contours or directing organs – that is to say without a brain or a nervous system [...] at the mercy of the most contradictory aims [...] irresponsible individual intelligences dominated by cliques, by alien pressures of a highly suspect kind and by group instincts, dissipating themselves to no effect.[20]

The Bolsheviks presented a sharp contrast: unified, disciplined, able to act as an effective pole of attraction at the decisive moment. This unity and discipline, according to Serge, was achieved in a particular way. It was the product (again) of a powerful radical democratic current which simultaneously both injected into the party a host of new members at every level of the organisation and infused it with a capacity for intense, often dramatic political debate. The new members brought a vitality, a temper, a dynamism to the organisation which, as Lenin himself recognised, was in danger of going elsewhere in the early months of the revolution.[21] At the highest level, of course, the coopting of Trotsky, the actual author of the theory of permanent revolution, into the leadership of the party was in one sense an implicit recognition of the party's decisive shift of strategy in 1917.[22]

The quality of debate inside the party, produced in part by this influx of members and in part by pressure from outside, was extremely high. Debates, as Serge both witnessed and described them, took place throughout the revolutionary period across a whole range of topics, from questions of tactics to art, culture and utopian speculation. Several debates centred not just on the line of the party but on the specific fates of individuals, not excluding those of the leaders of the party itself. One debate, for example, concerned the composition of the first post-revolutionary government and the possible exclusion of both Lenin and Trotsky from it.[23] Yet these debates were settled in a remarkably comradely spirit, without fear, intimidation or future prejudice. The unity of the party was in a real sense the product of its ability to contain, survive, even grow from these debates without resort to manoeuvre, splitting, expulsion or anathema.

Leninisms

It was this party and this revolution then that won Serge's commitment. His Leninism was thus a specifically revolutionary product, the fruit of the experience and observation of a Bolshevik Party whose vanguard status was validated in and by a revolution of a radically democratic character. At the same time, as many of the writings here show, Serge did not idealise either the party, the masses or the revolution itself. He recognised fully from the outset the terrible conditions that soon surrounded the revolution – civil war, foreign intervention, famine and disease. But he was not disposed to explain all subsequent deviations from the principles of 1917 as automatic consequences of the objectively difficult circumstances in which the revolutionaries found themselves. In his history and fiction of the period, as well as in the writings here, he showed an acute awareness of the limitations of all parties concerned in the drama of a revolution under siege from within and without. But his criticisms, unlike so many that have flowed from ex- and anti-communists ever since (and beaten out so insistently today), were articulated from within the framework he established in his fundamental commitment to the revolution of 1917, in the libertarian Leninism whose main lineaments have been sketched here.

It was the party's departures from its own norms and traditions, from the example it had itself set in 1917, that he condemned. Having credited the party in the first place with its achievements as a party of libertarian revolution, he criticised the role it subsequently played in its own degeneration. In a sense it was precisely because he had come to see the importance of the party, its centrality in and to the revolution, that he was able to identify so clearly the subjective factor at work. But these criticisms did not then or later undermine or invalidate his libertarian version of Leninism. This was strong and rich enough to acknowledge the real dangers posed by the emergence of an opposing version or tendency within Leninism, an authoritarian mentality which ran directly counter to the spirit of 1917. On occasion his focus was sharp enough to induce a sense of not only impending but present tragedy (as the title of the piece for *La Vie ouvrière* itself denotes).

As that tragedy unfolded, Serge's commitment was to be tested to the limit. As later chapters will show, the fundamentally libertarian character and inspiration of his Leninism, forged in these early years, was to bring him over time into often painful and difficult conflicts with some – Trotsky most tragically – who had been in part first cause and object of that commitment, but who developed a different vision and drew different lessons from it. None of these pressures and conflicts, however, could extinguish for Serge the original libertarian inspiration he had drawn from the revolution and Bolshevik Party of 1917. This was to provide him with his own, unique frame of reference from now on, a guide to theory and practice in the testing times that lay ahead.

THE DOCUMENTS

Victor Serge, Petrograd. Extract from 'La Ville en danger'[24]

An article by Trotsky
This evening *Izvestia* publishes a key article by Trotsky: 'Petrograd Defends Itself from Within as Well'. Two columns of cool and logical arguments; its logic is terrible and crisp.

As I read it I evoke his metallic voice, his regular gestures, his grave but deliberately simple martial bearing, the concentrated, self-assured, imperturbable energy that emanates from his whole person. No one but he could have written an article like that, styled so simply, powerfully and inflexibly.

From the military standpoint, he explains, the most advantageous course at present would be to draw the enemy into the city and fight him there. Since the telephone and telegraph network are in our hands, with strategic points fortified and defended with the participation of the working-class populace, Petrograd's maze of streets, canals and houses transformed into fortresses or places of ambush would become the cemetery of the White Army. There are still a few lines where he discusses the sparing of artistic treasures or of innocent victims 'the blame for whose bloodshed cannot in any case be laid to our account', but the conclusion has no ambiguity. If the regular army cannot fulfil its task, Petrograd must look to its own defence, within its own walls. 'Be ready, Petrograd! Perhaps it falls to you to write in these October days the most glorious page of your history!'

When a leader of the army writes like this, the nervous inhabitant, accustomed to the compulsory optimism of the authorities, believes that the worst has come. That evening the atmosphere is charged with anxiety. I have just been reading this article from an issue of *Izvestia* that has been posted up on the Nevsky Prospect.

A large and silent multitude has formed in front of the poster-newspaper. Suddenly we all give a jump: somewhere behind the Gostinny Dvor, on the other side of the embankment, a bomb has apparently exploded. But this is purely a nervous reaction which troubles nobody. Evening descends, grey and sullen with rain.

In the homes of the inhabitants conversation is marked by an onset of panic. It is said that aeroplanes have just bombarded Smolny; or that a bomb has demolished a house on the Sadovaya. None of it is true. Where do these rumours come from? They spring unconsciously from the fear and over-excitement of popular imaginations; and they are spread from one centre of gossip to another, unconsciously enlarged and distorted.

The organisation of the inner-city defence came about instantly. In order to prompt, it was necessary only to use the grid of the Communist Party to mobilise responsible and active members, a task of a few hours. Thanks to the exact inventory of its forces, to the centralisation of initiatives, to the close juxtaposition of the party machinery with that of government, all the city's energies are guided away from their habitual functions to concentrate on one project exclusively: the preparation for war in the city, which will be defended street by street and house by house.

Lev Davidovich Trotsky
Nevsky Prospect: here are two cars coming into view, stopping at a traffic block. In the crowd of passers-by, brief hints are exchanged. A name passes from mouth to mouth. Both cars are unenclosed. I notice the second one first, a large, neat vehicle with comfortable black padded

seating. It is occupied by between six and eight men in black leather jackets, rifles in their hands. Their headgear is striking: they are wearing helmet-caps made variously of felt or of a thick cloth shaded in field-green, coming to a rounded peak at the top and decorated with a big red star with its five points. It reminds one of the head-dress of Slav warriors in heroic times (but what times are more so than our own present?).

Trotsky, someone says. And I recognise him in the first car, wearing the same headgear pulled down to his eyes, and the grey greatcoat of all the army. With the creases in his brow, the spectacles in front of those dark, lively eyes, the small moustache, the dark goatee of a beard, he is recognisable at the first glance.

At this particular instant his eyebrows frowned, his manner was severe and slightly harassed... I know about his hunger for activity, his nights spent at the Smolny in the non-stop sessions of the Central Soviet Executive, his lengthy expeditions to the front, with the tales about him there which, while true, would turn into legend. At one spot in the south of Russia, during the cavalry attack led by General Mamontov[25] – who had recently sacked Tambov, Koslov and Eletz – Trotsky's train was surrounded by a Cossack detachment: it steamed on after a victorious battle over the attackers... In those days at the front, Lev Davidovich would go and crouch right in the first line of the trenches. Once he happened to arrive by car just as the Reds were being routed: the enemy was advancing, our own ranks were smashed. Lev Davidovich leapt on a horse and chased the fugitives till they turned and faced the enemy – or else himself led them back to the attack, I don't know which. This personal bravery is found rather imprudent, blameworthy even, in a leader and organiser...

In these tales of him that pass from lip to lip, what part is played by the popular imagination? It matters little. If some particular details are not accurate, others of a similar kind, less recounted, certainly are. The man who is here is the organiser of an army of revolution, an army he has conjured from the void: from the chaotic mobs of soldiery rebelling against the war, seizing trains by force, turning into peasants again and returning obstinately to their land...

In this journalist, theoretician and agitator, whose presence as an intellectual is what stands out now, we have a multiple personality, astonishing and powerful, whose advent was predicted by no one.

This high forehead, this head carried stiffly, perhaps in a forced attitude – for to command one must be very straight. Head held high, all the old fits of weariness thrown off by a vigorous movement of the shoulders – this small powerful mouth like that of a bird of prey, over a chin which, when at rest, looks scanty; the three punctuation marks, moustaches and beard, pointing up this faces's Mephistopheles look... I recall his orator's gestures, broad, precise, affirmative, his voice which hammers out sentences as a supple metal is hammered, giving off a clear sound; and his menacing irony like a rapier-thrust aimed at an invisible target and always finding its mark.

I have no intention of exaggerating. Chiefs impose themselves on me, I have no desire at all for their idolatry. In them I see the foremost servants of the proletariat, the ones whom one must follow, but also always look at face to face with the eyes of a free being. However, it seems to me that Petrograd knew that it was surely saved after this particular chief had come.

The Law of Iron

Today and here, Lev Davidovich Trotsky is the heart and soul of the resistance. If our assault-formations are mustering again here in some place, if trains loaded with meat and munitions and all the resources of this poor exhausted country are being summoned, organised and deployed methodically and in a mood to conquer, it is because they are channelled by his intelligence and directed by his will. An iron calling, this. The front in Siberia, the front in the Ukraine. Front of Poland and Latvia, front of Petrograd, front of Karelia, front at Archangel... Front of the civil war in the interior. An iron calling, that of a man who has to think of everything and, as a revolutionary, act mercilessly. This evening I have read an order signed by Trotsky commanding the immediate arrest of and detention as hostages, of the families of Red Army officers and soldiers who have crossed over to the enemy. There follow the names: arrested today Marfa Andreevna and her daughter Vera, wife and daughter of——, a traitor who has joined the enemy...

To kill or be killed: the Commune too, that Commune which inscribed on its banners such dazzling hopes, knew of this ancient law of iron [26]

Victor Serge, Letter to Comrade Michel[27]

Petrograd,
May 29, 1921

Dear Comrade Michel,[28]

When I think about it, your arrival here, along with Sirolle,[29] strikes me as nothing short of providential. I count on the three of us being able to do a good job together – a job that only we can do. It's about that which I want to write to you briefly now.

Your knowledge of Russian will enable you to see all the realities at first hand for yourself – and show Sirolle around properly. I'm afraid that you're in for impressions which are going to be quite frightful. Even I, though I'm inured to it all, find that on some days I can't stay detached; sometimes I feel shattered, despairing, not knowing which way to turn – especially when I'm with our anarchist mates, poor buggers. In Moscow a whole lot of infinitely painful impressions will hit you. At any rate, you'll soon know how terrible is the phase of 'after the revolution', in which we are situated, and how difficult it is to talk about it to friends who on their own can get no real idea of the scale of the problems and their awful depth. Soon, either here or in Moscow, we'll talk again about your impressions. I am putting myself entirely at your disposal to help you to get to know Petrograd; and on certain questions (the anarchist movement), I've assembled a whole mass of documents which will be useful to you. But as soon as I get to Moscow I'll be very keen to know your first impressions and your first opinions; actually, it might be useful if you could let me know what sort of documents or other information will help you most – or more generally, how I can assist you in any particular, concrete way.

Just now I want to tell you two or three other things which I haven't been able to highlight enough, perhaps, in our hasty conversations.

First, the heart-breaking, indescribable bankruptcy of the Russian anarchist movement. In Moscow you will find two anarcho-syndicalist groups (one around Maximov, the other around Shapiro), which are not only enemies of each other but joint enemies of the anar-universalists who are themselves split into two groups in a state of mutual excommunication;[30] plus an Anarchist-Communist Federation which stays out of this recrimination (directed by old Karelin from room 119 or 219 at the Hotel National – now the First House of the Soviets; do see him and give him my greetings, he's a very interesting man despite the tide of disparagement that runs against him),[31] and the loonies who've invented the language AO (!)[32] and a number of other tiny groups. You'll see all these buddies of ours, equally sincere and devoted at heart, slandering each other, hating each other, and getting themselves into some fucking prison through various stupidities committed. I suffer and you will suffer too, knowing the absurd and criminal persecution that has been visited on some (notably our heroic Voline),[33] but here is the first conclusion I want to offer you in advance:

It is our own fault, as anarchists, that, with fatal consequences for the revolution (now perhaps likely to die off from Statist centralisation, dogmatic orthodoxy and military deformities), we were unable to perform our role there, organise a mass movement in it on practical foundations, form within it an intellectual elite that was serious and capable of eliciting respect. As a whole we anarchists have behaved like kids or lunatics, and have been swamped by the least interesting elements amongst us. For a long time others have had to take up the responsibilities that the anarchists were incapable of assuming, and to do the work that we could not do. These others succeeded magnificently in these tasks for two or three years. They are no longer good enough for it, and there is no way of patching things up. My conclusion on this is that in this country we have to begin a long-term project for the future – and in other countries to avoid any fresh beginning of similar faults. To be precise: we need a new anarchism, equipped with a practical programme, enriched with all the experience of the proletarian revolution, capable of guiding the movement of the masses. Its basis, like that of the reorganisation of production itself, can lie only in syndicalism. And there must be a resolute break with old habits of ideological piousness. It is less important to be 'pure', than to be revolutionary.

If we can manage to push some healthy elements, abroad and in Russia, along this direction, we will have a real achievement. For the central error of the present Russian regime is its establishment of a whole bureaucratic-state mechanism to administer production, instead of (as in syndicalism) leaving this to the workers organised by industry. And its major misfortune is that it has fought against every individual initiative, every opposition, every criticism – however fraternal and revolutionary – every infusion of liberty, by methods of centralised discipline and military repression (in short, has let itself be guided by an approach foreign to the spirit of anarchism). The results of this are now before our eyes. What we must do then is at all costs to preserve the anarchist spirit, and to nurture it by giving it a practical base in revolutionary syndicalism. Outside that perspective I can see nothing. I hope that we shall reach some understanding on this common ground.

All this is strictly between us – Sirolle included of course. Destroy this letter or make sure that it isn't left lying around.

I was ever so pleased to meet Souvarine[34] the other day, slightly different from the sort of man I expected. His mind is so clear, and wide-ranging. There we have a Marxist of excellent pedigree with whom it is good and pleasurable to work.

Au revoir and best wishes to you and Sirolle,

                                                                    Victor Serge

Victor Serge, 'The Tragic Face of Revolution'. Extract from *La Vie ouvrière*[35]

Surrounded on all sides by its enemies, wearied by years of struggle in isolation, wasted inwardly by famine, the Russian Revolution is still the object of ferocious polemics which, unfortunately, do not all proceed from the reactionaries' side.

There are certain revolutionary tendencies which are blinded by singular hatred in all that concerns Russia's revolution. Usually they lack both a reasoned understanding of it and the power to understand. At the present moment when the ideas of Communists are being travestied, the better to be attacked, it is no bad thing to repeat once again a number of elementary truths concerning the most serious problem-areas of social transformation...

The Permanence of Danger

The dominating element in the whole course of the Russian Revolution, from its very first day to the day we are in now, has been the danger, the omnipresent danger, the danger of its death.

The revolution did not commence, in the way envisaged by all the revolutionary theoreticians, in a society at the peak of its capitalist development, one abundantly rich, in which the working class, once it attained consciousness of its interests and its historic mission, would only have to expropriate a tiny platoon of plutocrats in order to find itself in possession of a marvellous productive apparatus and of warehouses full enough to ensure immediate 'affluence for all', on the lines of the old utopian formula...

The revolution commenced instead in Europe's most backward country, from the standpoint of industrial development and of the general cultural level; in a country of illiterate peasants where the proletariat was no more than a numerically weak minority; in a country whose railway network was the least developed of the whole continent; in a country, finally, invaded, devastated and drained of its strength and very blood during three years of imperialist war when it still lay beneath the archaic despotism of the Tsars.

And, in this country, the revolution of the peasants, soldiers and workers found itself isolated. Its appeals met with no response from anywhere. First the Central Powers and then the Allies contrived to wage against it an undeclared, undeclarable war of treachery, followed by open war; they succeeded in creating an endless famine through their blockades, in the meticulously organised murder of an entire people, without any sign of rescue appearing from the proletariat of other countries, without the performance of their most elementary duty towards that revolution by the 'revolutionaries' who are nowadays so generous with their ill-minded criticisms against it.

For years now, the survival of the Russian Revolution has depended on a constant miracle, in the most literal sense. At the end of September 1919, Kolchack was advancing towards the Volga, and Denikin had captured Orel and was marching upon Moscow. Yudenich was at the gates of Petrograd and the Kadets, Social Revolutionaries and several other groupings were within Moscow hatching conspiracies. In mid-March 1921 the province of Tula was being ravaged by the bands of the Social Revolutionary Antonov; other bands were severing communications with Siberia; and the cannons of Kronstadt were in full blast. I am recounting only those moments which I myself lived through. And now, we have famine over the Volga region, the Crimea, Kuban, the Ukraine, every zone over which the counter-revolution has passed. And Red Russia is more alone than ever before.

There are certain truths which every critic should keep constantly in mind when he examines the doings of the Russians, when he permits himself, in the relative comfort and ease of revolutionary newspaper-offices installed in bourgeois society, to criticise that formidable experiment in social transformation of which the masses and the militants in the Western countries are still kept in almost total ignorance. Alone and confronted by limitless tasks, the revolutionaries of Russia have not known a single day in which they did not have to conduct the violent defence of their very right to exist. And that explains a great many things.

The Russian Communist Party

This miracle of armed resistance and victory in the Russian Revolution – whose work is it?

The revolution conquered because it conformed to the profound aspirations and interests of the large masses of workers and peasants. But these large masses, seen as a whole, are nevertheless very backward. Only a minority possessed a clear consciousness of aims, a firm practical will, and organisation. If this minority had been disunited, or lacking in discipline and doctrine, by which I mean positive leading ideas, it would have succumbed. That cannot be denied. That is the obvious truth. It won because it was strengthened by that powerful iron frame: the party.

What is the Communist Party in a time of revolution?

It is the revolutionary elite, powerfully organised, disciplined, obeying a consistent direction, marching towards a single, clearly defined goal along paths traced for it by a scientific doctrine. Being such a force, the party is the product of necessity, that is the laws of history itself. That revolutionary elite which in a time of violence remains unorganised, undisciplined, without consistent direction and open to variable or contradictory impulses, is heading for suicide. No view at odds with this conclusion is possible.

This party took over power. Which is to say, it necessarily assumed responsibility for the food supply, for organisation, for interior and external defence, for administration on a country-wide scale, etc. This was its imperative duty, and on this point too we are still merely stating what is patently clear. But, once it was in power, the party found a new danger.

While its best activists were dying in battle on seven bloody fronts over four years, along came the time-servers who always flock towards power, and joined the party. Excesses were committed in its name. Pre-revolutionary mentalities and miserable egoisms looked for cover under its banner. That much is true; but not of any importance. For in its mass nature it remained both working-class and revolutionary. Through its leaders it remained faithful to itself and its past. By its measures of discipline and purification and through its Spartan morality it conducted a fierce (and successful) defence against its internal enemies. Seen from close quarters, such a battle is clearly very painful, but it bears the stamp of true greatness.

Leaders and Masses
This party of masses has leaders who are called to their positions by history: men formed by twenty years of struggling and learning, who have known hunger, exile, calumny, ideological battle; and who, from obscurity on the eve of October 1917, have emerged as leaders because only they, in the tempest of their time, kept a clear view, showed the way forward, dared the decisive acts.

Their right does not depend on force. Whatever force they have – and yesterday it was only the word, written or spoken – is that of intelligence and will. People have followed them because of their capacity to see far and keenly. These leaders, it is true, are able to break the resistances of the less clear-sighted, for here lies the revolution's whole defence: but what enables them to do so is the trust and the confidence of the masses which at the present time strengthens them.

Multitudes are sometimes under the sway of irrational instincts and physical impulses. Among them anxiety and malaise, discontent and despair, may be instilled by suffering, fatigue, famine or the influence of the past. This is particularly so when these masses are weary and exhausted after long years of struggle. At such moments, leaders may appear to be standing firm against the masses' wish, and to be committing violence against them. But it is in these moments that the leaders embody the genuine higher interests of the masses; and, if they remain firm and straight, pulling the masses along with them in advance, it is because in their hearts the people know that is what the leaders stand for.

The same observations hold true of the party, and of the relations between party and masses.

All this has been put in a very abstract way, but could be illustrated easily with telling examples. All those who, in the last few years, have had any contact with the Russian people will know the unanimous respect accorded by them to 'Vladimir Ilyich', as well as the limitless trust he enjoys in the party, even among the harder or less definite oppositional groups.

Kronstadt

February 1921… There had already passed four dreadful winters of civil war, including two of famine. The population had been decimated by war, typhus and hunger, and was now at the limit of its strength. Then came Kronstadt.

Bukharin and Lenin defined this movement of discontented sailors as a 'revolt of the peasant, petty-bourgeois mentality', which has no aspiration towards Socialism and whose only ideal is the peaceful cultivation of a small land-plot by each individual for himself; the rewarding commerce of country fairs; the free speaking of a rural democracy which, if it ever came to be realised, would constitute in its obscurantism and conservatism a powerful bulwark of reaction.

What slogans did the movement adopt? Two principally: 'Freedom of small trading'; and 'For the soviets against the party'.[36] The first of these represented the interests of the countryside, unwilling to offer its produce to the revolutionary city at give-away prices (the city, meanwhile, was keen to sell at the highest price possible). The second is getting exploited by the Social Revolutionaries, by the Mensheviks, by the anarchists, even by certain Communists who have been drawn into the conflict, whether through blindness or provoked by elements even more suspect, such as foreign intelligence operators, *[35] former officers, etc.

---

* The French press, and particulary M. Serge de Chessin, had announced the Kronstadt mutiny one month before it actually occurred. [Serge's note.]

This bloc both seals the unity of all the Communist Party's political opponents and transmits the rebellion, against this stoical, obdurate party, of backward elements in a totally exhausted population. The party is determined to hold fast: not so the others, who would have gladly surrendered for the sake of a swift delivery of white bread...

What forces were there behind this movement? What personalities, what new leaders were preparing to take over from the Bolsheviks? Chernov was hurrying out to Reval, Wrangel was telegraphing from Constantinople. In Berlin the Kadets were jubilant. On the house walls in Petrograd, chalked slogans of death to the Jews! appeared overnight. Let us suppose briefly that the Kronstadt mutiny had turned out to be victorious. Its results would have been immediate chaos, the terrible kindling of a civil war in which this time the party of the revolutionary proletariat and the broad peasant masses would have been locked in combat. Within a short time a handful of liberal lawyers and Tsarist generals, fortified by the sympathies of the whole bourgeois world, would have drenched their hands in the blood of the Russian people in order to pick up the abandoned power. Thermidor would have come.

The Repression
In the whole tale of these events it has happened more than once that men utterly sincere in their dedication to the revolution, passionate idealists, have inflicted the gravest possible harm upon the cause they wished to serve.

No one can seek to deny the sincerity of the convictions of the left Social Revolutionaries who, for the purpose of ruining the Brest-Litovsk treaty and making war against imperialist Germany, tried in July 1918 to take power by force from the Communists whose coalition partners they had been till then.

No one can deny the sincerity, either, of the convictions of those anarchists who, while others of the anarchist creed were getting killed at the front in the defence of the Soviet regime, took up arms against that same regime. It is not the sincerity of any such convictions which is in question: it is the basic interests of the revolution's survival. And, however painful such a necessity may be, it must be stated openly: the revolution has the right and the duty to defend itself against those who, even with the best intentions, try to shoot it in the back.

The terrible necessity for domestically conducted repression is now one that no revolution in history has managed to escape up till now.

Where the revolution comes to power in an uncivilised country and as the successor to an Asiatically tyrannous autocracy; where there is a civil war continuing from an imperialist war which for years has coarsened the sensibility of the masses; where the atrocities of White terror multiply, where the threat of death is everywhere permanent – then this frightful necessity of repression is bound on occasion to involve itself in errors. No power and no party has succeeded completely in avoiding these. No grouping, even on the revolutionary side, of those who took part in the civil war can boast of being unstained by such deeds.

Nevertheless I am convinced that, when the reckoning is made, the Russian Revolution has proven to be more fortunate and less bloody in this regard than has been the case with either its predecessors or its enemies. A worse scale of cruelty can be found with Cromwell in England or in France with the like of Carrier (at Nantes) or Lebon (at Arras), to take only the most notorious practitioners of terror. Events in Finland and Hungary, and with Kolchak's and Denikin's forces, show what reaction is capable of. The revolution employed terror only in an infinitely slighter degree and when it was faced with extermination. On this point I could cite some revealing statistics.

I have discussed above some of the tragic aspects of the Revolution, If these features were better appreciated, I am sure that, among many sincere revolutionaries at present misled by sectarianism or influenced by malicious campaigns, the spirit of distrust, criticism (often inaccurate and inopportune because ill-informed) and personal resentment would (give way to the desire to come) at any cost to the assistance of the people that has made the revolution and the men who defend it alone.

Kursk, March 12th, 1922.   Victor Serge

Victor Serge, 'The Problems of Dictatorship'. Extract from *La Vie ouvrière*.[38]

Let us suppose that in a great industrial country where syndicalism – a Red syndicalism – is powerful, the expropriation is accomplished. Whether they wish it or not, and whatever may be their reluctance to begin by founding a state – the Republic of Labour – the revolutionary proletarians exercise a dictatorship, possess an army and prisons, nominate plenipotentiaries (for it is certainly necessary, at one time or another, to negotiate with the enemy and even with friends...). A minority with initiative has shown the example, suggested the resolutions, launched the slogans, aroused the energies. This minority – let us suppose it to be syndical – now through force of circumstances assumes the bulk of the responsibilities. The masses follow them, assist them, and also create — but with a smaller degree of consciousness. Is it not indispensable for militants of this initiating minority, who all know, appreciate and understand one another, and have a stock of common ideas, to concert together before acting, to seek to bind together permanently their efforts towards a single common goal? Now that they are exercising power — they who only yesterday were perhaps the adversaries of all authority, they run the danger of being swamped by unstable or dubious elements; they also run the risk of being corrupted or exhausted in the new situations for which they have no precedents. Is it not wise for them to equip themselves with a discipline, for them to control one another in a comradely spirit?

That is what they will do. For that lies in the very logic of the facts which has been verified by the history of the Jacobins and the Bolsheviks. In other words, these syndicalists (it matters little whether they call it a Federation, a League, a Union or something else), will form a 'party'.

And it is this proletarian party, the organisation of the most hardened, most conscious revolutionary minority, which will in fact exercise the dictatorship before long...

These are the problems which the revolutionaries hostile to any dictatorship in principle will have to confront 'practically'. Can they bring to these problems of theory, which tomorrow may become practical matters replete with menace, any other solutions but those we have outlined?

2 The Correspondence

Introduction by D.J. Cotterill

When in August 1939 Serge wrote his final anguished letter to Trotsky demanding satisfaction for the harsh criticism to which he had been subjected in the *Bulletin of the Opposition*,[1] it proved to be the poignant dénouement of a train of events begun with such promise in the April of 1936, following Serge's return to the West 'on a direct line' after his Orenburg deportation. Contact had been initiated by Serge with his first act on arriving, writing to Leon Sedov (Trotsky's son) asking as a matter of urgency to be put in touch with Trotsky, which he hoped could be achieved without their letters being intercepted, for he had 'so much to tell Lev Davidovich' about their mutual comrades still in prison and exile in the USSR.[2]

Leon Trotsky was equally anxious to correspond, and his reply to Serge's first letter contains this warm personal greeting: 'I can't tell you how happy NI [Natalia Ivanova, Trotsky's wife] and I were to get it, and to learn that you're abroad at last [and ...] have kept your feelings of friendship for us'. Adding that he hoped this was just the beginning of their contact, Trotsky even suggests that Serge should visit him in Norway if possible, so that they could 'talk, fully, freely and *to our hearts' content*'. Failing that, he declares his intention to be an indefatigable letter writer.[3]

A total of 41 separate items of correspondence between Serge and Trotsky are included in this chapter, comprising 23 letters from Serge and 17 letters and 1 telegram from Trotsky, dating from 1936 to 1939. The bulk of this correspondence, some 35 letters between April 1936 and March 1937, a period of close cooperation between the two men, contrasts sharply in both tone and content with the remaining letters of 1938 and 1939, which are essentially a reflection of the increasingly bitter and open polemic waged by them, over the Spanish Civil War (examined in Chapter 3), the Kronstadt rising of 1921 and Serge's relationship to the Fourth International (as detailed by Weissman in Chapter 4). It is a contrast brought more sharply into focus when one considers

Trotsky's open letter of 5 March,1937 defending Serge against the attacks of the Communist press, principally those of his former friend and colleague Jacques Sadoul.[4]

If this initial promise of collaboration and personal warmth between the two old comrades, which so quickly deteriorated into total estrangement, is 'a measure of the effects of defeat, persecution and exile on even the most noblest spirits',[5] this introduction will seek to show through the medium of their personal correspondence how political differences worked in equal if not greater measure.

Persecution and provocation there was, however, and nothing better illustrates its morbid effects than the suspicions that Trotsky harboured of Serge's release from the Soviet Union. Despite the considerable personal intimacy and informality of Trotsky's opening letters he was at the same moment writing to a European comrade, Lilia Estrine/Dallin,[6] asking her to 'watch Serge very closely: watch his body language, his style, any suggestions that he was acting as an agent', for he says 'If Stalin had released Serge, then he must have thought he could have used him.'[7] Trotsky found it difficult to accept that Serge's release had been brought about by a group of intellectuals exerting pressure on Stalin, principally in the controversy surrounding the raising in 1935 of Serge's 'case' at the PCF-inspired International Writers Conference at the Mutualité in Paris. A brief look here at the controversy and the circumstances surrounding Serge's release will place Trotsky's fears in context and do much to tell us about the pervasive atmosphere of suspicion into which Serge had emerged.

Serge and his family had suffered a steadily increasing level of persecution from the Stalinist regime in the period following the defeat of the Opposition in 1927. He was arrested in 1928 and imprisoned for a brief period, arrested again in 1933 and, after refusing to sign a concocted confession – an act that Serge later believed helped to save him when his case for release was pressed – was sent into internal exile to the town of Orenburg. Having been expelled from the party in 1927, and unable to have a single word printed under his name in the USSR, Serge published a prominent series of works in France, notably *Year One of the Russian Revolution* (1930) and his trilogy of novels, *Men in Prison* (1930), *Birth of Our Power* (1931), and *Conquered City* (1932), whose success provided a platform from which his friends petitioned the assembled intelligentsia at the congress in Paris. 'How can we complain of the political prisoners in the jails of Mussolini and Hitler, when we have prisoners of our own?', was the impassioned plea on Serge's behalf by the Italian Gaetano Salvemini.[8]

Whatever the justification for Trotsky's suspicions about Serge's release, and he was by no means the only one to doubt the straight-forward explanation,[9] he does seem to have discounted the problems that Serge's 'case' must have posed when placed before the assembly, in the light of the subtle policy changes now evident within the Comintern. For the PCF had, since the destruction of the German Communist Party, taken over as the largest Communist Party outside the USSR and on its shoulders now fell the responsibility, within the Comintern, for resistance to Fascism. With the consolidation of Hitler's power rendering the USSR vulnerable to attack from Germany, Stalin was compelled to seek allies from among other Western democracies; and the focus of activity shifted to France and Spain. To facilitate this, Stalin somewhat belatedly manoeuvred the Communist International, now almost totally an extension of the Soviet Union's foreign policy, away from its long-held hostility to the Socialist parties of Europe, abandoning the so-called 'Social Fascist' rhetoric of the 'third period' to usher in a new era of cooperation with the Socialists that came to be known as the Popular Front, whose most conspicuous success was the election in April/May 1936 of the Blum government in France (an event that features largely in Serge and Trotsky's later discussions).[10]

The mobilisation of intellectual support both nationally and inter-nationally was a principal component of Popular Front strategy. Identification with the cause from these quarters could confer upon it much-needed legitimacy and kudos.[11] It is clear that Serge's continued status as a deportee in the Soviet Union touched Stalin's policy at the point he least wished to be embarrassed, before such influential opinion. Put simply, Serge's status had now become potentially more damaging than his proposed freedom, and it was better to let the man go than suffer the continued embarrassment of a discussion of his situation surfacing at inopportune moments. That, and the absence of a concocted confession are more likely to have saved Serge and his immediate family than Stalin's need to 'use' him. Serge certainly looked upon it that way, as he recalls in his *Memoirs:* 'I am conscious of being the living proof of the unplanned character of the first trial and, at the same time, of the crazed falsity of the charges brought up in all the trials.'[12] Once free Serge could be of little use to Stalin, for unlike those in the 'dock', he could use his skills as a writer and his new-found freedom to strike back. Not that the Soviet Security Police(GPU) had forgotten Serge: the letters bear eloquent testimony to the many visa and passport problems he was to suffer, right up until his final exile in Mexico. Throughout the rest of his life he was to undergo consistent vilification in the Stalinist press for, sadly, the corrosive effects of persecution and provocation were never absent from the Oppositionist milieu in which he moved, and ultimately this contributed to his final break with the French comrades in 1938.

Despite his perhaps all too understandable reservations, Trotsky soon saw in Serge an irreproachable comrade and the letters quickly begin to fly back and forth between Brussels and Oslo, sometimes crossing in the post as the two men became impatient for a reply.[13] While Serge saw it as his duty to get as much information as possible to Trotsky and his followers in the West about conditions inside Russia, Trotsky was anxious to orientate Serge to his followers in Belgium and France:[14] 'Have you met the Belgian comrades yet? What are your impressions of them?' He hoped that Serge would, 'over a period', be 'able to get to know the publications of the Fourth International', so 'that we'll be able to have an exchange of views on such matters'.[15] Trotsky was keen for Serge, as a comrade full of authority, to be drawn as soon as was practicable into the fold of the Fourth International, whose creation Trotsky considered his most important work outside the Soviet Union'[16] and with whose groups and activities Serge's problematic relationship forms the principal content of the correspondence.

Indeed the whole concept of a Fourth International was problematical. It had not been created in any formal sense of the word, (nor would it be until 1938). Trotsky himself was forced to admit that he did not 'know what it means to 'found' the IVth International'.[17] In the years that immediately followed his expulsion from the Soviet Union in 1929 he had not rushed to call for either a new party or a new International, steadfastly opposing those of his comrades who suggested such a line.[18] Trotsky would only break with the Third International and adopt a 'new' line in 1933, when the failures of the Comintern in Germany and the situation inside Russia demanded a critical rethink of his position.

Trotsky had, despite his unbending opposition to Stalin and the 'third period' policies of the Comintern, remained wedded to the belief that 'with all their flaws and vices the Communist parties still represented the militant vanguard of the working classes'[19] and that 'The Opposition's place was with that vanguard'. While persecution had driven the Oppositionists out of the movement, they should maintain their struggle to regain their place within it.[20] This position was sustained by the belief that the Soviet Union remained a workers' state, for despite the bureaucratic deformation of Stalinism, what:

determined the social character *of* the Soviet state was the national ownership of the means of production. As long as this 'the most important conquest of October', was unimpaired, the Soviet Union possessed the foundations on which to base its socialist development.[21] [*emphasis added.*]

With his innate loyalty to the conquests of that revolution and its potential undiminished, Trotsky held the view that the party could be reformed from within.

However, the baleful influence of the Comintern with its policy of 'Social Fascism' aimed at the German Socialists (SPD), coupled with the abject failure of the German communists (KPD) to grasp the significance of Hitler, even as he attained power in January 1933, led, as Trotsky had often warned, to the destruction of the German left. He then concluded that 'it was no longer possible to fight the 'imperialist West', much less Stalinism, within the framework of Stalin's Comintern',[22] for 'an organisation which has not been wakened up by the thunderbolt of fascism [...] is dead and cannot be revived'.[23] In July 1933 Leon Trotsky called for the formation of a new International, and by October of that year had conceded that the Opposition would have to see itself as a 'new party in the USSR as well'.[24]

Throughout this period and up until his expulsion from the USSR in 1936, Serge had remained in either precarious freedom in Leningrad or internal exile at Orenburg, with very little or no news of Trotsky and political events in the West. 'On the Fourth International, we had practically no news to judge from', he wrote to Trotsky; 'it was I who made known the little news that got to us.'[25] On the vital question of the new International he assures Trotsky that 'Since we had no illusions about the IIIrd [International], we did not have to debate the principle of the IVth';[26] though he qualifies this with his express belief that the International's benefits will be agitational rather than revolutionary, given the prevailing political situation.

Despite this, Serge had no preconceived ideas about what could or could not be achieved by groups or individuals, and Trotsky seemed happy to allow him time to work out his political position:

> I can fully understand that, having arrived abroad, after years of incredibly harsh sufferings, you're not rushing to define your position and you don't want to give anybody the right to 'pigeonhole' you according to your former connections or on any other grounds.[27]

Trotsky felt that Serge would better serve the 'Fourth' by not involving himself in mundane day-to-day politics. He tells Serge: 'I think it would be quite unreasonable to expect you to waste your energies on *current* politics. In the final analysis, your books will make a far greater contribution to the cause'.[28]

Current politics were soon to engulf them, however, for Serge's emergence from the Soviet Union that spring corresponded with a quickening of the struggle in the West that was to embroil him fully in the politics of the Fourth International.

Serge had been in Brussels a little over a month, and was working hard to unify support around a campaign for political prisoners in the USSR, when the elections in France gave the Popular Front a sweeping electoral victory. This was quickly followed by Franco's military rebellion against Spain's own Popular Front government, and the first of the political trials in Moscow. All had far-reaching consequences for Serge's relations with Leon Trotsky and his followers in the new International. Spain and its tragic civil war were to prove continually divisive, while persecution by Stalin, as an outcome of the 'show trials', resulted in Trotsky's removal further from the centre of European political activity. Moreover, the organisational failures of the Fourth International, then in the process of formation, in meeting the challenges presented to it forced upon Serge a critical rethink of the revolutionary position. For Trotsky, Serge, in doing this, eventually went too far in challenging the very essence of the Bolshevik legacy. Here the correspondence reveals significant 'fault lines' in the Serge – Trotsky relationship. These manifested themselves initially as differences on tactics and organisational matters, but they were, as will be argued later, the product of the men's differing political temperaments and Serge's independent turn of mind, now allowed greater scope for expression outside the Soviet Union. These differences became apparent first over the role of the Fourth International during the spontaneous strike wave that greeted the election of Blum's government in France, and subsequently widened over the movement's attitude to the Popular Front and Spain as these broader political tensions multiplied. It is therefore along the course of these 'fault lines' that we begin to understand Serge's experience of the Fourth International and his eventual rift with Trotsky.

In France 'The Front', known as the 'Rassemblement Populaire', had come into being following long and tortuous negotiations between the Socialist, Communist and Radical Parties in the aftermath of anti-Republican attacks on the Chamber of Deputies on 6 February 1934, which raised the spectre of a successful Fascist coup in France – although in fact, its creation owed as much to the changed priorities of the Comintern following the debacle of Germany. That, coupled with the success in 1935 of a Bastille Day mass meeting in establishing the popularity (with the workers) of an anti-Fascist front, had:

> opened the way for the negotiations which led to the signing of the programme of the Rassemblement Populaire in January 1936, which in turn was followed by the re-unification of the trade union movement in a single CGT in March 1936, and finally by the election victory of May of that year.[29]

The strike wave began hesitantly enough in the middle of May, when workers at the Breguet aircraft factory in Le Havre struck and won concessions from their employers; this was quickly followed by strikes of aircraft workers in Toulouse a few days later, and by the end of the month such actions had spread to the car and engineering factories around Paris. Thereafter the scale of industrial action grew to staggering proportions. In June 12,142 strikes were recorded, involving 1.8 million workers (though this is possibly an underestimate); more strikes were recorded in that month alone than had taken place in the previous 15 years.[30] The sight of tens of thousands of French workers greeting the arrival of a government, which they had so recently voted for in such large numbers, with strikes and factory sit-ins, was undoubtedly a profound embarrassment. This was especially so for the communists, who in moving right in an effort not to upset the negotiations that forged the agreement had seemingly fallen out of step with the workers, who had moved to the left.

For Trotsky, who had long held the view that the situation in France was pre-revolutionary, the strikes seemed to justify his assertion to Serge on 9 June that 'A massive strike like this is undoubtedly the beginning of a revolution.'[31]

Trotsky had no illusions about the nature of the Popular Front, whose policies he attacked as offering 'no programme at all', which couched its limited demands 'in vague general terms: against wage cuts, for increased social insurance, for collective bargaining, "against inflation", etc',[32] but which rejected 'the struggle for power in order to create the workers' state'.[33] He dismissed it as a 'coalition of the proletariat with the imperialist bourgeoisie',[34] whose leadership, should it 'succeed in remaining on its feet in the course of the entire approaching and decisive period [... would] inevitably give way to fascism'.[35]

While neither the consequences of the workers' actions nor their significance for the future of revolutionary work were a source of dispute between the two men, the timing certainly was. Trotsky could not accept Serge's assessment that all the strikes showed was that the workers were just emerging from a 'phase of depression and extreme fatigue', or indeed that 'The full recovery may take several years'.[36] In reply to Serge's letter of 16 June he wrote, 'It would be excellent, of course, if history allowed a further 'several years' for this, if only (let us say) two or three years. But I am not so sure that this will be possible.'[37] He considered that the situation in France could develop at a faster rate than in Spain (where a Popular Front government had come to power that February). While he believed that the strikes were symptomatic of the workers' inherent distrust of the Front as essentially a reformist project: 'In France the bourgeoisie is immeasurably stronger' and 'may not give the proletariat any chance of compensating so rapidly for its leaders' bankruptcy'.[38] All that, Trotsky informed Serge, necessitated the formation of a new party as 'an extra-urgent task', in both France and Belgium. He was convinced that once the working class had come to see the Front as doomed to disappoint its revolutionary aspirations, it would need to turn to the Fourth International as the only political grouping capable of fulfilling them;[39] for 'even though it may have to be numerically small [...] without any party at all, the revolution is absolutely doomed'.[40]

However, when the government made its first appearance in the Chamber on 6 June, Blum brought forward proposals for three Bills: concerning the 40-hour working week, collective contracts and holidays with pay.[41] Furthermore, Blum called the unions and the employers to meetings at the Hotel Matignon on 7 and 8 June and again on the 10th, at which the employers effectively conceded to all the unions' demands. Thus when the Collective Contracts Act confirmed and completed the so-called Matignon Agreement,[42] the 'Party leaders lost no time in exhorting the proletariat to return to work',[43] with Thorez the Communist Party leader claiming, 'We must know how to end a strike' in speeches at Lille on 14 June. The strike wave then began to recede and despite further outbreaks during the rest of the year the impetus was essentially lost. In the months that followed, the employers took time to reorganise; by the autumn of 1936, through their new organisation the Confédération Générale du Patronat Français, they determined to rescind as much of the Matignon Agreement as was possible.[44]

Trotsky's hopes had rested upon the workers under the influence of the POI adding a political dimension to the economic demands of the strikes, which they distinctly failed to do. As Jacques Danos and Marcel Gibelin point out in summing up the Trotskyists' role, despite seeing their numbers and their relative influence growing in the months that followed: 'the weakness of the Trotskyists [...] in June 1936 made pure fantasy [...] those accounts which saw the POI [...] as the fomentors of the strikes, or as the *agents-provocateurs*'.[45] Moreover, while the employers' clawing back of the workers' newly won rights was broadly in line with what Trotsky had expected, and despite the continued decline of the Popular Front, due to the inherent tensions within it that Trotsky had clearly identified, the essential weaknesses of the Fourth International in influencing the masses remained – as Serge's later letters testify.

But what of party formation? Despite his reticence about a new 'International', Serge in no way wished to be discouraging; however, since his return to the West his experience of the Trotskyist groups was at best, mixed. Of the Belgian comrades he knew little save that 'their clannishness, with its morbid psychology, makes a dismal impression'.[46] With Hennaut's followers insisting on the preservation of their faction as a condition of joining the larger Belgian grouping, the French divided into two hostile parties and the Dutch about to split,[47] Serge was concerned that the whole of European Trotskyism could be marginalised from the workers by charges of sectarianism. So following his discussions with Trotsky's American emissary Muste, who had come with offers of cooption on to the founding committee of the Fourth International, Serge outlined his thoughts on the way forward.

Serge believed that by working 'towards a unification of forces', the Trotskyists could attract those sympathisers whom they presently could not, due to a lack of authority. To do this it would be necessary to cleanse their 'behaviour and eradicate all dirty procedures of a Stalinist sort', produce their publications in good French and open their pages to those 'sympathisers', who could be recruited later.[48] Furthermore, in his observations on Trotsky's 'A New Revolutionary Upturn', Serge posed the question of the correct attitude that the Fourth International should adopt towards the Popular Front, which Serge believed would only become the 'step' to Fascism that Trotsky supposed if the workers within it allowed themselves to be pushed around and provoked. Serge's outlook was more optimistic. In believing that the working classes were raising their consciousness through the strikes, he thought they could create a useful 'transitional tool' out of the 'Front' that would allow them 'to enter the later phases of the struggle with greater possibilities'. He was anxious for the Fourth International not to repeat the mistakes of the Communist International's 'third period', for he saw the possibility of sections of the Socialist Parties moving to a revolutionary position, which could be sustained only if: 'through our criticism and pressure we [...] help them in this more positive direction'. In crystallising his ideas under the slogan 'Transform the Popular Front from an instrument of class-collaboration into one of class struggle', Serge believed the Trotskyists must keep an open line to the old parties, for 'We must not forget that in France and Belgium' the parties of the 'Fourth International will only be able to present themselves as a real force by uniting the revolutionary workers who today belong to other political organisations'.[49]

In his response on 30 July, Trotsky criticised Serge's approach as 'too artistic and psychological, *ie*, not political enough', and he reacted disparagingly to Serge's suggestions on both organisation and tactics. While he agreed with Serge that a new Trotskyist party could attract people from the Socialist and Communist Parties, he could not accept his other comments, which he regarded as 'fundamentally incorrect'. Trotsky could not understand how it was that Serge, 'such a fine historian of the Russian Revolution', did not realise that everything he had said about the Popular Front applied 'to the bloc of Mensheviks and Social Revolutionaries with the Kadets [the Russian equivalent of the Radicals]', who had only been overcome in Russia after an uncompromising struggle. This stemmed, so Trotsky thought, from Serge's unfamiliarity 'with the history of what we've done here during the last seven and a half years'. But, despite this barely contained irritation, Trotsky was confident that once Serge had 'checked [his] *a priori* views against living political experience' their conclusions would coincide.[50]

It is clear from these exchanges that the differences between Serge and Trotsky, though not yet insuperable, were largely based on an assessment of what could be usefully gained via the dominant political movement of the period, the Popular Front. For Trotsky, this could be nothing other than a cover for profoundly anti-revolutionary alliances, but if anything he was too optimistic in assessing the strength of his movement in its ability to attract the workers at the expense of the established parties within the Front. That said, the same charge could ultimately be laid against Serge's ideal of a unifying force influencing those in the Front and creating a leading role for the Fourth in the process. This incompatibility of outlook was to be graphically illustrated by the Spanish Civil War, which revealed significant antagonisms, principally over the role of the POUM and its leader Andrès Nin in the 'revolutionary' atmosphere which surrounded the Catalan theatre of operations.[51] That August, however, with the official PCE line firmly against social revolution, there was much common ground between Serge, who believed the anarchists and syndicalists to be the Opposition's class comrades in revolution, and Trotsky, who agreed '*entirely* on the necessity for amicable cooperation [...] against Stalinist scoundrels and traitors'.[52]

Progress along this favourable political route was severely affected by the news from Moscow on 14 August: a thunderbolt announcement of the first of the major 'show trials'. The indictment of the principal accused, Zinoviev and Kamemev, on charges of terrorism included the fantastic claim that, from Norway, Trotsky was 'despatching terrorists and assassins to the Soviet Union'.[53] At the end of the trial, and despite the obvious fabrication of the charges, Trotsky was placed under house arrest. Serge, doing all he could to refute the charges brought up in the trials and support Trotsky, found it 'painful to think that Norway, one of the most civilised and freest countries', could take such punitive measures against a political refugee.[54] With Trotsky continuing in his refusal to sign undertakings to refrain from involvement in political questions, and the Norwegian authorities under pressure from the Soviet Union as to the future of relations between the two countries, Trotsky was eventually interned under restrictive circumstances. His final letter to Serge from Europe on 6 September had to be despatched through his Norwegian lawyer, Punterwald. A state of affairs such as this, as intolerable to Trotsky as it was embarrassing for Norway, was resolved only by the offer of asylum in Mexico, arranged by the painter Diego Rivera. Trotsky accepted, rather than suffer the possibility of a more restrictive internment in Norway.[55]

During Trotsky's period of enforced absence from active politics, the situation in Europe deteriorated markedly as the tensions within the Popular Front movements of both France and Spain produced a sense of perpetual crisis. In France, Blum would fall from power a little less than a year after taking office; in Spain, the spontaneous revolutionary response to Franco's military rebellion was being tempered by a Republican government under the slogan: 'Before the war is won the revolution must be crushed'.[56] By the time Trotsky had arrived in Mexico on 9 January 1937, Serge had already accumulated considerable differences with comrades of the Fourth International over Spain, following his attendance at their international conference in Amsterdam. Serge was devastated by the manoeuvring of the International Secretariat against the POUM; claiming that while 'addressing diplomatic compliments' to the Spanish party, the Secretariat was 'organising a split within it'.[57] In refusing to support Serge's call for solidarity with the POUM, the International Secretariat was, he wrote to Leon Sedov, 'weighed down by such a mass of mistakes' that it would end by pushing the POUM 'even further from the IV' [sic],[58] when the IS should be, he wrote to Trotsky, establishing 'truly comradely relations with it'.[59] Notwithstanding his seeming rapprochement with the POUM in the autumn of 1936, Trotsky was angered by the continued policy of the POUM and its leader Andrès Nin in accepting the Popular Front electoral programme and by the party's entry into the Catalan government, a course he believed would lead straight to disaster; he chose therefore to support the anti-POUM majority of his followers in the Fourth International. In time, the government in Valencia, along with its Communist allies who were playing out an ever more deadly game against the anarchists and syndicalists, would in May 1937 purge the POUM and murder Nin, in conditions of near civil war among the loyalist forces behind the lines in Barcelona.

Disagreements such as these, were to tinge Serge's view of the Fourth International as a 'sectarian movement, run by manoeuvrings from above, afflicted by all the mental depravities against which we had fought in Russia'.[60] The split over Spain was to set the tone for the rest of Serge's involvement with Leon Trotsky, which, if it was to stimulate debate on revolutionary tactics once the rift between them became public, was also to lead them into serious disagreements over Bolshevik history.[61]

At the same time that Serge was experiencing difficulties within the Fourth International, the success of his book *De Lenine à Staline* prompted a campaign of slander against him by the Communists in France. Jacques Sadoul, a former colleague from the Comintern, saw fit in the pages of *L'Humanité's* edition of 2 February, to grub up the scandal of Serge's involvement in the prewar trial of the Bonnot Gang. In his article Sadoul accused Serge of complicity with 'robberies, burglaries and murders', and claimed that as a 'valet of the pen' it was logical that having sold his services to Bonnot's 'tragic gang', Serge should then sell them to the 'gang of Trotsky'.[62] Despite his burgeoning differences with Serge, Trotsky was moved to defend him publicly in an open letter published in *La Lutte ouvrière* on 26 March 1937.

The Serge that Trotsky defended in this piece, as someone who had 'remained in the ranks of the Opposition without hesitating' and 'whose name will be forever linked with the renaissance of the working class's struggle for liberation',[63] is unrecognisable in the Serge whom a little later, Trotsky decided, had taken up a position 'on the left-wing of its implacable adversaries'.[64] For as Weissman shows in Chapter 4 below, the raising of the Kronstadt controversy of 1921 as a direct parallel to the events in Spain had by then plunged both men into an open polemic that touched even upon the revolutionary morality of the Bolsheviks themselves.

Moreover, shortly after Serge wrote to Trotsky on 18 February 1938 offering his condolences for Leon Sedov's untimely death, Trotsky was accusing Serge of siding with those who, like 'the bankrupts of anarchism, united with the bourgeoisie and the Stalinists against the workers, found nothing better to cover their bankruptcy with than by raising a campaign on the issue of ... Kronstadt'. Furthermore Serge, in publicly expressing his open solidarity with the POUM and contributing to pub-lications 'mortally hostile' to the Fourth, was 'consciously moving to a complete rupture and implacable struggle'.[65] During 1938 and 1939 Trotsky broadened this criticism. A piece in the *Bulletin of the Opposition*, entitled 'Victor Serge and the Fourth International', accused Serge of being an 'opponent' whose political inconsistency had turned into 'a series of personal combinations, if not intrigues'. And, following what seems a wilful misreading of Serge's Partisan Review article 'Marxism in Our Time', with 'Intellectual Ex-Radicals and World Revolution' in *La Lutte ouvrière*, he castigated Serge for confusing his own crisis with a crisis of Bolshevism and Marxism.[66]

By the time Serge wrote his penultimate letter to Trotsky, penned on 18 March 1939, almost a full year from their last personal exchange, the gulf between them had become wider. In this letter Serge gave a powerful rendition of their personal disagreements, which were 'very great indeed', but which 'I pointed [...] out to you immediately upon my arrival in Belgium'. Furthermore, in a puissant critique of the failures of the Fourth International, Serge held forthrightly to the view that it was impossible to build an 'International while there are no *parties* [...] But there are no parties here. It is a dead end.' In a situation where only small groups managed to hold on 'in this deadlock', where there was no influence or common language with the working-class movement, no such organisation could be constructed from:

> intolerance and the Bolshevik-Leninist doctrine, for in the whole world there are no more than two hundred people (except the surviving inmates of Stalin, perhaps) who understand, who are in a position to understand, what Bolshevism-Leninism is.[67]

Serge's response to these dilemmas was, in its consistency with his long-stated views on their mutual aims, a total refutation of Trotsky's charges of political 'changeability'. His words are worth repeating here at length, and indeed should be borne in mind when reading the documents in Chapter 4:

The solution, I believe, lies in an alliance with all the left-wing currents
of the workers' movement (its platform: the class struggle and internationalism); in free, comradely discussion of every issue, without abuse
and mutual recriminations; in the creation of an International Bureau
of committees and similar bodies – such a Bureau to be composed of
the representatives of local movements and to work towards concrete
goals; one must abandon the idea of Bolshevist-Leninist hegemony
in the left-wing workers' movement and create an international
alliance, which would reflect the real ideological tendencies of the most
advanced sections of the working class (I am convinced that in such
an alliance the Bolshevik-Leninists would have a greater influence than
in their own high and mighty International.)[68]

Serge by now, through his dissonance from the Fourth International, his publicly stated convictions and his continued involvement
with all complexions of the working-class movement, was operating
semi-detached from the rest of Trotsky's comrades. His eventual rupture
with them, he informed Trotsky, occurred over the identity of the
suspected agent-provocateur within the Paris-based organisation. In an
effort to have the matter investigated, Serge succeeded only in unwittingly bringing suspicion on to himself, and in offending the comrade
over whom he had voiced concern. While these events forced Serge's
break with the group and ended investigations into the affair, the
conviction that there was '"foul play" around the group' remained.[69]
The actual 'agent', Comrade Etienne [Zborowski], who ran the Paris
organisation after the death of Leon Sedov, apparently with full
confidence, was to remain undetected. He was only unmasked in the
US in the 1950s.[70]
But a final and yet more sinister twist was to be added to the
Serge–Trotsky relationship. Can we detect in this the hand of the
'agent' Etienne? Despite all disagreements and disparagements, Serge
had continued faithfully translating Trotsky's books into French, and
in March 1939 his translation of *Their Morals and Ours* appeared. Trotsky
was immediately incensed, not by the translation itself, but by the
publicity prospectus or *prière d'insérer* included with it. This, in a travesty
of Trotsky's philosophy, implied that: 'For Trotsky, deceit and violence,
if they are placed in the service of a justifiable end, should be employed
without hesitation.'[71] His response was to pen a furiously worded
denunciation under the title 'The Moralists and Sycophants against
Marxism', in which he held Serge or 'one of his disciples' responsible
for the offending insertion. It is a sustained polemic against Serge and

his supposed confederates, which encompasses all of Trotsky's anger and frustration at years of perceived betrayals and which concludes: 'The moralism of V. Serge and his compeers is a bridge from revolution to reaction.'[72]

Within the scope of this introduction, it is sufficient to say that this affair brought the personal correspondence between Serge and Trotsky to an end. A fuller account is given in Chapter 4 below, in the context of Serge's open polemic with Trotsky. For Serge was to receive no reply to his letter of 9 August 1939, in which he took issue with Trotsky over the content of 'The Moralists and Sycophants against Marxism': 'You subject me to a harsh criticism in it, ascribing to me the article (*prière d'insérer* to 'Leur Morale' [sic]) which I have not written, nor edited, nor do I know its author'!.[73] It is clear that by this time Trotsky, despite having 'not lost all hope of seeing [Serge] return to the path of the Fourth International', considered him an 'adversary, and a hostile one at that'[74] no longer worthy of a personal response.

While the mischief created by the affair of the publicity for *Their Morals* was almost certainly the work of the agent 'Etienne', it could not of itself have succeeded in further dividing Trotsky from Serge; that it did so was a measure of the distance that now lay between them. The presence of Etienne and the actions of the GPU could serve only to cloud further waters that were already muddy. Therefore, in the view of the present editor, the origins of these disagreements are to be found less in the machinations of the Kremlin and the Soviet secret police than in what Serge identified within Bolshevism when he joined the party in 1919, and what he retained of that identification even after he was expelled from the party in 1927 and subsequently from the USSR in 1936. It was neither the GPU nor Etienne who created the differences between Serge and Trotsky on either the Popular Front or the role of the Fourth International, but rather the substance of Serge's assessment of revolutionary socialism's prospects, and those of the Fourth International in particular.

Serge's dissensions from Trotsky's line quite clearly stemmed from his scepticism over the creation of a new International opposed to the Socialist and Third (Communist) Internationals, at a time of defeat and retrenchment for the workers' movement. If this scepticism is an indication that 'Serge was less fixated on the role of the vanguard party', as Richard Greeman believes,[75] it is, I contend, very much the product of both men's differing political sensibilities, resulting from their different political origins. Trotsky's views were formed from within the Russian movement, forced by circumstance to adopt the constraints of a clandestine organisation, both in its Menshevik and Bolshevik strands, while Serge's were imbued with the experience of the Western movements, both Socialist and anarchist, operating beyond those constraints. Serge's earliest attraction to Bolshevism was more than a simple exaltation of revolutionary vanguardism, or a recognition of the correctness of Lenin's tactics at the time. It was rather that he saw the promised fulfilment of his long-cherished hopes through the libertarian and international aspects of Bolshevism. And indeed, it was, as Philip Spencer points out in Chapter 1 above, 'the party's departures from' these 'norms and traditions'[76] that stimulated Serge's criticism and his alignment with the Opposition as the best option for defending the revolutionary project from the Stalinist bureaucracy and the corruption of 'Socialism in one country'.

Nothing of the persecution he underwent, or any of the defeats suffered in the Soviet Union, dimmed Serge's adherence to these libertarian and international aspects of the revolution. He returned to freedom in the West with these ideas intact, and his esteem for Trotsky high. However, Serge's hopes for a renewal of revolutionary socialism in the West following its reverses in Russia were soon to be clouded by his perception of the political climate as unpropitious for revolution, and by his subsequent recognition of the failure of the Fourth International either to work with the main strands of the workers' movement to further its aims or to act as a pole of attraction for the workers. For Serge, a new International could not be brought about without the parties to create it. Instead what he found within the 'Bolshevik-Leninist' movement in Europe, and France in particular, was a small collection of militants and a few hundred more sympathisers, all engaged in intrigue against each other. His criticisms of the Fourth International sprang from this.

Yet, if Trotsky's aims in founding a new International were, as Deutscher claims, not to 'gather around him a retinue of lyrical admirers' but to 'set his followers, as he himself was set against every power in the world: against fascism, bourgeois democracy, and Stalinism; against every variety of imperialism, social-patriotism, reformism, and pacifism; and against religion, mysticism, and even secularist rationalism',[77] then one would have thought that even Serge's dissonant input would have been welcomed. For it is equally true that in his suggestions and corrections to Trotsky's line Serge sought enmity with neither Trotsky nor his followers, but simply to aid the movement as it wrestled with its difficulties. In so doing, Serge acted in accordance with the same motivations that had prompted his defence of the Bolshevik cause in Russia itself, with what he termed his 'double duty': which sought to protect the revolution from its own internal excesses as much as from its external enemies.

Sadly, however, Serge found within the Fourth International a mirror image of all the worst aspects of the Third International it had left behind. Trotsky, by demanding, 'of his adherents unshakeable conviction, utter indifference to public opinion, unflagging readiness for sacrifice',[78] created an organisation which Serge believed thought only through Trotsky's head[79] and which brooked no disagreements or dissension, even when, as in Serge's case, this was done in utmost faith to Trotsky himself. For Serge, comradely criticism and fraternal discussion comprised the mental exercise which kept the 'revolutionary organisation' healthy and fit for struggle. When that had died within the Soviet Union the prospects for Serge's libertarian and truly international vision of Socialism did not die with it. But to find the same error repeated in the West forced him to conclusions which took him on a divergent path from that of Trotsky and his followers.

As we have seen, by 1939 Serge was admitting to Trotsky his belief that they would hold greater influence within the left-wing workers' movement if the idea of a Bolshevist-Leninist hegemony within it was abandoned. By this, Serge was not implying a renunciation of Socialism or revolution, but a rejection of those stratagems which had palpably failed to work as they had been applied in the West. What this argument did imply, however, was that the tactics of Lenin and the Bolsheviks had been correct for a particular country (Russia) at a particular time (1917), but that the situation as it presented itself in the West now required new thinking and tactics. This was a prospect that Trotsky could never have entertained,[80] as Serge must have sadly realised, and it was not to be.

Trotsky's death in 1940 at the hands of Stalin's assassin would further deepen Serge's sense of isolation from Trotsky's movement, which was to remain with him during his own final exile – spent, paradoxically, in the same Mexico City where Trotsky had met his end. During those years Serge was to see the emergence from war of a Europe shaped by Stalin's cold calculations, which led him 30 years after the revolution and only weeks before his own death in November 1947, to pose the problem thus:

> What, after its ten exultant first years and its ten black years following, is left to defend in the Russian Revolution? An immensely important historical experience, the proudest memories, examples beyond value; these would already be a lot. But the doctrine and tactics of Bolshevism require a critical analysis. There have been so many changes in this

chaotic world that not a single Marxist – Socialist, for that matter – concept could be applied today without being updated first. I don't think that in a system of production where the laboratory is taking precedence over the workshop, the hegemony of the proletariat can assert itself, unless in moral and political ways which in fact imply a renunciation of hegemony. I do not think that the 'dictatorship of the proletariat' will reappear and be viable in the struggles of the future. No doubt there will be revolutionary dictatorships of one kind or another in the future; I am convinced that the role of the workers' movements in these cases will be to guarantee the democratic character of these regimes – not just for the sake of the proletariat alone, but for the sake of all workers and even nations. In this sense, proletarian revolution is no longer to be our aim; the revolution which we are waiting to serve can only be *Socialist* – in the humanising sense of the word – and, more precisely, *socialising*, through democratic, libertarian means. Beyond the borders of Russia, the Bolshevik idea of the party has failed completely.[81]

THE CORRESPONDENCE

Prefatory letter: Serge to Sedov (in French)[82]

Brussels, April 21, 1936

Dear Comrade Lev Lvovich,

I've been here in Brussels for four days – actually expelled from the USSR, getting here on a direct line from the Orenburg deportation where I left behind some of our friends. Friend Mikh.[ailovich] Eltsin[83] and several comrades less well known made me responsible for sending their most affectionate and loyal fraternal greetings to Lev Davidovich, and also various messages. I also have some infinitely painful news: the death of Solntsev[84] (in hospital at Novosibirsk, in January, as a result of a hunger-strike). About all this, about all that I've lived through, seen and learned in these last years of depressing struggle, I have so much to tell Lev Davidovich. How can I get in touch with him without my letters being intercepted by some intelligence service?

Write to me at *Poste Restante, Central Post Office, Brussels*, using my name (a pseudonym anyway). Again an important question, with a practical warning. 1. Do you know who (Senin) Sobolevicius[85] was and what became of him? 2. I've acquired the conviction that *agents provo-*

cateurs have penetrated the circles of the Communist Opposition in the West very deeply, even in Lev Davidovich's immediate circle in 1932–33, and I think it likely that this situation (with its danger) still continues.

Please as a matter of urgency send Lev Davidovich my most heartfelt greetings. Tell him at once that in the depth of all the prisons and all the far foul places of deportation in the 'sixth of the world', men whom they will not break by physical means are thinking of him all the time as the surest of revolutionaries, are watching, waiting, interpreting avidly every word from him. I must add that for some years now almost nothing has reached us.

I personally am very happy to make contact with you. I shake your hand fraternally.

Victor Serge

PSs. Do you know anything about a Frenchified Russian named [———][86] whose real name is [———]? Isn't he somewhere abroad?

I'd like a word of clarification too about [———]. These questions are to help me clear up some questions about provocateurs. I think that provoc.[ation] is the worst danger we face. It is that, anyway, which makes any Oppos.[itional] activity impossible in the USSR.

Letter 1: Serge to Trotsky (in French)

Brussels, April 22, 1936

Dear comrade,

I have just written to Lev Lvovich in Paris asking him to send you a few words. I have been in Brussels four days – expelled with my family from the USSR. *I have a mass of information to get to you.* But first a fraternal salute, the warmest, truest and sincerest possible, from a handful of deported and imprisoned comrades who are heroes and whose entire thought is still tender towards you – you of whom for years we have known almost *nothing*.

Can I write to you freely, or almost freely, at Vexhall?[87]

Shortly before my departure from Orenburg (I left there on April 12) we became extremely anxious about your health. I've not read anything by you for years, but our friends in Paris are going to send me recent publications.

I'm a bit exhausted physically, not at all exhausted, I think, in morale. Solntsev died in January at Novosibirsk as the outcome of a hunger-strike. Lado Dumbadze[88] has been deported to Sarapul, he is in grave danger, everything possible must be done to save him. *Boris Mikhailovich E.[ltsin] was with me at O.[renburg]. His son Victor*[89] *is at Archangel*. Both of them send greetings to you with all their hearts.

My thoughts too have turned to you constantly from the abyss of these black years. And I shake your hand, in all firmness and in fidelity to the strangled revolution.

Victor Serge

Address: Poste Restante, Central Post Office, Brussels,
V. Kibalchich or c/o Charles Plisnier,[90] 18 Pl.
Louis Morihan, Brussels.

Letter 2: Trotsky to Serge (in Russian)

April 24, 1936

Dear Victor Lvovich,

I've just received your letter (I sent you a telegram). I can't tell you how happy NI[91] and I were to get it, and to learn that you're abroad at last, that you're in good spirits and have kept your feelings of friendship for us.

I was deeply affected by the news of Solntsev's death. I have a vivid recollection of him and always recall him with great affection. My closest associates have one after another died a tragic death – Glazman, Butov, Blyumkin[92] and now Solntsev...

Do you know what would be the ideal thing to happen for us just now? It would be for you to come and spend some time with us here, so that we can talk about everything fully, freely and *to our hearts' content*. I *very much* hope that this is just the beginning of our contact with you. If you can't come and visit us here immediately, let's hope it can be later. It would bring us enormous pleasure.

At the very least we look forward to your letters, let them be as detailed as possible: on our side, we promise to be indefatigable letter-writers to you.

Could you write a few words on Solntsev for the next issue of our Russian *Bulletin*,[93] and a summary of the essential facts, about yourself and the general situation, that need to be told? I understand that it isn't easy to write so soon after your arrival, but I mean no more than a *brief informative piece*.

How have you settled down in Brussels? What are your personal plans? Any chance of paid literary work in the *near* future? I'm sure that you will produce a book on the USSR which will sell throughout the world.

I'm now finishing a theoretical-political book on the USSR[94] (200 printed sheets.)[95] I'd be very glad to have your opinion on it. But can you be bothered with it now? But if you're agreeable to reading it, I'll send you the manuscript at once.

Have you met the Belgian comrades yet? What are your impressions of them? I want you to pay particular attention to Lesoil,[96] he is a very serious and reliable comrade. I don't know Dauge[97] personally, he has moved closer to us over the last year. Do you ever see Godefroid,[98] the youth movement's secretary? I don't know him personally but I don't trust him. I'd be very glad to have your opinion of him.

But, above everything else, write to us about yourself and your family, particularly and especially about your material situation. It's so good that you are out and abroad!

I hear that you're in touch with Ch[arles] Plisnier. He sent me a poem of his, *unexpectedly* dedicated to me (contemporary 'left-wing' poets usually dedicate their productions to *Gosizdat*[99] and its masters). I did write a few words back to Plisnier, but perhaps not very tactfully. They might have seemed unduly magisterial to him (I certainly didn't intend that impression). It does worry me now; if I'm wrong to worry, please reassure me when you get the chance.

Do you know anything about our son Seryozha?[100] Well, I'm sure that you'll be writing everything that you do know.

I do hope that over a period you'll be able to get to know the publications of the Fourth International and that we'll be able to have an exchange of views on such matters. *A great deal* can be done in Belgium today, if only Dauge and his group would follow Lesoil and not Godefroid.

You can write to me with complete 'frankness' at the address you have, to the extent that one can anyway entrust one's 'secrets' to the post.

Warmest greetings to you and your family from N Iv.

a fraternal embrace,
yours, Leon Trotsky

Letter 3: Trotsky to Serge (telegram, in French)

Kibalchich. Poste Restante Central Post Office Brussels
Fraternal greetings
Letter follows – Leon
25/4/36

Letter 4: Serge to Trotsky (in French; published in part in the Russian-Language *Bulletin of the Opposition* [Paris], no. 50, May 1936)

Brussels, April 25, 1936

Dear Comrade Lev Davidovich,

I have already written to you on my arrival in Brussels. I feel that not an hour or day must be lost in acting on the information I have. Here then:

1. Our comrade Solntsev, imprisoned in 1929 after his return from America, first served three years in prison, then an extra two years. He was released at the beginning of 1935 and deported to the frontier of Siberia – I don't know precisely where but I was in contact with him indirectly – to a village where it was impossible for him to find work so that as a result he suffered material poverty. At the end of 1935 he was again arrested, without any conceivable legal excuse, and soon afterwards sentenced to 3 or 5 years' imprisonment. He refused to serve this sentence, undertaking a hunger-strike of about twenty days to defend his 'liberty' as a deportee. He succeeded in this demand; and the NKVD agreed to send him to Minusinsk where his wife and son awaited him, both deported. It was a harsh journey, travelling by stages with people condemned to various sentences. On it he fell ill, had an emergency operation in the hospital at Novosibirsk and died there last January (1936).

2. All the Trotskyist deportees in the Tara area, ten or so comrades including Gerstein, were arrested in January–February. This means that a case is being mounted against them which can end only with their being sent for many years to concentration camps.

3. Lado Dumbadze must be rescued. Wounded in the civil war, with serious injuries dating from another period, he is paralysed in both arms. After a prison sentence, he was sent over '34–'35 from Suzdal[101] to Butirky,[102] from Butirky again to deportation again at Suzdal, in other words transferred from prison to prison and town to town, without obtaining any real medical care and getting iller and iller. In the end he was deported to Sarapul where he is alone and an invalid, living on a monthly allowance of 30 roubles. It is virtually impossible for him to dress or undress himself; there is no one to help him, letters to him are obstructed, and he himself can hardly manage to write a short letter, it takes hours of painful toil. – I have read one of his letters, a tragic document; but if we cannot get medical care for him or other improve-

ments in his existence, Lado Dumbadze is doomed, his heroism will enable him only to die well.

I think we must conduct wide publicity over the suffering and death of Solntsev, and Dumbadze's suffering, resistance and danger. My sources of information are completely reliable and for my part I shall do everything possible.

I am waiting for some sign from you before I can write more fully. The friends to whom I owe my rescue have asked me not to make any public demonstration at present, so that I don't get deprived of permission to reside in France or Belgium.[103] It has been extremely difficult for them to obtain asylum for me. I'm still not very clear about my situation here.

I have read Tarov[104] and Ciliga:[105] on the whole they understate what is happening. The reality is even worse.

Victor Serge

Letter 5: Trotsky to Serge (in Russian)

April 29, 1936

Dear Victor Lvovich,

I'm rather sorry I put 'letter follows' in my telegram, since that might have made you wait for a letter from me and postpone writing a letter of your own. Do I have to tell you that we are waiting with burning impatience to hear from you?

I'm writing now to give you information and my own impressions of some of our common acquaintances and old comrades. I'm referring to Souvarine[106] and the Paz couple[107] first of all.

When I arrived in Turkey I did everything I could to reach an understanding with Souvarine, whom I always valued as an experienced political worker and journalist, though never over-appreciated him as a *revolutionary*. The letters between him and me soon revealed that we had nothing in common. Souvarine has a purely analytic mind, ie, formally analytic and negative. When people of this mental disposition join a serious creative group and are loyal to the line of a great tradition, they can be of considerable service to the movement. But Souvarine's character does not permit him to belong to any group. At the same time he is utterly incapable of developing an independent political line of his own. In his search to establish an independent political line passing directly from Marx to himself and by-passing Lenin and Bolshevism on the way, he made an unwitting discovery of – Menshevism. His book on Stalin, which I've only looked through, is valuable for its scrupulous selection of factual matter, but theoretically and politically, I'm sorry to say, it is barren.[108]

As far as my information goes, Souvarine attaches considerable importance to the fate of the Mensheviks in the USSR: he challenges us on whether we are bound to defend them or not. He often made bristling attacks on us because we never made any commitment on this question. At the present time there is no real significance in the issue of repressions against the Mensheviks, not even for the bureaucracy itself: the overwhelming majority of the Mensheviks have accommodated themselves perfectly well with the Stalin regime and assist it to persecute our comrades. All the information that we have confirms that they have recruited no new forces. The only issue remaining is that of a dozen or more 'scapegoats', whom Stalin needs in order to prove that he doesn't just persecute Bolsheviks.

Politically, the question of the Mensheviks can be posed correctly only on the international scale. In all parts of the world, the Social Democrats are allying with the Stalinists, and this alliance is being sealed by ruthless persecutions against us internationalists, partisans of the Fourth International. The preparation for a *Union Sacrée*[109] in the event of an imminent war is beginning with the 'union sacrée' between the Second and the Third Internationals against the real revolutionary vanguard. At the present time you can see this in operation over the world, the Mensheviks are expelling our people from the party[110] and, where possible, from the trade unions, so as to be able to finger them to the imperialist police tomorrow, at the moment of the war-mobilisation. There can be no doubt that in every country the GPU is drawing up lists of the names of internationalists, and is quite willing to share its information with the police of 'friendly governments'. As an individual, Dan[111] is of little interest to us. But he belongs to the same international mafia as Vandervelde,[112] Léon Blum[113] etc. Politically speaking the problem for us is not how to defend a dozen Menshevik 'scapegoats' whose sufferings serve no purpose except to bolster Stalin's prestige, but rather *how to defend ourselves against the treacherous blows of international Menshevism and international Stalinism*, while waging a merciless campaign of denunciation against them. This is the only significant question, and Souvarine is totally blind to it. That's why he's so ready to distribute his demands for justice impartially between the Mensheviks and us. Such being his position, there is not and can't be anything in common between our politics and his.

I must tell you in passing that Ciliga, the Yugoslav Oppositionist, who started with an ultra-left position, has also strayed on to the path of being the Mensheviks' friend. His line of reasoning is, more or less: the USSR is not a workers' state but a capitalist-Bonapartist one; for the USSR, democracy would signify progress; the Mensheviks are for democracy; therefore, the Mensheviks are our allies. It is useless to try to disentangle this bundle of misconceptions, if only because (as I said above), we cannot define a policy towards the Mensheviks on the basis of 'a single country'.

The task of the proletarian vanguard in the USSR is not the practising of philanthropy towards the Mensheviks but the preparation of the revolutionary overthrow of the Bonapartist bureaucracy. People may ask what would be the policy of the Fourth International's party towards the Mensheviks if it took power. We can make no commitment whatever on this question. It will all depend on the international situation, the alignment of forces, the policies of the Mensheviks themselves, and so forth. If Dan's allies in the Second International imprison and kill the new Liebknecht,[114] then of course we shall not exactly pat the Mensheviks on the back. But all this is music of the future.

There is no need to dwell on the Pazes. Magdeleine P. campaigned for your release: it is the sole praiseworthy action of her whole life. As for him, one can't even say as much to his credit. He is a conservative bourgeois, hard-hearted, narrow and utterly repellent. He joined the Left Opposition at a certain time only because it gave him a halo absolutely without cost (a decisive factor for him) and without committing him to anything. Since my own attitude to the Bolshevik-Leninist movement is a little different from this, Paz could only continue to be a Platonic follower of my ideas so long as I hadn't myself arrived outside the USSR. The split was inevitable, and I reproach myself only for having been too patient and for wasting time corresponding with both the Pazes.

You've probably heard about my conflict with Rosmer[115] too. It's now old history and not worth telling you about in detail. At any rate, Rosmer is a figure of an entirely different calibre. There just was a time when we disagreed on one particular matter,[116] and he despite his normal tact and reticence flared up and refused not only to work out an agreement with us but even to talk things over. That was why we didn't see each other during our time in France. But we still keep all our esteem and warm feelings for both Alfred and Marguerite,[117] and I think it is the same with them. Rosmer has written an excellent book on the working-class movement during the war.[118] He is one of those that one can count on absolutely in any time of new ordeals. I have no doubt at all that our personal relations will be resumed and become stronger than ever.

And now something else. I feel that you arrived in Belgium at a particularly favourable moment to form a judgement on the sort of activity we've carried out there, our methods of approach and our internal differences. Just now Belgium is an extraordinarily valuable testing-ground. Lesoil, Vereeken[119] and Dauge represent three different currents in our *international* movement. Spaak,[120] who is now a government minister, who came to see me in Paris for a 'consultation' (a few months before he sold out), told me that he found Lesoil and Vereeken to be the two best workers in Belgium. I hope you've already met them, as well as Dauge, and will let me have all your observations and impressions.

My main fear, as far as things in Belgium are concerned, is the conciliatory, wait-and-see attitude towards Godefroid of Dauge and some of the others. Godefroid poses as the friend of the expelled members, but may well change sides at the last minute and help Vandervelde to isolate us from our public. This is just the role played so shamefully in France by Marceau Pivert,[121] not without assistance from our own comrades.

Enough for now. Warmest regards from N Iv. and me to you and your family.

A comradely handshake,
yours, LT

PS. Have you any news of Alexandra Lvovna?[122] Or of Maria Lvovna[123] and the children?

I have the opportunity now to issue through the biggest American press agency[124] any communiqué I like on the USSR (in an appropriate tone of course). Maybe you could draft a statement on the political prisoners and deportees? It could be drafted as a letter from you to me. But there is still the question of using your name. I don't think you can remain 'in the shade'. It would take away 9/10ths of the value of your exposures, and the French and the Belgian Stalinists will reveal your identity anyway. I think it would be better to work openly. But I may not be properly aware of what your position is or of all your various plans.

Letter 6: Serge to Trotsky (in Russian)

April 29, 1936

Dear Lev Davidovich,

Your letter of April 26[125] gave me incredible pleasure. The thing is that very alarming rumours about you have been spread recently among the deportees. Our thoughts turned constantly to you. (By the way, at the time of Rakovsky's capitulation, the NKVD officers in private 'chats' with followers of the 'general line' put out the rumour that LD [Trotsky] had applied or was going to apply for permission to return to the USSR on certain conditions... They had no success whatsoever.) I venture to write to you in Russian, please forgive the clumsiness of my syntax and my mistakes – I shall normally write in French. I am going to give you in a series of letters a complete briefing on everything I know, including every characteristic detail. Today's reply is '*en style télégraphique*'.

I spent three months in the inner prison in Moscow with no definite charges brought against me. My books were brought up as evidence against me and I was supposed to confess that I had carried on some sort of clandestine work in the USSR under your directions. Rutkovsky conducted the investigations, a number of my friends were arrested simultaneously. I'll write about all this in greater detail later. They made an attempt to base the charge against me on a *false* testimony of my wife's sister Anita Russakova.[126] (This was in 1933: at present this poor, completely apolitical and defenceless girl, arrested again in 1935, has a sentence of five years' deportation to Vyatka – actually I believe in order to hide the disgusting concoction of my case, formally for – 'technical aid to the Trotskyites'). During the investigation I became convinced that there were definitely some provocateurs in the International Secretariat[127] and somewhere in the French *Ligue Communiste* and that a certain Sobolevicius (Senin?) who had visited you in Constantinople and in 1932 brought me greetings from Lev Lvovich was either a provocateur or else, when he was arrested, behaved worse than a provocateur.

In the three years of my Orenburg deportation I met a number of remarkable comrades, who at various times gave me messages and errands to send to you but above all sent their most heartfelt greetings to you. I'll be writing to you in detail about all of them. For the moment I give you their names:[128] Vass[ily] Fed[orovich] *Pankratov* (in the isolator now at Verkhne-Uralsk); Khanaan Markovich *Pevsner*, arrested in connection with the 'Wrangel officer affair'[129] of 1928, now in the Chelyabinsk isolator; Vas[ily] Mikh[ailovich] *Chernykh*; Bor[is] Mikh.[ailovich] *Eltsin*; Lisa *Svalova*; Yakov *Belenky*; Faina Abr[amovna] *Upstein*; Yakov *Byk* (still in Orenburg); Boris Ilyich *Lyakhovitsky*; and Al[exei] Sem[yonovich] *Santalov* (now in a concentration camp). All these comrades are dedicated, firm, convinced Communist – Oppositionists and some of them are professional party activists of exceptional calibre. I managed to exchange a few letters with Grig[ori] Yakovl[evich] Yakovin[130] before he was arrested. He seems to be in Suzdal now.

I have, because of other pressures, got to postpone sending you their messages for a couple of days. My financial situation is quite good, ie I can carry on for some time and work on my book. I have my mentally disturbed and utterly exhausted wife[131] with me and our two children. My son Volodya,[132] who is fifteen and draws rather well, is now making a copy of his portrait of Boris Mikhailovich Eltsin, which he proposes to send to you.

I have in fact been deported from the USSR but in a hypocritical manner: I've been given a passport valid for three months, without the right to travel back to the USSR! I was not allowed to stay overnight in Moscow. Both in Moscow and at the frontier they took away all my personal papers: completed manuscripts, photographs, etc. – 'for censorship'. I don't know if I can get all this valuable material back. I don't know yet if I can visit you with this passport or whether I'd be able to afford such a trip in the near future. Here I am required to abstain completely from all political activity and I haven't yet found out what the actual limitations on my 'freedom' are. All these matters are to be sorted out in the next few days.

I've already written to you, as an urgent priority, about Dumbadze. I saw an absolutely tragic letter from him, with the words spelled out in a child's printed letters. Dumbadze describes his hopeless situation at Sarapul, where he is lonely and with nobody to help him even to get dressed or undressed. 'I spent four hours working on this letter,' he wrote.

The comrades asked me to pass on a number of questions to you. I was slightly afraid that we in deportation, cut off from the comrades who can breathe freely, might accumulate considerable disagreements with them. But, after I read your article in the *Bulletin* no. 42 of January 30, 1935, I think that this isn't so. I'll come back to all these topics in more detail later. This is only a hastily jotted letter.

I remember how joyfully the comrades who remained under the GPU's heel saw me off when I left Orenburg. The mere thought that someone was going to give their fraternal greetings to you meant so much to them. Deportation and prison have already steeled remarkably dedicated and staunch revolutionaries, who face their systematic suffocation with extraordinary fortitude. All the comrades I've mentioned are like that.

A warm handshake from us to you and N Iv.

Victor Serge

Letter 7: Serge to Trotsky (in Russian)

rue Joseph Bens, 134
Uccle, Brussels.
May 6, 1936

Dear Lev Davidovich,

Have received your letter of April 29. I wrote to you on April 22 and 26[133] and a longer letter on the 29th.

It surprises me and worries me that your telegram *hasn't arrived, nor has the first, extremely serious letter from Lev Lvovich*...(I've already received a copy of the letter). Frankly, I think somebody is taking an active and imprudent interest in me.

I am surfacing from chaos: I have a room and can breathe. Tomorrow I'll begin sending you information regularly and working in general. Up to now it was impossible. (You probably know I have an eighteen-month-old daughter and a mentally unbalanced wife).

I basically agree with your characterisation of Souvarine. I would like to add though that he is an excellent *pamphleteer*, dominated sometimes by the power of his own words. As to the Mensheviks, I think you are quite right from the angle you discuss, but the question can be posed on a different plane as well. I'll write you a special letter about this and all the other uncertainties between us.

My situation is complicated by the fact that Belgium gave me asylum only on the condition of my political neutrality, or (more precisely) of my non-interference in Belgian politics – which doesn't worry me at all – and of my 'abstention from aggressive activities which could cause international difficulties for Belgium...'(*sic*!!). Yesterday I had a very civil but rather unpleasant discussion on the subject with a senior official. They seem to be seriously afraid of objections from the Stalinists. Yet, as a writer I am completely free in what I say in my books, and won't allow myself to be bound hand and foot. I haven't decided yet whether it would be possible, under these conditions, for me to publish a series of articles under my own signature. Maybe the forthcoming elections will result in a more favourable atmosphere for me. Otherwise, you can make references to me, and so on, but I won't be able to put my name to the most basic statements without risking immediate deportation – where to?

I saw Alexandra Lvovna shortly before my arrest in 1933, in Leningrad. Maria Lvovna was there too, I know nothing about her but would be very surprised indeed if she was still free – it's virtually impossible.

Alexandra Lvovna has been deported to the northern region of west Siberia 'near' Tobolsk (I'm not sure, perhaps 'near' Tomsk), she's living in terrible conditions. I know this for certain from comrades who've been there. Forgive me for writing so cursorily and hastily.

Warm handshake and my cordial greetings to NI.

My son is working on the portrait of Boris Mikh[ailovich] Eltsin for you.

VLK

Letter 8: Trotsky to Serge (in Russian)

May 8, 1936

Dear Victor Lvovich,

I've received two letters from you, the last one being of May 6th. Write in Russian or French, whichever suits you. Your Russian is irreproachable.

The first question: do money and parcels *from abroad get to the deportees*? I've sent them several times but never had any replies. Do you know anything about it? It is one of our most important propaganda points: the deportees are refused work and at the same time aren't allowed to receive money from other sources. We must win the right to send them money.

Now about your 'political' visa status. Of course one shouldn't interfere at all in internal political matters or cause any distress to 'friendly governments'. We signed a similar undertaking when we were given Norwegian visas. All this means is that one shouldn't commit any illegal acts, take part in 'conspiracies', or prepare 'acts of terrorism', etc. Any other interpretation of it is senseless. I don't intervene in Norwegian political life at all, but I openly contribute to publications which appear legally in other countries. I think you should act openly and so, by direct action secure, the same status for yourself. It might be possible for you to move to France. On the other hand, anything could happen to you there. It would be better to be active in France while living in Belgium. That's my first impression.

Elections are going to be held here in October. The Norwegian Labour Party hopes to win an absolute majority. It's not out of the question that you could move here. But only as a last resort, since Belgium has such enormous advantages for you: the language, a city, cheap living.

Maria Lvovna was at Kirov, Odessa region, with her children. If she's been deported, which is certainly so, what has happened to the children?

They were probably put in an institution, if not thrown on to the street to become waifs. No family would dare offer them shelter.

Maybe, when you feel able to write, you could draft something very short for our press about Alexandra Lvovna. Better coming from you than from me. I've said in my autobiography everything that matters about my relationship with her (if you need to use it).

You know that Stalin and his GPU villains have tried several times to link the Opposition with 'terrorist' acts. These efforts of theirs still go on. They'll be directed against you once you come out in public.[134] That's why it's so important to expose this line of GPU activity in advance through an article or interview. We've got to take the rug from under the feet of these practitioners of the amalgam.[135]

Once more let me say: you should face out the authorities with a *fait accompli*. Since the Socialists are in the government now, you won't get deported. Anyway, where could they send you? You're not planning to do anything illegal after all. The Belgian Constitution does not compel anybody to praise Stalin, especially where the foreign press is concerned.

What do the doctors say about your wife's condition? Any hopes of recovery? What can be done for her? Write and tell us all about it, maybe there is some help we can get. We have some doctors among our friends, and money could be raised. *Write in as much detail as you can!*

A few years back, we were 'rich' (*History of the Russian Revolution!*). Now we are going through a severe crisis. But I hope that in a month or two our situation will get better. In any case we do have friends whom we can call upon. So write to us in complete frankness.

Have any of your books been published in America? Only America pays any money for literary work. But to start with, you should create a *boom* [written in English] around your name! What about doing an interview for the American press? Once your new book on the USSR is out, I believe that it might be possible to promote your previous books in America as well.

I have an idea! At present I'm working on a long introduction to the second (cheap) edition of my *History of the Russian Revolution*. This introduction is a description of the USSR, about 200 printed sheets. *I must bring in a couple, or more, of quotations from you in this introduction*, even if only from personal letters (on the bureaucracy, contradictions between the bureaucracy and the people, the violent suppression of the Opposition, etc.). I could directly state that you are preparing a book. Think it over and send me something suitable as soon as you can. *This is of great importance practically* as my publisher is offering large publicity for the book.

I would be very grateful to your son if he sends me the portrait of Boris Mikh[hailovich]. Could you send us a photo of yourself? One for us and another for our press.

A warm handshake. Salut.
Yours, LT

PS. We'll make another enquiry about the non-arrival of the telegram. There was nothing controversial in it, just '*Salut fraternal. Lettre suit*'.

Letter 9: Serge to Trotsky (in Russian)

May 15, 1936

Dear Lev Davidovich,

I'm not answering your letter of May 9[136] now through lack of time and strength. I've already written a good fifteen pages today. Thank you for your concern. I'm sending you an extremely disordered account of our small Orenburg group[137] and a few items about other people. I apologise for the clumsiness and haste of this information, but I can see that postponing it from one day to another in order to do it better tomorrow is no good either. My next letter will deal with current attitudes, controversial questions and the repression in general.

I found out yesterday in Antwerp how one can send parcels and money to the USSR. Its a grim picture. Parcels are very expensive, money is sent through black-marketeers, also at great expense and with no guarantee of delivery. I used to receive something regularly myself, through the foreign-currency shop which no longer exists. *But I never heard of anyone else to whom anything got through...* It needs further thought and something should be worked out – it is imperative to organise aid. I've now remembered that Ida Shumskya[138] is very hard up and worn out. I read a very sad letter from her.

Use anything of mine you like for the *Bulletin* or for other purposes. The only thing is that I don't yet feel it is possible to *sign* – just my anxiety over being deported from here. But I do agree with you that I have to win the right to speak out and I think I'm going to win it.

My wife is slightly better but the picture is still gloomy... I'm expecting Alfred[139] to arrive any day now.

My heartfelt greetings to N Iv.

A comradely handshake,
VLK

Letter 10: Trotsky to Serge (in Russian)

May 19, 1936

Dear Victor Lvovich,

I am waiting for your reply to my last, hand-written letter, in which I made some practical propositions. Of course, *you shouldn't in any way feel bound by these proposals*. If, for whatever reason, you find them inconvenient, do write back and say so with complete frankness. From here I can't properly appreciate your circumstances, and still less your personal and political frame of mind.

It's politics now that I want to take up again. In *L'Action socialiste révolutionnaire*[140] of May 16, I found a reproduction of your letter of April 21 to *La Révolution prolétarienne*.[141] I won't conceal from you that this upset me. Not so much because you turned to a syndicalist group but because you turned *only* to them. If that means that politically you feel closer to syndicalism than to Marxism, then there is nothing left for me except to register the profound difference between us. Nevertheless I like to hope that this is not so, and to explain your writing to them by the fact that, on the information that you've had, it is this group that carried out the main campaign for your release.

I am afraid that, on this point too, you have a rather inaccurate view of the true dynamics of the struggle as it has been conducted over recent years. The *RP* group, Paz and the rest played the role of *liberals* who in favourable circumstances are good for a speech or an article, or for getting a petition going through influential persons. Magdeleine Paz did the same for me as well to try to get me a visa for England. That is her natural role. The people from *RP* never rose an inch above that role. But take our own comrades – they penetrated into the public meetings of the Stalinists, distributed appeals, raised 'scandals' during the most solemn sessions, were frequently beaten up, and in short caused a great deal of embarrassment for the Stalinists and their friends like Barbusse,[142] Romain Rolland,[143] *et al.* Only a few days ago, during Bukharin's visit to Paris,[144] a group of Bolshevik-Leninists broke in while he was addressing an audience and scattered an appeal in defence of those imprisoned in the USSR. They were, of course, thrown out of the hall. It is solely through that type of revolutionary action that liberals have been able to reap a certain degree of success; reforms (such as your release) always come as a by-product of revolutionary action struggle.

Ciliga, who is straining to unite all and sundry for the defence of those imprisoned in the USSR – and whom, of course, we don't oppose on this point, though we don't share his illusions – also turned to the *RP* for help. They promised him that their representatives would make a special speech on this issue at a trade-union congress. Ciliga wrote a rapturous letter to me. The rapture turned out to be premature: no such speech got made. The *RP* group is now on the cosiest terms with the reformist faction of the trade-union bureaucracy, which is in alliance with the Stalinist regime. To slip an article into a little magazine is one thing, to speak out in the middle of a hostile meeting is quite another matter. The *RP* group is a completely conservative, non-militant sect which has no political significance whatever. They have their own circle of gradually disappearing readers, for whom they publish their little review. The spirit of revolution flew away from them long ago.

I can fully understand that, having arrived abroad, after years of incredibly harsh sufferings, you're not rushing to define your position and you don't want to give anybody the right to 'pigeonhole' you according to your former connections or on any other grounds. The situation in the working-class movement is extremely complicated at present, and it can't be easy to get your bearings. *My letters have no other purpose but to improve the information you are getting.* I'm ready to wait very patiently for the time when you'll be able to determine your own position vis-a-vis the different political groupings.

PS. May 20, 1936: As I finished this first page, I received your long letter with its description of the Orenburg deportation. Many thanks for this work of yours. I have already extracted from it everything that can be published, almost the whole piece in fact, but with a few deletions. The text has been reproduced in several copies and is being sent to different countries (without your name on it, of course, so as to spare you any trouble with the police).

As far as the American press agency is concerned, I shall write a statement for them myself, based on your material, and send it off at once, again without naming you. From London the despatch will be cabled to hundreds, if not thousands of American newspapers. There are no restrictions on the length of the message. I'll let you have a copy of the cable when I get the chance.

I beg you sincerely again not to take the first part of my letter as some sort of grudge or 'reproach'. I only want to remove any conventionality from the very start. Even if we are divided by some serious disagreements (which I trust is not so), the best way to overcome these is by absolute *franchise* – to spell out that French word in Russian letters.

Comradely handshake. Greetings from both of us to your family. I'd be very glad to know how you found Alfred.

yours,
LT

Letter 11: Serge to Trotsky (in Russian)

May 23, 1936

Dear Lev Davidovich,

I have your letter of May 21,[145] and though I have to dash off now I want to send you few lines immediately. I'm going to write more tomorrow. I'm sorry to say that I haven't settled to a normal routine of working life yet, and the sharp changes in my wife's condition interfere not only with my working but with living.

On sundry matters:

1. When I got to Belgium I began to resume contacts, first of all along the lines of old personal friendships. I wrote a number of letters, of which one was to *Révolution prolétarienne*, where Jacques Mesnil[146] works, the person I feel closest to. I am not a syndicalist, I think there can be no misunderstanding on this question. But I believe that the revolutionary-syndicalists are our natural allies on many occasions and that amicable, non-sectarian relations with them are the obvious course. Naturally, that does not exclude complete freedom of criticism and so on.

My contacts with the comrades of *La Verité*[147] in Paris were established later. I must add a very unfortunate feature of this liaison. Our comrades, from *La Verité* for example, did not manage to maintain contact with me, whereas others did manage. This is a matter of people's ability to work, their efficiency and various other factors. Many times in Russia I went along with various attempts to establish contact with comrades, and these efforts always ended in failures, betrayals and provocations. That is how it was with Marenko, with NI Karpov, Preobrazhensky, Sobolevicius and others;[148] while the contacts which I based not on formal organisational links but on personal ones, on friendships, even those with considerable disagreements, held up remarkably well and were fruitful in every regard. I'm not going to deduce a theory from this experience, I just want to explain to you that, despite the clear positions I hold politically, I don't have and at present can't have a narrow organisational approach to contacts.

I wanted to come out as a writer publicly not with the letter to *RP*, whose publication did not seem all that significant to me, but with two other letters, to Magd[eleine] Paz and to André Gide[149] – that is, to the literati, the people of literary interests. In both these letters I speak with unfailing clarity about *my* comrades in Russia, and in that way define my own position.

I don't want to *anticipate* my later letters (which are absolutely necessary) but may I say that on the Russian question I take your formulations to be fundamentally precise and correct. I don't yet dare to make any definitive judgement on questions of international policy. Yesterday I had a talk with Rosmer on this subject. (He'll be here for another couple of days.)

I have only one thing to add, dear Leon Davidovich: I am glad to read *all* your letters. I don't and can't have any susceptibility. If, on any occasion, you need to come down heavy on me, as they say it *there*, do so by all means. I promise absolute *franchise* [this is in French in the original] on my part – that should go without saying.

2. As I was moving into my flat here, some people who have rented a flat at the same time as I were moving into theirs on the first floor. It now turns out that somebody is keeping watch on us quite undisguisedly from the windows of that flat. It is not the Belgian police of course – they couldn't care less – but the doing of the GPU. Let them carry on, but we'll take the fact into consideration. Do you know that your telegram and an important letter from Lev Lvovich never reached me?

Till tomorrow then. Warm greetings to N Iv.

A comradely handshake.
VS

Letter 12: Serge to Trotsky (in French)

Brussels, May 27, 1934[150]

Dear Leon Davidovich,

I have just reread your recent letters so that I can answer them all better. The conditions of my work are still pretty bad because of the state of my wife, who is acutely ill one day in two, or two in three, which stops me from organising our existence. I have to do everything myself. After her general improvement, which nonetheless is on its way, I hope things turn out better in the long run. The psychiatrists have diagnosed schizophrenia but I tend to believe it's less serious than that. The only treatment is a quiet life. I think we'll manage to have that.

It seems to me that I am going to find it quite difficult to earn a livelihood. I can keep going for a while, perhaps even for some months, by practising the strictest economy. Since I've been looking for literary jobs (translations etc.) Lev Lvovich has suggested to me that I translate some of your writings. Even apart from my need to find jobs like this,

I'd be very happy to collaborate with you in this technical way, have no doubt about that. But I must make one objection: I don't want to take work away from comrades like Parijanine.[151] I've written to Lev Lvovich saying so.

They've written to me saying that I've been given a French visa, but no official letter confirming this has reached me yet. So soon I shall be going to Paris for a short stay, eight to ten days, and I shall be seeing all our friends there. Alfred passed through here, we had a long talk about you; he was very touched by the note you wrote about his book – a great book, truly.

I've sent the two open letters to the press, one addressed to Magdeleine Paz, to whom I owe an enormous debt, the other to André Gide. Both of them deal with the part played by our comrades in the USSR and with what's happening to them. The second is a sort of message to the intellectuals who have rallied to Socialism late. At present, except for other letters of a secondary nature and form, these are going to be my only public activities. I share your opinion completely when you say that, while respecting the conditions on which asylum is granted, one must not let oneself be gagged on matters concerning Russia. In my own case I think it's a question of tact, and that a form of action less blustering and perhaps less pointed in its expression will be more useful than any other, bearing in mind above all complete frankness *in its essentials* as well as its general character. I am going to write very quickly a short book which will, most likely, be called *Defence of the USSR in 1936*.[152] I'm giving myself a month to do it. I'll be sending you the manuscript, perhaps even before it's finished, and if you can quote from it or use it in any other way, that will be a big, big help to its circulation. At the present time I shall be working on a large work, a personal account of our struggles from '27 to '36, in a literary and emotional form which will be as fully worked as I can manage.[153] Lastly, I've sent Lev Lvovich copies of some material on the repression in the USSR, to help the campaigning of the Paris comrades. When combined with the documentation from Tarov and Ciliga, my material will be a very solid resource which can be used very effectively.

About this campaigning:

I feel it must be broadly based, firm, persevering, unceasing and reaching into all quarters that can be influenced. The aim is twofold: to rescue our comrades who embody the living traditions of October, and to raise in a particular manner the issue of proletarian democracy – in the shape of freedom for Socialist opinion in the Soviet Union.[154] In that way we touch Stalinism at its most vulnerable point before the working class and the intellectuals, just where it can't at any price show itself frankly, where it has to lie and contradict itself by its actions every day; and against it we're mobilising both the intelligence and the perceptive sense of the masses. Then too, there is going to be, we can be sure, a period of some vacillation in the working out of the new Soviet Constitution.[155] If our campaign is waged energetically at this moment, it can bring serious results. – Don't believe that I have any illusions on this score. I've read your article on the proposed Constitution,[156] and find it to be one of your best recent articles. All I expect from the bureaucracy is a number of measures designed to deceive world opinion, in a thoroughly Jesuitical piece of double-dealing. But this trickery has to be unmasked, and there may be some way of changing these feeble adaptations of Stalinism to Western democracy into distinct points of its retreat. In the present state of the oppression of the Soviet proletariat, the smallest chance of breathing a little, however deviously acquired, will count for quite a lot.

To be a success, our campaigning must avoid being sectarian. It has to address itself to the whole of the working class by putting the question of freedom of opinion for all the different shadings of the Socialist approach (including the anarchists). From which follows the necessity of mentioning the Mensheviks exactly like all the others. I have no objection to what you wrote recently about Menshevism and its counter-revolutionary nature (my only reservation being that Social Democracy isn't homogeneous and that a left wing in it is bound to define itself and come over to the revolution in the end). I think we were right to reduce the Socialists of counter-revolution to a position where they could not hurt us during the civil war, but the problem today is quite a different one. When certain Soc[ial] Dem[ocrats] carried out a sabotage policy during the revolution's [period of] mortal danger and roused the backward layers of the working class; when a Black Guard of uncontrollable armed bands[157] was formed in the capital of the revolution, it was necessary to disarm both enemies. But seventeen years later, when the intervention and civil war, the party and soviets have all ceased to exist (except formally in the latter cases), there is no other question of public emergency except that of making up our minds whether we, in the midst of persecution and imprisonment, are going to deny to our cell mates the rights of speech and thought which the bureaucracy is denying to all of us. Any such attitude of denial would be indefensible, and amount to our political suicide. Alternatively, while recanting none of the traditions of October, we can and must engage in a practical rediscovery of what workers' democracy means, proving that we fear neither debate nor rivalry and that we are not in any way the kind of people who build an enormous prison for anyone who disagrees with us. I'm writing all this to you because I've been told that you oppose collaboration with all parties and groupings in this particular matter. Actually I don't know what your views are. Ciliga did send me a copy of a letter he sent to you on this topic, but I don't want to try unravelling your ideas through the medium of his.

Before letting you know my impressions of the West, dear Leon Davidovich, I must tell you again about our comrades in Russia. The comrade A. of my last letter[158] is Eltsin, and B. is Chernykh. As far as my information goes, we are very few in number at present: a few hundreds only, in the region of 500. But those five hundred comrades there will not give way, they are tempered characters who have learnt to think and feel for themselves and who accept calmly the prospect of a persecution without end. In the isolators our comrades are numbered in tens, compared with hundreds of Zinovievists, rightists and doubtful Stalinists there. Among ourselves there is no great unity of viewpoints. Boris *Mikh[hilovich] Eltsin* said, 'It's the GPU that has created any unity that we have...'. We are divided, roughly equally, into two main tendencies: those who think that everything must be reconsidered, that errors were committed from the outset of the October Revolution – and those who consider that the Bolshevism of the first years is beyond criticism. The former are inclined to take the view that on organisational questions you were right against Lenin when you were on the same side as Rosa Luxemburg.[159] In this sense, there is a 'Trotskyism' whose connections go back a long way indeed. (I personally share this opinion, with the qualification that Lenin's organisational principles did establish their validity for a particular period and particular country, one peculiarly backward). We are also divided about equally on the problems of Soviet democracy and dictatorship (the former tendency being supporters of the broadest possible workers' democracy within the dictatorship; my impression is that this grouping is by far the stronger of the two). Inside the isolator a group of proponents of state capitalism, (*goskapisty*) has detached itself; they argue that state capitalism, a state of affairs to which Hitler, Mussolini and Stalin are all evolving, is the worst enemy of the proletariat today.[160] There are not many of them but they include some of the most capable comrades.

The entry of our comrades into the Socialist parties did not provoke any sharp debates as far as I know. At Orenburg it was I who made it known to the others. The only question raised was whether our comrades would be able to keep their distinct political identity inside the Socialist parties. If this condition was met, we took the view that it was quite right to join the large mass parties.

On the Fourth International, we had practically no news to judge from. Again it was I who made known the little news that got to us. Since we had no illusions about the IIIrd I[nternational], we did not have to debate the principle of the IVth. But we did pose the question in these terms: is it *possible* at the present time to use a new revolutionary International as the rallying point for groupings which will be serious enough to give it some solidity? On that point we all had our doubts; we thought that, while the hour for *founding* a real rev. International had not yet struck, as an agitational slogan the idea would be very useful.

The unexplained defection of Rakovsky[161] and Sosnovsky[162] had no effect, practically nobody followed them. The more recent capitulations of Kasparova[163] and her son were seen as the result of physical weakening. It's becoming increasingly difficult if not impossible to hold on, that's all. At first a number of comrades interpreted Rakovsky's telegram as an initiative for a united front and rallied towards it (B. and V. Eltsin, Byk)[164] but as soon as they read R[akovsky]'s long declaration in *Pravda* they saw sense. Generally speaking, there are no authorities any more, the old are discredited and the young want to think for themselves. By the old I mean the Oppositionists' generation of '23–28, of whom only a few wonderful cadres remain, like Yakovin and Dinglestedt,[165] and who anyway are young. In the isolators and elsewhere it is the Trotskyist dissidents of 1930–33 who are mainly to be found. Only one authority is left: yours. In Russia you have an incomparable moral standing, and absolute devotion.

I am in disagreement with the *Bulletin* when it classes as Trotskyist the thousands who have been expelled from the party, imprisoned or deported under that label. After Kirov's death[166] they arrested all the ex-Oppositionist capitulators and a lot of people were picked up really at random. The bureaucratic apparatus works so indiscriminately, with its pre-established categories, that the classifications scarcely have any resemblance to reality. Viewed from close quarters, the vast majority of these so-called Trotskyists are absolutely worthless: informers, alcholics, part-philistine. We certainly have genuine reserves as big or even bigger elsewhere in the party and even outside the party.

Have I discussed Article 168 with you? All those expelled from the party after the checking of their files were promptly arrested and condemned on the basis of Article 168 (abuse of confidence), which is going to mean concentration-camp or deportation sentences for them.

About 200,000 people are being processed in this way just now: the prisons are bursting with them.

Dear Leon Davidovich, in two or three days I'll talk with you again about more general matters (the workers' attitude of mind, etc.). Here is a portrait of BM Eltsin by my son. My lad is only fifteen, the artist must be given some licence. The picture is a good likeness, except that Boris Mikhilovich is generally full of good humour, zest and sardonic wit. Vlady sketched him at a bad moment of depression and fatigue, which does him a bit of an injustice.

Are you still without any news of your son Sergei?

Our friendly greetings to N Iv. I shake your hand firmly.

Victor Serge

Letter 13: Trotsky to Serge (in Russian)

June 3, 1936

Dear Victor Lvovich,

I've got two letters from you: one in Russian of May 23 and one in French of May 27.

First, about personal matters. I read an article by the late Academician Pavlov[167] on how successful the new treatment for schizophrenia was with prolonged, chemically induced sleep. Do Belgian doctors know about it? I suppose in any case that such therapy can be carried out only in an in-patient clinic. NI and I were very pleased to hear of the general improvement in your wife's condition. We can easily imagine the extraordinary pressures of your situation.

As far as literary earnings are concerned, America offers the main hope. First of all you must publish the big book which you're drafting or getting ready to write. I'm certain that you could get it published there. I think too that you could make your way into the large-circulation American press with a series of articles on Soviet literature and Soviet arts in general. A book by Eastman on this theme[168] came out a year or two ago. Do you know it? Do you read English?

I'd be delighted if you were to be the translator of my book into French. You won't 'steal' work from anybody by doing that. And I couldn't possibly dream of a more qualified translator. I'll be waiting impatiently for your book *The Defence of the USSR in 1936*.

I'm afraid that you've been writing in Russian just for my convenience. Don't bother, write any way that suits you best. I understand your handwriting just as well in French as in Russian, without effort that is.

Now on political questions.

1. About *La Révolution prolétarienne*. You know that I've had long-standing contacts with this group since the war. I got to Constantinople with the firm intention of working with them and put a good deal of effort into establishing political and personal contact, particularly via Rosmer, who from the outset was more sceptical of the endeavour than I was. He turned out to be right. You say how necessary it is to be on friendly terms with 'revolutionary-syndicalists'. Quite right, but where are they? *La Révolution prolétarienne* is neither syndicalist nor revolutionary. It is just a small group isolated from everything that is alive. Monatte became old and withdrew.[169] Louzon[170] is a hare-brained petty bourgeois, a belated caricature of Proudhon. He has some assorted knowledge, which does more harm than good to him and his readers. Those from the grouping who do any syndicalist work crawl on all fours before Jouhaux[171] and Co. and detest our own movement. This group is dead. That is the conclusion I have come to, and not lightly, not on first impressions, but on the basis of my experience, a patient experience at that, over several years. I should add that a year ago, on my personal prompting, the French comrades tried once again to get a joint action going with *La Révolution prolétarienne* against the menace of social-chauvinism. Nothing came of it, because these people are incapable of struggle and don't want struggle, don't understand what struggle is. This doesn't exclude 'personal links', of course. But you will soon see for yourself that there is absolutely no reason to regard *La Révolution prolétarienne* as 'revolutionary-syndicalists'.

2. If I understand your letter from Paris[172] correctly, you are dissatisfied with our attitude towards Andreu Nin[173], which strikes you as 'sectarian'. You don't know, and had no way of knowing, the political and personal history of this relationship. You can easily picture how I rejoiced when Nin managed to get abroad and out of Russia. For several years I corresponded with him with great zeal and care. Some of my letters were veritable 'treatises', for after all the question at stake was a living revolution in which Nin could and should have played a leading part. I should think that my letters to Nin, over the period of two or three years when they were written, could make up a 'volume' of several hundred pages. From this alone you can see the importance I attached to Nin and to amicable relations with him. Nin in his replies affirmed agreement in the realm of possibilities but was extraordinarily evasive where practical tasks were concerned. He posed abstract questions on

the soviets, democracy and so forth, but never said a word about the general strikes which were sweeping Catalonia at the time. It goes without saying that no one is compelled to be a revolutionary. But Nin placed himself at the head of the Bolshevik-Leninist organisation in Spain, and in so doing assumed serious obligations. In fact he did his best to slide out of those obligations while at the same time, in his letters to me, throwing sand in my eyes. Believe me, my dear friend, I have a certain intuition in such matters. All that I could be accused of, as far as Nin is concerned, is that I let myself be deluded on his account for far too long. By allowing this I gave him the opportunity to wrap himself in the banner of Marxism-Leninism while cultivating passivity and confusion, qualities of which there is already enough, even without him, in the working-class movement of Spain – I mean among its leadership. If, instead of Nin, there was one serious worker-revolutionary, someone like Lesoil or Vereeken, gigantic strides could have been accomplished there during those years of revolution. Motivated by the ambiguity of his position, Nin systematically supported all those in other countries who, on any pretext at all, would pick a fight with us, and usually ended up as unadulterated renegades. How did the final rupture occur? Nin resolutely opposed the tactical entry of our comrades into the French Socialist Party. Then, after long vacillations, he declared that the French were correct and that the same should be done in Spain. But, instead of that, he joined in with Maurin's[174] provincial organisation,[175] which has absolutely no perspectives but lets him lead a quiet life. Our International Secretariat wrote him a crtical letter. Nin responded by breaking off all contact and publishing a statement to this effect in a special bulletin. If I wasn't so concerned to avoid wasting your time, I would send you the complete file of my correspondence with Nin; I kept copies of all my letters. I am quite sure that you, like various other comrades who became familiar with this correspondence, would accuse me of excessive patience and 'conciliationism', rather than of sectarianism.

3. I can easily imagine that *La Révolution prolétarienne* or the Paz couple could more readily maintain contact with you than *La Verité* has managed to do: the former have better facilities for contact, more leisure, material means and practical experience. Don't forget that we have a membership of inexperienced youth who are beset by numerous impediments. You speak of provocateurs. I don't doubt that there were some and still are some. The provocateurs have nothing, of course, to discover from the circles around Louzon or Magdeleine Paz. Instead they take considerable pains to penetrate the Bolshevik-Leninist groups who preach the general strike, build the workers' militia and

conduct a fierce anti–patriotic agitation. How can a movement like ours possibly stay free of provocateurs? I am very far from any justification of the slovenliness or inefficiency of our young comrades, with whom I am constantly at war. But no one can fail to see that many of their liabilities are the reverse side of their inestimable merits – they are *revolutionaries*, while the Louzons and the Pazes are passive, conservative philistines.

4. Let's move on to the position in Belgium. We are accused by some of being too intolerant towards Vereeken. If Lesoil's group had not entered the Belgian Socialist Party we would not have achieved the modest but definite success we have at present. Vereeken, for his part, refused point–blank to enter. Should we have capitulated to him and lost the chance of making a substantial advance? (Our success could have been much more marked if from the start we had adopted a firmer and sharper policy towards Godefroid.) In this situation, a break with Vereeken became unavoidable. But I always believed, and said and wrote so to the comrades, that at the next turning we should find Vereeken with us. Today I have hopes that we'll join forces with him[176] despite his sectarianism (again the obverse of his really valuable qualities).

5. On the subject of our defence campaign for Stalin's political prisoners: I'm sending the statement I wrote which has already been cabled through the Associated Press to the United States, where it will appear in toto or in extracts in hundreds of newspapers. Unfortunately I had to draft it in German as my English isn't good enough. As you can see, I am not afraid to resort to a bourgeois agency and press on a matter like this. What kind of 'sectarianism' is that? I am ready to say, and on the appropriate occasion will say, in the public press, that the politics of encouraging the Popular Front internationally, even preparing the fusion of the two Internationals, while at home keeping the Mensheviks in prison, is the height of infamy. Repressions against the Mensheviks are not being prompted by the necessities of the revolution but by the necessities of internal camouflage: 'After all, we're arresting not only the Bolshevik-Leninists but the Mensheviks too, we are therefore faithful to the tradition', etc. Having said this, it is hard to imagine a more stupid act than that of Ciliga, who went to the Menshevik press to publish his article. I discuss the position of Ciliga in a separate document which I enclose with this letter: from the very beginning, I may say, to judge from his letters to me, I gathered that he was no more than a Menshevik in a state of high exaltation.

6. Your observations on the deportees and your various assessments are of course immeasurably worthwhile, particularly to me. I cannot,

however, subscribe to your generally contemptuous attitude to the thousands of recently expelled Trotskyists, Zinovievists, *et al.* It is indeed very likely that philistinism is rife among them. But in the era of Thermidor, the philistine is the dominant character-type. In the majority of cases, capitulations are provoked by rather philistine causes, reflecting both the epoch and the milieu. Yet the bureaucracy would not, without very serious political reasons, be so set on expelling tens of thousands of party members. There is a book by the American worker Smith,[177] who before turning into a frenzied enemy of the USSR was an idealistic Stalinist (he gave all his savings to the Communist Party before leaving to reside in the USSR): he says that it was those who acted as the most fervent devotees of 'the line' and the loudest denouncers of the Opposition at factory meetings, who turned out to be clandestine Oppositionists themselves. The majority of that sort of people continue with this 'double game' inside prison or in deportation (your letter hints at this too). At the present time we cannot expect to have a mass Opposition theoretically as educated and personally as courageous as the Oppositionists of the first two waves, who were active in debates, read political material, and so on. Yet in spite of this, it is not a pure accident that the GPU classifies part of the expellees as Trotskyites, another part as Zinovievists, a third section as right-deviationists, etc.

7. On the IVth International. Actually I don't myself really know what it means to 'found' the IVth International. There are groups and organisations in different countries, which campaign politically under that banner. They are trying hard to work out a concerted position on all major international events. They are trying to produce a common programme whose theoretical and practical premises will be conditioned by all the experience of past struggles. A future Ryzanov[178] will, with sufficient leisure, be able to solve the problem in retrospect: when, precisely, was the Fourth International founded? We, on the other hand, simply have to continue and develop our work.

Well, that seems to be all. In your present personal situation you are going to find it quite hard to get through this letter and the 'appendices' on top of it.

I find the portrait of BM Eltsin very well crafted, and recognise one of his expressions there. Lacking any other way of expressing my deep gratitude to your son, I enclose a photo of myself for him.

I would be very, very happy if you and I could reach an understanding on the *main issues*. I haven't the slightest intention of dragging you into petty day-to-day bothers. If you get your books written – with that talent of yours, which I only discovered when I was out of the USSR – you'll do far more good to the movement than in any other way.

Firmly and warmly embrace you,

L Trotsky

Letter 14: Trotsky to Serge (in Russian)

June 5, 1936

Dear Victor Lvovich,

There were a few things I left out of my last letter to you. First about Nin. If you think he could come back to us, why don't you try to influence him back? I personally don't entertain any hope of converting Nin into a revolutionary, but I could be wrong. Do verify my impression if you feel it necessary. I personally would welcome such a second opinion. Of course, the issue can't be resolved through mere verbal assurances from him (in this respect he is very lavish) but only by definite actions. Nin at present is in alliance with hardened adversaries of the Fourth International, who cover their petty-bourgeois hatred of revolutionary Marxism with empty phrases about 'organisational' disagreements, as if serious people could ever break with revolutionaries and join opportunists on account of secondary disagreements. If Nin wants to come back to us he must openly unfurl the banner of the Fourth International in Spain. Any excuses in this matter are of the same order as Blum's prevarications with regard to the class struggle: 'generally a good thing but not for the present time'. Blum's policy is class collaboration but his 'theory' acknowledges class struggle. Nin acknowledges the Fourth International verbally, but in deeds he helps Maurin, Walcher, Maxton[179] and other allies of his to wage a fanatical struggle against the Fourth International, a struggle of exactly the same kind that the pacifists à la Longuet or Lebedour[180] waged against the revolutionary-internationalists, partisans of the Third International, during the last war.

As far as the Pazes are concerned I'd rather not add anything to what I've said. But I feel it is my duty to warn you that on no account should you make any arrangements through them for the publication of your literary work. I give you this piece of advice because *I learned to my own heavy cost* the consequences of not following it. In any case, if they make any proposal to you on that front, I'd like to know about them before any final decision, so that we can unite our efforts to ensure the maximum success for your new book.

Best greetings,
yours,
L Trotsky

Supplement to the remarks I made on Ciliga's letter

The letter is in such flagrant contradiction with the political methods of Marxism that it's quite hard to decide which refutations would be the most important. Ciliga asks: if it's permissible to side with Blum against Fascism, why not with Dan against the Stalinist 'reaction'? I've already done a brief analysis of one aspect of this 'argument', here is another. Blum in comparison with the Fascists is the lesser of two evils, but can it be said that the Mensheviks are the lesser evil when compared with the Stalinists? Certainly not. If we only had the choice between the Stalinists and the Mensheviks in the USSR, we should definitely choose the former, as the Mensheviks could serve only as a stepping stone for the bourgeois who would destroy the planned economy and establish a regime combining a truly Russian Fascism with a Chinese economic chaos. *Economically* the country would be thrown back fifty years. Planning is the only way forward to secure the country's independence and future development. The Stalinists are also preparing the demolition of the planned economy, but in a very different time-scale. We may hope that the proletariat will manage to overthrow the bureaucracy before the latter demolishes socialised property relations. Those who wish to do so may call the Soviet regime 'state capitalism', but if one looks at the other five-sixths of the world it is clear that only that regime is still capable of developing the productive forces. To disregard this fact because the bureaucracy is so vicious means taking the stance of a liberal, not that of a revolutionary Marxist.

Letter 15: Serge to Trotsky (in Russian)

June 6, 1936

Dear Leon Davidovich,

I've received a registered letter from you of June 5 which begins with the words 'There were a few things I left out in my last letter to you'. What 'last letter' did you have in mind? I haven't had anything from you for a long time, and *don't know if you received* my long letter of May 27 with the portrait of BM Eltsin. All this is a great worry to me. I suspect that I'm under GPU surveillance but the disappearance of letters is worse than surveillance.

In any case, here is an absolutely secure address for me.[181] Write without putting my name on the envelope.

Was your last letter registered? If so, get an enquiry going.

Comradely hand-shake,

VS

PS – Soon – in about a fortnight, I think – I shall be going to Paris for a short visit.

Letter 16: Serge to Konrad Knudsen[182] (postcard–in Russian)

Today I received the letter from LD which I was worried about.

Warm greetings,

VS

June 6, 1936 – Brussels

Letter 17: Trotsky to Serge (in Russian)

June 9, 1936

Dear Victor Lvovich,

I've just got your letter of June 6 in which you express concern about the letter of mine which you hadn't received. I hope that it was simply delayed by one day because I'd registered it. Just in case, I enclose a copy of it. There was a photo of mine for your son enclosed with it, as a memento of my gratitude for his portrait of BM Eltsin (a very good portrait, which I liked very much).

That same long letter had a hand-written PS which said more or less this: I have no egoistic design to draw you into current day-to-day practical work. Even though in the last few years we've registered considerable success in forming new cadres (the most difficult job, and the least visible from the outside), we haven't yet grown out of the 'infantile disorder'[183] stage. Only when I got out abroad did I acquire the opportunity to appreciate your literary talent and artistic gifts. That is why I think it would be quite unreasonable to expect you to waste your energies on *current* politics. In the final analysis, your books will make a far greater contribution to the cause of the Fourth International than any participation by you in day-to-day work. That is my general assessment. Naturally, this does not preclude the possibility of your taking part, as an older, authoritative comrade, in some important meetings, associations and so on. All this is only hypothetical, of course. You'll make your own decisions as you get a better idea of what has been done and is being done on the international scene.

In *Spartacus*[184] and in the last issue of *Action socialist révolutionnaire* I found extracts from your letters to Paz and Gide. I do regret not having the full text. These letters would give me the chance of making quite indispensable quotations in my book on the USSR. Don't you have copies of the letters in full? (I'd return them to you once I'd used them.) Or maybe they've already been published in full somewhere else?

You are off to Paris. I do envy you a bit. Two or three times a day I turn on the radio to listen to the birth-pangs of the French Revolution. A massive strike like this is undoubtedly the beginning of a revolution. How all those leaders (Blum, Jouhaux, Salengro,[185] Cachin,[186] etc.) must be trembling before the advancing revolution, wriggling and lying and imitating Kerensky,[187] Tseretelli[188] and Dan with every word and gesture: this in spite of the higher level attained by the French school of rhetoric! The next few months in French politics may seal the fate of both France and of Europe for many years to come. I'd be very glad to know about your Paris impressions.

A German publisher who is sympathetic to us wants to bring out a theoretical Marxist journal* under my editorship. He offers me complete freedom, of course, and knows that the journal would be the theoretical organ of the Fourth International. I plan to start in the autumn, and hope that it will be possible to publish a parallel edition in French. I count firmly on your participation in the HQ of this forthcoming journal. Naturally I would like to attract Alfred on to it, but I absolutely wouldn't want to come up against his refusal (I hope that won't happen). That is why I'd like to make the first overture to him *through you*. If Alfred is agreeable in principle, I shall write to him personally.

Comradely hand-shake,

yours,

L Trotsky

* A monthly

PS Have just received your postcard about the safe arrival of my long letter, and the offprints of your letters to Paz and Gide.

Merci. Everything is OK

LT

Letter 18: Serge to Trotsky (in Russian)

Brussels, June 16, 1936

Dear Lev Davidovich,

I've had some very difficult days. My wife got worse. I was getting ready for a trip to Paris, everything seemed agreed with certain 'minister-comrades', but my visa was held up at some offices or other. In the meantime, unexpected difficulties arose here with the Belgian police. I hope to get it all sorted out within a few days and be in Paris by the end of the week. I'll write you my impressions from there.

Your letter of June 3 contains nothing I object to. I seem to have no great illusions in groups or people. Yet I do believe that we have to mobilise everyone who can to the slightest degree be mobilised. Besides, something completely new has begun now. All those who have a single revolutionary vein left beating in them must come to life soon. The wonderful strikes in France and here show clearly that the working class is recovering after its phase of depression and extreme fatigue, and is entering a new period of struggle. In such a situation one may hope for anything, so long as one does not expect an immediate all-round upsurge. This is the beginning, the first step out of bed, which indicates the recovery of the patient. The full recovery may take several years, but that is what one should work towards during these years of preparation for the revolution. Right now, I think, so much depends on the Oppositionists in France. The moment has come for them to found a really viable and efficient organisation. Will they be capable of doing that?

Here the situation isn't so good as in France, or rather much worse. I heard of the project to launch a new party in the Borinage[189] by merging the existing groupings. I am convinced that it is premature to talk in terms of a real party. There are no people for it. There are some in the provinces, but the party cannot be provincially based. One has to start by creating a viable group and take things from there.

I shall write from Paris, or afterwards, about the campaign in defence of Stalin's prisoners. I did what I could for my own part. I wrote a big (anonymous) report on the repressions, added some new names to the list of those persecuted, and raised the issue, modestly so far, before the wider public. I sent the report and other material to L.[ev] L.[vovich]. I believe that we have to conduct two big parallel campaigns: one among the intelligentsia, which is of course weak and susceptible to corruption but is bound to undergo some differentiation which will be to our advantage; and the other – among the workers. I am not in agreement with Ciliga's ideology, but I hope that he will not turn out to be 'a

Menshevik in a state of exaltation'. He represents a tendency which is very widespread among the deportees and prisoners. Its starting point is sympathy towards decentralisation, but it moves out towards the unknown, perhaps towards Menshevism, though it is impelled not by a liking for rotten bourgeois democracy but by a thwarted revolutionary instinct. We must take this psychology seriously so that we don't lose a number of valuable personnel.

I hope that my two open letters didn't provoke fierce objections from you. They are drafted somewhat diplomatically, despite my distaste for diplomacy. A first I thought of addressing the second letter to R[omain] Rolland, who had shown some concern over my case. But once I became familiar with some of his statements, it appeared impossible for me to treat him with any kind of indulgence; one had either to stay quiet or else take an implacable stand against that old man, who has wiped his slate clean of all his past. I chose to stay quiet. I've read your article about him, very restrained I thought, an article by Martinet and another by Emery.[190] There is nothing I can really add. Gide responded with a very friendly personal letter and a request for a meeting with me, which couldn't take place because of visa trouble. He assured me that he isn't blind, doesn't want to be blind, and wishes only to choose the best means of serving the revolution ... We shall see. I am a sceptic in this particular case. He received my letter just before his departure for the USSR, where he is now. Our conversation will continue when he comes back. I believe that if this representative of the cultivated, upper-class intelligentsia comes back after his tourist strolls in the USSR to take a public stand in favour of the Stalinist repressions, he won't in the least degree deserve the same 'tolerance' as old RR, whose life has had a couple of fine pages.

You are absolutely right on the *main point*: my priority in my present situation is to write my books in the form that is most congenial to me. Apart from some less important things, I am now working on the *Défense de l'URSS* and on a long draft about the struggles of 1923–36, written in the form of a *'Témoignage'* about living people. Ideologically, both these works will be completely explicit, the second being entirely devoted to our comrades. About the material side of my situation: I think I can arrange to get translation work through L.[ev] L.[vovich] in Paris and also get some other commissions from there. For the time being I have only a meagre income from the literary work I do for the provincial Socialist newspaper in Belgium (*La Wallonie*). I'm carrying on negotiations about the book, and hope that with help from you the *Défense de l'URSS* (more of a think pamphlet than a book: it has to be ready soon) can be promoted on the Anglo-American 'market'??

I've just finished reading Comrade T's *Ma Vie*, I can hardly tell you with what consuming interest I read it. Two comments: the translation is very poor, undoubtedly *below* the translator's abilities.[191] I suppose he worked in a great hurry. Pity – the book loses by it. Secondly, may I voice the hope that one day you will find the time to recount the tragic (for us, the younger ones) history of the Comintern at the time of the Balkan (Bulgarian) revolutions.

Let me tell you of a first-rate idea I've had about your work in general. Many of your best writings are dispersed in books which are almost inaccessible to the working-class reader (expensive, not easy to get hold of, hard to read because of theoretical arguments and the younger reader's lack of familiarity with our history, etc.). I think that it would be extremely valuable, and not too difficult, to publish your *selected writings* from certain years – historical, theoretical, memoirs – in one book of a standard size. I would be happy to lend a hand with such an edition in terms of editorial work, translation, etc. It would make a book very convenient for propaganda work. I'm convinced that publishers could be found very easily.

I recall that by some miracle, soon after its publication, a dozen copies of *My Life* appeared in the International Bookshop in Moscow!!! No doubt somebody got deported very far off for that mistake. A copy of it was then passed from hand to hand, completely dismantled so that each page could be read and hidden seperately. But *all* the pages, creased and soiled, were there! Someone lent me that copy *for one night*. Later on it must have landed up with the GPU.

A sympathetic Belgian comrade has asked me to pass on the enclosed questions to you, and expressed the hope that you would find time to look at them one day (in outline they strike me as being so interesting that I want to think about them myself).[192]

I enclose the portrait of me – not a very successful one – made by my son. It's got a certain likeness and has captured one of my expressions. In addition I enclose a small photo with the 'artist' himself in the foreground. He, incidentally, is leading a very intense and active life now. He was sixteen yesterday. Deportation taught him a great deal: the experience of real living conditions in the USSR, contact with true Communists. In every milieu where he had lived before then, the Communists were noticeable for their negative features even by comparison with philistines.

We were all pleased with your photo – you look quite healthy and vigorous on it. There are persistent rumours down here that you are ill, very ill, and so on. The 'latest news' which appeared in thick print in Paris the other day was that 'T. is dying!!' Perhaps this request will seem immodest to you, but I'd like to have another copy of the same (or else another) photo of you (with permission to reproduce it) for my 'study'. Volodya put his in his room. All I have is a postcard of you at Alma Ata produced by the Rieder publishing house. At Orenburg Volodya drew a copy, on a much larger scale, of the portrait of you which had appeared in the Rieder's[193] advertisement in *Le Monde*. We left this drawing with Eltsin. He gave another comrade a reproduction of the photograph of you taken by the Tsarist police.

With warm greetings to N Iv. (have you had, after all this time, any news of Sergei Lvovich?) and a firm handshake.

Victor Serge

PS. I have recently sent you a cheap edition of my writings: the short story *Mer Blanche*, 1936,[194] and *Poèmes*, some of which date from Orenburg.

[Enclosure of manuscript by 'a sympathetic Belgian comrade', (in French), with Serge's copy marked 'sent to LD, June 16, 1936' in his own writing]:

Questions
The Socialist revolution will find in Western Europe a basis more suitable than in Russia:
   in respect of technology
      of trade-union organisation
      of democratic traditions
      of the accumulation of material assets.

It seems then that on certain points it must not be a repetition of the struggles of Russia's revolution, that it can and must be conducted differently.

How, to what extent and with regard to which points should we take account of the experience of the Russian revolution – including Stalinism?

On which points should we revise and innovate by reference to this experience, and how?

How do you envisage the beginning and the course, as far as they can be predicted, of a Socialist revolution in Western Europe?

Do you think that it is linked with war or with the danger of war?

Letter 19: Serge to Trotsky (in Russian)

June 24, 1936, Brussels

Dear Lev Davidovich,

I wrote a long letter to you on June 17 [sic]. I have various problems with the local police and some inexplicable (or only too explicable) pro-crastinations with the French visa. Nevertheless, I shall get to Paris in the near future and maybe move there.

I suppose that you've got enough information from the newspapers on what is happening here. I only want to convey my principal impressions to you.

The movement started, quite spontaneously, in Antwerp. It overtook all the leaders and expanded on a scale unprecedented in the history of the Belgian workers' movement. It is symptomatic that the trade-union 'leaders' and the organisers of the Parti Ouvrier – smart fellows – have decided, after a brief hesitation, to support the movement. Some seasoned reformists have undergone an instant quick-change and now comport themselves – remarkably. *Rexistes*[195] – our local Fascists – at first demanded repressive measures, and then entered the battle … on the strikers' side! Small shopowners in various districts have also decided to lend their support. *The petty bourgeoisie* has in general got into an almost revolutionary mood and sympathises with the workers. I should think that this will remind you of the characteristic days of 1905 or 1917. Wherever one goes, the same talk can be heard in the same tone: 'Enough feeding workers with promises, enough government commissions! They're absolutely right', and so on.

An old Catholic, a good acquaintance of mine, said to me, 'This is undoubtedly the beginning of new social relations. All this distinctly smacks of revolution…'

The right wing and the business circles are in utter disarray (in France too). The proof of this is the granting of the 40-hour week through Act of Parliament, even though it creates immense difficulties for export industries. In France this may be *politique du pire* – but here it's a clear symptom of disarray.

About the comrades. I know very little about their activity. But their clannishness, with its morbid psychology, makes a dismal impression on me. I've been told that two small Brussels groups of Communist-Oppositionists came to a big workers' meeting with two different leaflets of almost identical content! It can be imagined what effect this has on the Belgian workers with their habituation to the spirit of unity. Sectarianism means that the work doesn't get done, or rather means the sabotage of any revolutionary work. I was told that Lesoil's paper is withering (from lack of cash), but he does not want to merge with others into one common organ. The young people from Hennaut's[196] group (highly intelligent doctrinaires), of whom there are only 12 in the whole world, are demanding the right to preserve their 'faction' as the precondition for entering into a large grouping!! They are not satisfied with the mere possibility of defending their theoretical position, they want this formal, factional approach! And so on and so forth! All this strikes me as an astonishing loss of touch with reality. The new epoch in the working-class movement, the proletarian giant's emergence from depression and slumber will *force* these people to alter their position and their attitudes. Only on that condition will they become capable of doing work, of maintaining an active political life.

A very suspicious and even dangerous personage has arrived here from Moscow – the Italian ex-Bordigist Ambroggi,[197] whom I used to know. According to the evidence of very serious people and of the attendant circumstances he probably came to work for the NKVD or the Italian OVRA, or both.

Warmest greetings to you and N Iv.
VS

Letter 20: Trotsky to Serge (in Russian)

June 24, 1936

Dear Victor Lvovich,

I have received your last long letter, the portrait and the photograph. Thank you for it all.

NI enjoyed *Les Feuillets bleus*[198] very much. I haven't started it yet: I am still finishing my book[199] and have to spare my eyes. I look forward to reading it, once I've given some rest to my eyes which are badly over-strained.

I'll write at greater length when my Russian assistant arrives: just now, must confine myself to a few lines for the same reason (the eyes!).

We were very disturbed by the news of the worsening of your wife's condition in the last few days. Couldn't it be a reaction to the move, to a change of surroundings?

You write that under the influence of the last mass movement, many of those who have seemed hopeless may come alive again. Undoubtedly! Try to shake up everyone that you can. I shall be delighted to alter any of my judgements, formed on the basis of patient experience in the last seven and a half years.

I've seen too little of you, and too long ago, to be able to say whether the portrait of you is a good likeness. But in any case there is something deeply *individual* about it, which alone reflects great credit on the artist.

Friendliest greetings,

yours,

L Trotsky

PS. *We haven't heard anything from Seryozha or about him.* Ciliga met him in Krasnoyarsk by chance, but what happened to him *since* nobody knows. *Pravda* has started a new fierce attack on the 'Trotskyites' — in connection with the new constitution.

Letter 21: Trotsky to Serge (in Russian)

July 3, 1936

Dear Victor Lvovich,

I haven't so far replied to your last two letters of June 16 and 24, apart from sending you a short note — I explained the reasons for it then. I want to make up for it now. I don't know where you are at present, in Brussels or in Paris, so I'm sending this letter to both addresses.

You write that in the time of great events one should mobilise everyone who has 'a single revolutionary vein' beating inside them. I fully agree with you, and think it's a great asset to the cause that you, as a 'newcomer' abroad, are therefore in a position to approach a number of people without any preconceptions or accumulated personal bitterness, and test to see if there is any such 'vein' beating in them or not. I mean Rosmer in the first place, of course. Personally I have no doubt that everything that matters is 'beating' within him all right. But would he be willing to *move closer* to our movement? I'd be very happy if he did so. It isn't a matter of drawing him into mundane day-to-day work, of course. But he'd be an extremely valuable or rather irreplaceable member of our editorial team, particularly on that monthly journal which I'm planning at present. I'd like to have for that publication not only Rosmer's name but that of Martinet. Please find out from them if they agree in principle, and I'll then write to them about it in more detail. The monthly will appear in German first, but we're going to put out a magazine in French of the same kind, in parallel. If you can nominate any other contributors for the editorial board, please let me know at once.

There can be no disagreements between us on the enormous significance of the June events. You offer the hypothesis that the 'convalescence' of the European proletariat may take several years. 'Convalescence' coincides in practice with the formation of a new revolutionary vanguard. It would be excellent, of course, if history allowed a further 'several years' for this, if only (let us say) two or three years. But I am not so sure that this will be possible, unfortunately. In France, events may develop much faster than in Spain. In Spain, in fact, the working masses had to start the second revolution completely from scratch, because the seniors who call themselves the leaders killed off the first one. In France the bourgeoisie is immeasurably stronger and more intelligent, and it may not give the proletariat any chance of compensating so rapidly for its leaders' bankruptcy. That is why the formation of a party is an extra-urgent task in France, as well as in Belgium. I wouldn't intervene to stop the Belgian comrades from declaring a party, even though it may have to be numerically small. Of course a small party may not have enough time to become a large one. But without any party at all, the revolution is absolutely doomed, in Spain as well as in France and Belgium.

Now about Ciliga. I would be only too glad if you or any one else managed to bring him back on the revolutionary path. But up till now the fact remains: he collaborates with the Mensheviks and subjects us to unrestrained criticism in their organ, at a time when the Menshevik-Socialists of France, the friends and associates of Dan, confiscate our French publication and prosecute our friends. To take a place on the other side of the barricades is not a trifling offence.

You enquire whether I took too critical a view of your two open letters. The one addressed to Gide I find superb. An element of 'diplomacy', as you put it (I would rather say, an element of *conventionality*) is inevitable in this case and does not spoil the letter at all. I'd like to cite this letter in full in my book, if you have no objection. There are some fine lines in your letter to M Paz, but the recipient disgusts me so much with her rhetoric, hypocrisy, insensitivity, etc. that it casts a shadow over your letter too. I am waiting impatiently for your book *Défense de l'URSS*.

The French translation of my autobiography is not only 'slovenly' but a disgrace from beginning to end. It is not a translation but a mockery: not a single phrase is mine. I nearly took the matter to court, but French courts always decide in favour of the proprietor, the publisher in this case. In the end I summoned Parijanine out to Prinkipo, where he spent a month with us, and we worked every day together on the translation of my *History*, which was translated into a written French much better than the autobiography.

You suggest compiling a selection of my articles, or extracts from my books and say you'd be willing to do this yourself. Naturally I can only welcome this idea, if only you can find a publisher ready to pay you properly for your work. A few years ago the publishing house of *La Nouvelle revue française* suggested something of the kind, but I was completely absorbed in the *History* at the time. You can, of course, have a free hand with my 'copyright permissions'.

(Now I'll answer your questions one by one). We know nothing, absolutely nothing about Seryozha. You can well imagine how this affects Natalia Ivanovna.

In order to define better my position on the June events and the perspectives from this new situation, I am enclosing, *for your personal attention* and possible critical comments, my draft theses on the subject.[200] The theses will become the topic of collective discussion and only then published.

Now about Belgian politics. I don't know Hennaut personally but I did try in the past to come to an understanding with him. He seems to be a completely hopeless charlatan. Such people will join us when it becomes impossible not to: you cannot persuade them with words. As far as Vereeken is concerned (you call him Lesoil by mistake) he is an inveterate sectarian, despite his many valuable qualities. I am in correspondence with him, and I try in every way to bring him back. Lesoil, now, isn't at all sectarian: unfortunately, though, he is seriously ill and also very much depressed; he needs a long rest. The young Dauge displays a lot of energy, but he suffers from a stomach ulcer, which completely paralyses him from time to time. It really is too bad!

About the Italian Ambroggi I know this: he openly called himself a Bordigist during Bordiga's last visit to Moscow. It was as a 'Bordigist' that he came to see me, but I could never understand why he came and was rather surprised that nobody interfered with him. At least one of these scoundrels should be exposed openly one of these days.

Friendliest greetings.

Yours,

LT

PS. An American comrade, Muste,[201] is due to visit you in about eight days from now. He's a very worthwhile and serious comrade. He was up here for about a week participating in our work and discussions.

I'll be really pleased if you and he get on. He used to be a Calvinist pastor: now – a revolutionary Marxist. He is travelling with his wife.

Yours,

LT

Letter 22: Trotsky to Serge (in Russian)

July 6, 1936

Dear VL,

I enclose the draft version of the appeal in defence of political prisoners and deportees in the USSR.[202] Couldn't you try to collect signatures to it (you can alter and adjust it in any way, if necessary)? I think the quotation from *Pravda* is very important – it sounds particularly sinister ... It also demonstrates once again that the main targets of the persecution are *our* comrades.

You will, of course, do all you can. I am sending copies of the draft to several other addresses.

Yours,

LT

Letter 23: Serge to Trotsky (in Russian)

Brussels, July 14, 1936

Dear Lev Davidovich,

It's been several days now since I received your letter with the theses and the appeal. I'll write to you about both of these when my situation permits. I feel tired now, I've had some very difficult days. The most tiring thing of all is my wife's condition. We've been to a doctor – there's nothing to be done.

I shan't go to Paris for quite some time yet. While bureaucracies in Paris delayed my visa for a whole month, I got into some problems with the Belgian police (none of which have been settled yet). Then the three-month limit of my Soviet passport expired. I went to the Trade Mission to get our passports extended. They asked me to leave the documents and come back in a couple of days. Then, yesterday morning, I was told that by government decree I was stripped of Soviet citizenship. There is no specific reason, it seems. I demanded an extract from the minutes concerned or a written statement. They promised to reply in five days. They don't know for certain whether my wife and children have also had their citizenship annulled, but they think it must be so and are keeping their passports too. I wonder if my ill wife, sixteen-year-old son and eighteen-month-old daughter will also be declared enemies of the people?

Simultaneously, but unofficially, I also learnt that, even after they'd given permission in principle, *Glavlit*[203] has categorically refused to let any of my manuscripts be sent from the Soviet Union to me here. All my work is in detention, and so on, etc. (Gide promised to solicit for its release: he must be back from Moscow soon.)

I haven't decided yet how to respond to the forfeiture of citizenship. It is one more arbitrary act of bureaucratic police-authority, and I think it should be publicised with appropriate comments. I'll probably not make an appeal against it (what for? to whom?)but a protest to the V-Tsik[204] adapted for a wider public, ie. for the press. What is your view?

Lev Lvovich has put a specific proposal to me about the translation of your book.[205] I promptly notified him of my agreement today and asked him to send me the manuscript immediately: one mustn't lose a single day if the book is to be ready by the end of September as the publisher wants. The payment terms for the transaction are quite satisfactory: materially alone this work helps me out, while morally it will give me great satisfaction. I will consult you directly on all stylistic questions: the book will gain from this quite a lot.

My own book is growing fast and will soon be finished. Then I'll send you the manuscript, asking you to pay attention to a few passages which I'll point out. The character of this work of mine has changed for me after my conversations with young comrades. I don't know yet which publisher I'll offer it to and I'm afraid it will bring me no income (particularly bad in my situation), since our old Hasfeld[206] has his eyes on it... Wouldn't it be possible in that case to get some sort of income from an American translation?

About the book itself I'll write next time, just now I am utterly exhausted.

Our heartfelt greetings to N Iv.

A comradely handshake,
Victor Serge

Letter 24: Serge to Trotsky (in French)

Brussels, July 27, 1936

Dear Leon Davidovich,

After long discussions with our friend Muste,[207] I should like to give you my views on several questions in all frankness. I shall do so in an almost telegraphic style, without developing anything.

In France, opportunities for development and for organisation are considerable, but the internal difficulties are extremely serious. I have already met many of the comrades. The young ones are of high quality, much can be expected of them provided that they can develop themselves inside our organisation. The old cadres are really demoralised, in the deep sense of that word, through the effects of ten years of depression and splits. There is an urgent need to: put a stop to personal involvements; establish a collective, *strictly collective* leadership; insist that all those who join it display a genuine intention to get to work cooperatively, renouncing any claim to personal dominance; get people into it who have a moral authority and a political past (Rosmer would be no end of a catch here), already seasoned militants like N.[208] and R.[209], and a number of young fresh comrades, carefully selected, to bring in new ideas. I am not well briefed on all aspects of the Mol[inier][210] case but I take it that M. cannot remain in the leadership but cannot now be eliminated from the movement and ought not to be; he will therefore have to be persuaded to move to the second or third rank and stay there for some time.

The new party will be less numerous, less influential, less equipped with activists than its periphery, ie, the layer of sympathisers whom it cannot at present attract because it lacks authority. It has to create respect and sympathy among militants of all tendencies. In order to achieve this it has to change its behaviour and eradicate all dirty procedures of a Stalinist sort. It must adopt a polite and fraternal manner in debate, except of course towards riff-raff and actual enemies. Above all, it must attach prime importance to the quality of its publications, and write in French! In this respect things are really terrible at present. An editorial committee of at least passable quality must be set up, and anything in half-baked French and appalling taste must be cut out. That certainly can be done. All translations must be edited properly before going to the printers.

To infuse some life into and recruit more writers of an interesting kind, the journal must have an open-forum page in which contributions can be invited from people who may be recruited later on, or may simply provide help 'from the sidelines'. We totally lack the capacities required to create strictly orthodox publications. Any intention to create them, when there is no sign of any collective thinking that is at all influential, will only produce sectarian rags, barely readable and without any access to the working-class public. Our ideological intransigence must be expressed and developed in an atmosphere of free collaboration, without anxiety about secondary differences.

A good review can be very quickly got going provided that half of it is given over to a forum-section broad enough to attract the collaboration of people like Martinet, Dommanget,[211] perhaps Wullens,[212] Plisnier and Simone Weil.[213]

On principle I am against any outright ban on those who, over the last ten years, whatever stupidities they have committed or said, have remained loyal to Communism. I am thinking, for example, of somebody like Treint,[214] for whom, I may add, I don't feel any personal sympathy! In the period we are now entering, ideas are going to have to evolve and change. There is also a Lasterade[215] grouping, semi-Bordigist but in fact influenceable, with whom collaboration is possible if we leave it some degree of internal freedom.

To sum up, we have immediately to work towards a unification of forces at present dispersed (in the Fédération de l'Enseignement alone there must be several hundred sympathisers we can win if we attract their confidence), and towards a party ideologically firm and disciplined in action, but unsectarian and without a personality cult in its leadership, genuinely democratic and comradely in its manner, in which people will feel free to be wrong, and to think and speak freely. That will not result in any confusionism, quite the contrary.

Maybe certain political issues will have to be left open, without any definite resolution until the militants as a whole have clearly made their minds up. One of these, in my view, is the question of the nature of the Soviet state and of the defence of the USSR – matters on which enormous confusion reigns among the rank and file. Besides, the Russian question, while of great importance in the education of militants, is not the principal one before us.

I still believe, and it's very important to make this clear, that all questions about individuals and about the details in different localities should in principle be settled at the base, without your intervention. The comrades should be asked to give a proof of their maturity by relieving you of your concerns, and by refusing to allow the head of the movement to become embroiled in quarrelings which sometimes have no possible means of resolution.

Solidarity with Spain.[216] I suggest that the conference and the French organisation should immediately elect substantial delegations to leave immediately for Spain. One or two comrades should be sent there as official representatives of the party to the workers' organisations, several others as observers and reporters who would conduct broad propaganda aimed at the rank and file and the newspapers, and if possible a band of (?) 10 or 20 comrades at the disposal of the workers' front in Spain (depending on their skills, they could provide various services). They should leave illegally, and as soon as they have got there the fact of this initiative should be widely publicised. In addition, we could think of setting up an international workers' ambulance service, quite openly, and raise questions of passports, etc.

I hope also that the conference[217] will take seriously the question of the campaign to be waged for our imprisoned comrades in the USSR.

A strong and friendly handshake,

V

Appendix to letter 24: extract from 'A New Revolutionary Upturn?'

1. I do not think it is accurate to state that the working class *as a whole* is ready for struggle. It is only emerging, awakening, out of a long period of depression: it is the beginning of a process which will make it ready for struggle as a whole once it has fully recovered its energies. (I am working from the idea that its depression of the last ten years can be largely explained by the exhaustion of the working class in the war and in the postwar defeats.)

5. The parties of the Second International are not homogeneous. The events in Vienna and the Asturias and also the reactions of the French Socialist Party to the strike show that the Socialist masses are evolving towards revolutionary action. A section of the party activists is following and it could even be that certain Socialist leaders and key figures might learn something from history and avoid playing the role of Noske and Ebert.[218] Through our criticism and pressure we must, if the slightest opportunity offers itself, help them in this more positive direction.

9. If it is true to say that 'the People's Front', as a coalition with the bourgeoisie, is a brake on the revolution and a safety valve for 'imperialism', it seems to me both unjust, and above all far from expedient, to say that 'the Popular Front is a transition stop towards Fascism'. That much it could become, and will become *if* the working-class movement lets itself be manipulated, pushed around and perhaps even provoked by the bourgeois elements of the Front (or outside it). But one can be more optimistic. If the working class continues to improve its consciousness of the situation (an objectively revolutionary one) and if, as has happened in the strikes, it exerts enough pressure on the Popular Front, the latter can be a useful transitional form which will allow the workers to enter the later phases of the struggle with greater possibilities. As for the present situation, the Popular Front has already performed a great service to the workers by giving them the self-confidence which

produced the launching of the stikes, which, in their turn, gave a quite new political colouring to conditions in Parliament.

The proper attitude towards the Popular Front seems to me to be as follows:

- *support* for the implementation of working-class demands.
- *criticism* of vacillations, compromises and half-measures.
- *denunciation* of the bourgeoisie's game and of class collaboration.
- with, as a slogan, 'transform the Popular Front from an instrument of class collaboration into an instrument of class struggle' – which obviously implies, in a further perspective – a split with bourgeoisie or bourgeois-dominated elements and the regrouping of the working-class forces around a revolutionary programme which can assure them of the support of the middle classes.

In any case we must not use expressions reminiscent of the 'struggle against the Social Fascists' (third period, etc.). In general:

The awakening of the working class, the evolution of the Socialist masses, the total betrayal of the Stalinist leaders, the revolutionary situation all make necessary the formation of a workers' rev.-internationalist party and indeed offer real possibilities for its development. But it cannot be pretended that this party exists at present except in an embryonic state, with its initial components very weak. In the current situation, these elements must above all seek to acquire a moral authority, to work deeply within the masses and become linked to the masses. We must not forget that in France and Belgium these parties – of the Fourth International – will only be able to present themselves as a real force by uniting the revolutionary workers who today belong to other political organisations (CP, SP, syndicalists, anarchists) or else are still unorganised. Very numerous are the Soc. and Comm. workers destined to rally, in the course of the struggle, to the rev. organisation which knows how to make itself heard by them. A hypothesis of splits and regroupings within the old parties seems likely to me. We must always have a perspective of keeping our lines open towards the old parties.

In Belgium: we must take account of the existence of a Catholic proletariat which is capable of entering the class struggle. To the slogan of 'Popular Front with the Cath. and liberal bourgeoisie', oppose the slogan 'Popular Front with the Christian workers, expelling the bourgeois elements – class front'.

Letter 25: Trotsky to Serge (in Russian)

July 30, 1936

Dear Victor Lvovich,

I've received your letter of July 27, written after your conversation with our American friend. Unfortunately I cannot agree with you. I am afraid your approach is too artistic and psychological, ie, not political enough. Moreover, much of it stems from your insufficient familiarity with the history of what we've done here during the last seven and a half years. You actually accuse me of sectarianism. I cannot accept this accusation. I think that your own brief experience, if you had assessed it correctly, would completely refute your accusation. To unite people to help the political prisoners and deportees is much easier than to unite them for the social revolution. You have a name, you have a double authority as an old revolutionary and as a man just escaped from Stalin's noose. One might think that it should be easier for you to override sectariansism and unite broad circles in an international campaign against Stalin's butchers. Yet you complained in your last letter that your efforts had been in vain. You are not the first one to have had this experience. Is that just an accident? No, it is not. Our supposedly sectarian organisations also carry on a struggle in the defence of the deportees. They are the only ones who wage that struggle. But their attempts to broaden it – attempts with which I sympathised and which I aided as much as I could – have yielded no results so far. Do you think that those philistines, who cannot be stirred to action by such a burning issue as Stalin's repressions, can find themselves a place in a revolutionary proletarian party? I don't think so. General arguments against sectarianism are no good nowadays, *one must show in practice the possibility of a different route*. Up till now, all those who sought a different route simply departed to another camp. Such is the fact, my dear VL, and I am accustomed to basing my knowledge on facts, not on general speculations.

You started by accusing us of an incorrect attitude to the 'revolutionary-syndicalists'. I replied: the whereabouts of such is unknown to me. As far as *La Révolution prolétarienne* is concerned, it is no more than a home for the chronically disabled. You've been to Paris since then. Have you found revolutionary-syndicalists there? Give me their addresses, please. Did you find a revolutionary flame in Louzon's heart? If so, I am ready to do everything to establish closer relations with him. Point out concretely what is to be done. But, unfortunately, after your visit to Paris, you haven't said a word about 'revolutionary-syndicalists'.

Then you speak about the Fédération de l'Enseignement, which supposedly has a few hundred of our sympathisers, whom we could attract if only we could 'win their confidence'. Here again your approach is quite gratuitous and unfounded. I lived a whole year in France among those people (from the Fédération de l'Enseignement). I had countless talks with them, exchanged letters, we even held a small conference with all the leaders of the Fédération. Neither I nor my closest friends could become more intelligent, civil or beautiful for their sake. But we did all we could to engage them in our work. Their secret is quite simple, in fact: they are *petty-bourgeois through and through*; their little houses, little gardens and cars are a thousand times dearer to them than the fate of the proletariat, though they still retain some awfully radical ideas in their memory. I visited some of them at home, saw their style of life, not only saw it but smelt it. Excuse me, Victor Lvovich, but that smell won't leave me deceived. To have any hope for these people is to sow on stony ground. There are revolutionary elements among the young teachers. We are looking for a road. But the leadership plays a reactionary role, preventing the young from finding the road towards us. That is why I lashed these gentlemen in one of my recent articles and will lash them even harder at the first opportunity.

You name Martinet. I also mention him in my letter to you. If we manage to attract him – fine. You name Dommanget. I know him personally. He joined us, then drifted away. His historical treatises aren't bad. At best, he might once a year contribute an article on Babeuf [219] to our magazine. He is hardly capable of doing more than that. You name Simone Weil. I know her very well, and used to have long conversations with her. At one point she was somewhat sympathetic towards us, then she got disenchanted with the proletariat and Marxism and began to write preposterous idealistic-psychological articles in defence of 'the individual': in other words, evolved towards Radicalism. It is possible that she will turn left again. But is it worth talking much about? In any case your nominations don't contain a single new person. With all those people we've had a long and negative experience. All of them give thousands of reasons which prevent them from joining us or in general from carrying out revolutionary work: our style is no good, our translations are bad, our polemic is too harsh, and so on. These people talk about everything, except the most important things: *the programme, the strategy, the fight for the masses.* Do we have to adjust to this human garbage? No, that would be a fundamentally wrong orientation. One must find a way to *the workers*, by-passing ex-revolutionaries or even elbowing them impolitely out of the way.

Here is another example. A few months ago our comrades tried to set up a monthly trade-union paper together with the Enseignement people. So what happened? Nothing came of it. These petty-bourgeois (I simply can't find another word) have no taste for struggle. They are fully prepared to meet and chatter together on a revolutionary topic or form a mutual-admiration society for non-entities. But we won't go along with that.

What you say about my 'interference' and the need for 'collective' action I've heard many times. Do you know from whom? From those who demanded my interference but didn't get it because I did not agree with them. There are many of these. The echoes of their complaints have now reached you. You write of Rosmer. You know how highly I regard him. But why did he withdraw from us? He got into a conflict with Molinier. This conflict came to a head. I had nothing to do with it, didn't even know about it. Rosmer and Naville made an attempt to expel Molinier, but found themselves in a tiny minority in the organisation. Then Rosmer turned to me for support. I replied by saying more or less this: that even if it was clear to me that Molinier's expulsion was necessary, I couldn't do anything from here: *you must convince the majority of the organisation yourself.* After that Rosmer broke off his political contacts with us and left the organisation. I am willing to do all that is necessary to re-establish our collaboration. But I still don't think that he is a suitable person for the revolutionary Centre of our time. As a contributor to a magazine he is very valuable. But Rosmer is not a militant activist and he will immediately get into fierce disputes with the young revolutionaries at our Centre. You speak *a priori* while I speak on the basis of an uninterrupted experience of seven and a half years.

You also named Treint. Do you know that I called him to Prinkipo, that he spent nearly a month in our house, that I went through a fierce struggle with the Pazes, Rosmer, Naville and many others in order to draw him into our work? There was a time when he began to work with us. But, alas, he is a maniac, not in the figurative but in the most literal sense of the word. He broke with us not because we prevented him from expressing his maniacal ideas, but because we disagree with him. What could be done? A non-sectarian policy consists, among other things, in ridding ourselves in time of sectarians who prevent us from finding the road to the workers. That is why, at a certain juncture we got rid of the sectarian Vereeken in Belgium and won to our side, without him and against him, a considerable group of workers, whom he has gone and joined now. Maybe Treint will come back to us some day, too, when we are stronger. But to adjust our present policy to Treint, to maniacs and sectarians, would mean to block our own path to the workers. Let's look at the case of Nin now. Some people, including Rosmer, regard my ruthless criticism of his policy as sectarianism. In that case the whole of Marxism is sectarianism, for it is a doctrine of class struggle, not of class collaboration. The present events in Spain show how criminal was Nin's alliance with Azana:[220] Spanish workers pay with thousands of lives now for the reactionary perfidy of the Popular Front, which supported, with the people's money, the army led by the butchers of the proletariat. It is not minor details which are at issue, dear Victor Lvovich, but the very essence of revolutionary Socialism. If Nin comes to his senses now and realises how he disgraced himself with the workers, if he makes all the necessary conclusions, then we'll accept him as a comrade. But we cannot allow favouritism in politics.

From your corrections to my theses on the revolutionary upsurge I've taken up the one in which you point out that a considerable number of people will break away from the Socialist and Communist parties and move further to the left (there was an allusion to that in the text but not sufficiently developed). Unfortunately I cannot accept your other comments because I regard them as fundamentally incorrect. You, such a fine historian of the Russian Revolution, for some reason refuse to transfer its most important lessons to other countries. Everything you say about the Popular Front applies to the bloc of the Mensheviks and Social Revolutionaries with the Kadets (the Russian equivalent of the Radicals) as well. We, however, waged an uncompromising struggle against that bloc, and won only thanks to that.

Your practical suggestions on Spain are excellent, they fully agree with *our* line. But I wonder if you could find a dozen people outside our 'sectarian' organisation who would accept your suggestions, not only in words but in deeds. The fact that you make such excellent *practical* suggestions is a vivid indication that there is real common ground between us. I shall wait patiently until you have checked your *a priori* views against living political experience and draw the necessary conclusions. I don't doubt for a moment that your conclusions will coincide with ours, which we have formulated *collectively* in *different* countries, on the basis of the experience of great events. Despite our alleged 'sectarianism' we continually grow in strength and number, while our critics haven't been able to build anything.

Well, enough for today. I've responded to your frankness with complete frankness myself, and believe we shall carry on along this path to our mutual benefit.

A hearty, comradely handshake.

yours,
L Trotsky

PS. About the translation. I'll make corrections to the chapter on *the family*, better not translate it yet. I'll send you the end of the book on Tuesday, in five days' time.

Letter 26: Serge to Trotsky (in Russian)

August 10, 1936

Dear Leon Davidovich,

Forgive me for not replying to your letter of July 30 earlier. I started it a couple of times, but couldn't finish. As you can imagine, I am torn by various commitments and couldn't cope with my work. Since there are no substantial disagreements between us (for our assessments of the personal qualities and the working capacities of the comrades from *La Révolution prolétarienne* are not all that significant), these subjects could be put off till later. I am inclined to make the accusation of sectarianism not against you alone, but against the whole of our movement. I think I can substantiate it, alas, very convincingly. But today political work provides the way out of sectarianism! It was annoying, even sickening, to see how much paper had been wasted in personal squabbles about Molinier, while not a single pamphlet had been published about our comrades in Stalin's prisons! Hundreds of French workers know about these squabbles, *but don't know* the names of *Yakovin* and *Pankratov*.[221] This is outrageous. But the rising tide of the working-class movement should carry away such anomalies.

The most encouraging phenomenon is happening now. Everyone is rushing to Spain. I've received a desperate letter from Ver[eeken]: all his young people are rushing off, everyone is en route to Spain. He is asking us to intervene, to retain some of his people here. We shall try. The same in Paris. Two Italian comrades from Marseilles were killed near Saragossa (and once again – some incompetent work: what a lousy article *La Lutte*[222] devoted to them). Rosmer has left. Of the Socialists closest to us, Collinet.[223] Louzon has left. Batches of anarchists are going from everywhere. My son has been barely stopped after long conversations with me (he is sixteen, too young).

I approached the International Secretariat with a proposal on the anarchists and syndicalists. It is necessary to forestall a disastrous conflict, instigated by the Stalinist swine in Spain. Hernández[224] has plainly stated to the press – 'This will be a bourgeois revolution, not a social one (sic), and we shall make short work of the anarchists' (sic, papers of August 8). The anarchists killed the Socialist bureaucrat Trillas[225] in Barcelona. Among them there are loud voices to the effect: we won't allow Stalinism to set in, we'll shoot everyone first. A civil war might break out in the proletarian ranks. The Spanish anarchists have an indisputable overwhelming majority in the decisive industrial region – Catalonia. I propose to take the following line and issue this appeal:

1. We revolutionary Marxists consider it necessary to fortify the rear of the revolution by a firm policy. At the same time we declare that the dictatorship of the proletariat must and will provide real liberty for all the working people. We shall fight along with you to assure freedom of opinion and of different tendencies within the revolution. We solemnly promise to do our utmost to prevent the bureaucrats of every stripe from turning the revolution into a Stalinist-type prison for the workers.

2. We are partisans of complete democracy, combined with complete discipline in combat and in production.

3. We consider you, the anarchists and syndicalists, to be our class comrades and dedicated revolutionaries. We offer you our fullest cooperation along with uncompromising criticism and ideological struggle, carried out in a fraternal atmosphere.

4. We alone, on behalf of the Fourth International, can talk to the anarchists and syndicalists in this way. *Neither* Socialists, like Caballero,[226] *nor* Stalinists can adopt this line. We have an enormous advantage here, which might save the situation.

We must pursue this line in all our press. (Why didn't it report the remarkable death of the anarchist Ascaso?[227] I've tried to correct this mistake).

Your last letter made me think that you *haven't received* my hand-written letter in Russian in which I told you that I had been stripped of Soviet citizenship (along with the family) and that this has prevented me from going to Paris so far.

It would be extraordinarily 'strange' if that letter had not reached you. Let me know about it.

I'll go to Paris as soon as I get the document enabling me to travel for my visit to you. I'll write about that separately.

I suggested to our comrades, in connection with the events in Spain, to launch the slogan of *workers' control in the army*.

1. As the slogan for the establishement of dual power in the crucible of events.

2. As the slogan calling for agitation and exposure with the practical sense that every worker in the army must see himself as a representative of workers' control and show maximum vigilance.

The publisher asked me to submit the translation by instalments. (I was pleased with your radically new formulation of the question of the state. It is a major contribution to theory.) I shall wait for your comments before I send the first lot to the publisher.

A hearty, comradely handshake to you and N I.

VS

Letter 27: Serge to Trotsky (in Russian)

August 15, 1936

Dear Leon Davidovich,

After much hesitation, I've decided to send you the first part of my translation. I think it would be better to have all your comments *before* I produce the final version. I'll send you the manuscript of another hundred pages the day after tomorrow. Please try to go over it as soon as you can; the publisher wants me to submit the translation by instalments.

I have a good rapport with our young people. I've met many of them and my impressions are excellent. It's extremely annoying that the International Secretariat has been effectively disbanded at the time when we need it *daily*. There is *no* Centre now. We must quickly create some kind of efficient bureau, so as to be able to respond to events with practical actions.

Lev Lvovich wrote to me that he had passed on to you my concrete proposals to the International Secretariat on the attitude which should be taken towards the anarchists and syndicalists in the Spanish Revolution. This is a vitally important question, we must choose a line and follow it consistently. In Catalonia the anarchists and syndicalists have a decisive and stable numerical superiority: they make up between two-thirds and three-quarters against all the Marxist trends; the terms of their activity

– the superiority is even greater! They have a real party – the FAI.[228] There are elements among them which could cause mortal harm to the revolution. But these are a feeble minority (though a very active one). The majority of the anarchists are dedicated to the revolution, ready to die for it, but they are poisoned by their muddled ideology and, even more, by their hatred of the state-prison, created by bureaucrats. The policy which the Stalinists have adopted towards them – and not only towards them – can only be described as the suicide of the revolution. By stamping all their adversaries as 'anarchists' – a good bogey for the international bourgeoisie! They are preparing the liquidation of all the workers who are partisans of the social, ie proletarian revolution. The question of the anarchists and syndicalists reflects *all the peculiarities of the Spanish Revolution.* I think we must take the initiative here – only we can take the initative – in order to avert civil war in the ranks of the revolution and prevent the discrediting of Marxism by the Stalinists' treason. By stating our intention of collaborating with the anarchists and syndicalists on fraternal terms, which don't exclude implacable ideological criticism; by stating our determination to fight for a real workers' democracy, with full freedom of opinion in the revolution, we shall win the right to demand real discipline in combat and in industry, and shall be able to take the offensive against all the confusionists. In this way we shall conciliate a considerable section of the anarchists and syndicalists and sow the seeds of future work. Because, in the furnace of the revolution, many of them should come over to our side, if we don't repel them with a fallacious and outdated doctrinaire approach. I proposed to issue an appeal on behalf of the International Secretariat. But in fact there is no IS; when will it start functioning again? Have you received my letter of August 8 and the one before it (about the forfeiture of Soviet citizenship?).[229] The Embassy is keeping silent on the matter.

At least I have a complete set of the *Bulletin*. Extremely interesting, it's a pity that I got it so late. Otherwise I could have used it widely in *Defence of the USSR*.

Please, dear Leon Davidovich, write all you think about my translation without the slightest constraint.

My warmest greetings to you and NI.

VS

Letter 28: Serge to Trotsky (in Russian)

August 16, 1936

Dear Leon Davidovich,

I am worried about you. Drop me a line as soon as you can. What is happening around you?

I wrote to you yesterday, asking if you had received one of my previous letters.

I think that they are preparing the physical liquidation of Zinoviev[230] and others, and I'm very worried about many of our comrades. I've reacted immediately. I've written a refutation, which will be sent to the press on behalf of the Belgian and French organisations, and an article. I haven't got a copy of it, you'll see it in the press.

The passivity of our comrades with regard to the repressions in the USSR was criminal. It's time to arouse everyone to act *definitively*. *You must demand this from everyone*. It is extremely annoying that there is for practical purposes no Secretariat at present.

I am organising myself, wherever I am as best I can, a campaign against the repressions.

A hearty, comradely handshake to you and N I.

Yours,
VS

PS. Wouldn't it be possible to publish the chapter from my book, called '1935, the Year of Terror', pp. 34–39, widely in America or England?

Letter 29: Trotsky to Serge (in Russian)

August 19, 1936

Dear VL,

NI and I have just returned from a short trip to the sea – tried to take a rest from politics, but politics – and what politics! – caught up with us as soon as we left. We learnt of the attack on our flat[231] on the way. A car with two Fascists and then with four (including their propaganda chief) trailed us tail-to-tail for about 300 or 400 kilometres. At the seaside we were 'screened' by the police. We received a visit from the chief of the Norwegian secret police, who carried out a polite interrogation.

Then TASS issued its vile statement,[232] which baffled everybody here. I am now going to write about this amalgam.

What you write about Spanish, or rather Catalonian anarchists is absolutely true and I am extremely glad about our unity of opinion on this principal question of the present moment. Unfortunately we are only observers... The most important thing now would be to find organic forms of collaboration between the POUM and the unions in Catalonia (juntas, soviets, Committees of Action?), even at the expense of considerable concessions in organisational matters. But these questions can only be solved on the spot.

Your notes on the translation of my book show that you take your work too conscientiously. You have such a superb literary style that there is absolutely no need for you to check the 'liberties' of your translation with me. I fully approve all your chosen versions in advance. It would be a different matter if you had queries on the *meaning* of the text.

I did receive the letter with the news that you had been stripped of Soviet citizenship, but I didn't really think that this could prevent you from entering Blum's kingdom. Blum is the last one who reigns there, in fact.

'Sectarianism' in that general sense which you impart to the word, is simply a physiological factor of age-development and of extremely *hampered* growth (Fascism, the Comintern, the Soviet bureaucracy, the Popular Front, and so on). One should patiently (but not passively, of course) go through all these difficulties and stupidities.

I am in great haste. This is my first letter after a two-week break.

A most comradely handshake to you.

Yours,
LT

PS. I am very glad about your comments on the theory of the state. I had a feeling myself that I had succeeded in clearing up certain points.

Letter 30: Trotsky to Serge (in Russian)

August 22, 1936

Dear VL,

I've had time to read the first thirty-five pages of your translation – just now I'm up to my eyes in the Moscow trial – it is the last word in foulness, vilification and bureaucratic stupidity. I've no doubt that with the necessary effort we are going to expose all the provocateurs' work! But the battle will take up our time.

Your translation is *excellent*. Don't bother to send me any more, too much time is lost that way through the post. I endorse your translation in advance. I marked a few misspellings and similar corrections in red pencil on the first 35 pages.

I read the article by Fabre in *l'ASR*.[233] My young friends and I are delighted with it (despite its attitude towards bourgeois elements in the Spanish government). I agree with you *entirely* on the necessity for amicable cooperation with the syndicalists against Stalinist scoundrels and traitors. Your perseverance in this direction is of first-rate importance.

A comradely handshake.

yours,

L Trotsky

PS. I'm waiting for your comments, observations and conjectures on the trial, its various incidents, the provocateurs (I've already 'caught' one of them – Oldberg,[234] and so on). Apart from an interview, I'll be writing a pamphlet, which will expose this sewage down to its very depths.

PPS. Wouldn't you like to write a play, set against the background of the October Revolution? It could be a great success. A really appealing subject.

Letter 31: Serge to Trotsky (in French)

Uccle, August 30, 1936

Dear Leon Davidovich,

The reports in the newspapers have made me very worried about you. Please, can you immediately give me some quick information about your actual situation? Can you correspond freely? And continue your work projects? Is your security all right?

I find it painful to think that Norway, one of the most civilised and freest countries, could take measures against you which amount to a sensational and unprecedented violation of the right of asylum and of international protocol. The legal position seems absolutely clear to me. The refugee must refrain from any political activity within the country which offers him hospitality, but he keeps full liberty to express his views on whatever happens in his own country of origin and elsewhere in the world. Kropotkin was able for thirty years to publish a Russian-language anarchist paper in London in which there appeared celebrations of international terrorism. Kerensky and many others published Russian papers in various countries in which there was open discussion about politics in all nations ... The German and Italian exiles enjoy the same freedoms in various countries. Is Norway about to take the initiative in altering international law as it affects you by imposing a gag upon political refugees? That seems incredible to me. Is the government of one of the world's most reputable democracies going to let itself be kicked in the backside by the executioner of Moscow without blinking an eyelid? Impossible to believe it, although in our epoch anything can be expected...

The main thing is that you must be able to show up the judicial farce in Moscow. Since I'm going to have a long chapter about that in my book, and I have to finish the book very soon, I beg you kindly to send me everything that can be of interest on this subject: your interviews, etc.

I think too that the book of yours that I'm in the middle of translating cannot omit a discussion of these crimes and that, either in the preface or through a separate chapter, it has to contain an appreciation of the Stalinist slithering (a slither in blood towards the infamy of the Borgias).[235] As far as this goes, I've nearly finished the translation *but I am waiting for the final part of your manuscript.* Do you intend also to modify the chapter on the family? Or should I translate the text as it is?

I am giving great priority to this book and its publication as rapidly as possible, as in itself it is a sufficient refutation of the slanders put out in the trial.

About our comrade-Oppositionists in Russia: I am absolutely convinced that none of them are in deportation any more; they must all have been thrown into prison, and they are going to be under pressure to disavow you on pain of death. They *are all in peril of their lives.*

My wife is in a horrifying condition. My friendly best wishes to Natalia Ivanovna. A strong handshake, dear Leon Davidovich.

A couple of sentences in reply, quickly, please.

Victor Serge

Letter 32: Trotsky to Serge (in French)

Hurum, Sept 6, 1936

Dear friend V. Serge,

I've sent you back in time the first part of your translation, which I find excellent. It's essential now to get the book published *as soon as possible.* I certainly hope that the publisher knows where his interests lie. The book is an *a priori* refutation of the Moscow trial. Its appearance immediately would have vast importance too for the legal trial I am about to open (through my lawyer Mr Michael Punterwald[237] as an intermediary), against the Norwegian Stalinists and Nazis (the only target I can aim at from here).

It is very difficult for me to do the extra chapter on the trial from here. But if you yourself find it interesting to add a few notes or even *a translator's addendum* you have my consent in advance. I would be happy with this method of collaboration. You can, if you like, send the addendum to me here – I reply to you immediately.

Natalya's health, like my own, is more or less satisfactory. We are settling as well as can be expected in our new abode for purposes of work. The main matter now is the trial for which I must have the active help of all friends, all informed people, all the honest public. This flagrant crime must be chastised.

As I wrote yesterday to my son, all documents, testimonies, counsels and postulations must be channelled through my lawyer Punterwald.

Warmest greeting to you and your family from N and myself.

(sign.) Leo Trotsky

Attested in handwriting:
In fidem:
Michael Punterwald,
advocate.

Letter 33: Serge to Trotsky (in French)

September 30, 1936

Dear Leon Davidovich,

The book is completed, sent to the printers, set up and corrected and is due out any time now. In consultation with Lev Lvovich, I have added only a short piece of twenty lines about the trial and the significance that the book now has in this situation. If I had received your letter a little bit sooner, I would perhaps have been able to write better or more fully. But on reflection, I think that the book as it is forms a coherent whole and provides quite sufficient refutations for current purposes. As to the trial, quite obviously you must write a lengthy and detailed analysis of it which will make a book on its own and which will hit the fellow over there good and hard.[238]

As to my own activities, I've been very busy. I at once wrote a strong-worded pamphlet on the trial which I'll send you as it's been out in

Paris for a few days now. The reports of the trial in the Russian press are full of nonsenses, enormous lies and Jesuitical sophistries, to such an extent that a careful reading would almost be enough by itself to expose the criminal machinations of it all.

I am able to provide, for any commission of inquiry that may be set up, precise and associated testimony on the following points:

1. The GPU's methods of investigation.
2. The role of provocateurs in political cases and repression.
3. Repression in general.
4. The attitude of the Opposition in general, and about these trials.
5. The consequences of the Kirov affair in social life.

Although they are a little indirect, such testimonies could have their use.

I'm very anxious about our friends and comrades in Russia, whose situation must have become intolerable. But what can one do?

My wife is in the same distressing state and our situation is becoming oppressive. In three weeks or so I hope to get to France to find work and prepare for our 'installation' down there, which has become necessary since Belgium doesn't provide us with any material opportunities.

We wish the best in health, strength and work to both of you.

Victor Serge

Letter 34: Serge to Trotsky (in Russian)

Uccle, rue Joseph Bens 134
January 10, 1937[239]

Dear Leon Davidovich,

At last, according to newspaper reports and personal assurances I've had from a Mexican diplomat, you are at liberty and out of immediate danger. It was hard to have no news from you. In the first days of December I managed to arrange a Belgian transit visa for you. I very much hoped to see you but the most incomprehensible news was arriving from Norway. It is difficult to understand why the Norwegians took such a fright. I would like to know what lay behind that vile intrigue.

As soon as I get your address I'll send you the special issue of a magazine – *De Lenine à Staline* – which I have just brought out in a large circulation edition.[240] The book *Déstin d'une révolution*[241] will come out in February. I work tirelessly and with evident success. The Moscow trial has clearly swayed public opinion aginst the butchers.

There is no news from the USSR. It is terrifying to think about the position of our comrades in the isolators and concentration camps. I think we must devote the utmost of our effort to them, to their rescue, saving their lives, that is. As you're returning to work with renewed strength in new surroundings, you might be able to give this struggle a fresh start. In Paris our 'Committee for the Defence of Freedom of Opinion in the Revolution and for Investigation of the Moscow Trial'[242] is active, and I shall be able to lend it more energy in the near future, when I get there.

I've just learned that in September, apparently in response to my first public statements on the Moscow crimes, my elder sister was arrested in Leningrad, and also the sister and brother of my wife. All of them are apolitical and have lived in very difficult conditions; my sister was already exhausted. What's become of my mother-in-law in these circumstances – I cannot imagine. What bastards they are. It seems that, after our campaigns, the second trial is being concocted with quite a lot of difficulty. I am convinced that if they dare to stage it, it will be an unprecedented moral flop. But even without it, there is no way out of the existing situation.

About the translation of *The Rev[olution] Betrayed*, there seem to have been a considerable number of misprints, etc; after all, we speeded it up as best we could, had to work day and night with no one to rely on, for there is no one with enough knowledge of the subject and of the languages. However, the reader does not feel that he is reading a translation, and that is where my achievement lies, because in so many books the translation comes through and often quite unpleasantly.

I'll write to you about other matters as soon as I have some news about you. The most serious matter is that I and a whole group of comrades ran into considerable disagreements on Spanish affairs and the POUM with many other comrades.[243] In my opinion we must support this party in every way, re-establish truly comradely relations with it and not demand from it an orthodoxy which it cannot have. The main thing is not to conduct any factional sectarian work there and not to aspire to lead this revolutionary organisation from outside. In this respect a number of comrades have piled up a lot of blunders, aggravated the relationship and caused a highly undesirable reaction. Whatever you may say, the POUM represents a militant unit now, which behaves on the whole very courageously and reasonably and holds out great hopes in a situation of *very grave danger*.

My personal affairs are tolerable, partly quite good. My wife's illness is without change, ie very bad. I am thinking of moving to P[aris] in

February, from there I shall try to make it to Bar[celona] and – to you!!
I cherish this dream and it seems feasible in the future.

I'll await news from you with great impatience. For the time being
I am immeasurably happy for you and NI. After all, your migration is
like a release from prison, and there is now an ocean lying between
you and Yezhov's[244] agents...

Most heartfelt greetings to both of you.

Victor Serge

Letter 35

Prefatory note.
The following 'open letter' from Trotsky to Serge was printed in *La
Lutte ouvrière*, organ of the POI (official French section), on 26 March
1937. The French Communist Party had launched an intense campaign
of slander against Serge following the impressive impact of his *De
Lenine à Staline* on its appearance in January. On 12 February a huge
CP meeting of 8,000 workers in the Salle Wagram heard Fernand
Grenier, Secretary of the 'Friends of the USSR', condemn Serge as 'an
accomplice and receiver of stolen goods for the Bonnot gang, which
had killed so many unfortunate workers, bank employees and drivers'
(referring to the 'tragic bandits' case of 25 years previously). At the
crescendo of his address 'the workers booed Victor Serge', (*L'Humanité*,
13 February). Grenier had taken his cue from an article, 'L'avocat de
Trotsky', in the 2 February edition of *L'Humanité*, by Jacques Sadoul
(an acquaintance of Serge's from Russia in the early 1920s), who
charged him with 'an established complicity in a long and bloody series
of robberies, burglaries and murders' in the Bonnot years. The article
claimed that because of his doubtful record of 'banditism' he had been
relegated by the Comintern to 'subordinate tasks such as secretarial work
and literature'. Moreover, as Serge was 'a valet of the pen', it was 'logical
that having sold his pen to Bonnot's tragic gang he should sell it to the
gang of Trotsky' (or, as *L'Humanité* put it on 28 February, 'place his
pen in the services of Trotsky and the Gestapo').

The defenders of Serge (for example, Georges Pioch in *La Flêche*, 27
February) were able to recall what *L'Humanité* then the organ of Jean
Jaures' idealistic Socialism, had said of Serge during the Bonnot trial
itself: that only 'very inconclusive' charges applied to him and that 'the
good faith of this ideologist is certain and he should never have been
prosecuted' (issues of 4 and 26 February 1913). But the Stalinist
L'Humanité returned to its libels on 3 March, recounting a story about

an 'important theft committed by Kibalchich in Belgium' before the
war 'to the prejudice of a revolutionary organisation', and alleging that
Serge had been sacked from his translator's job in the Soviet Union
because in his rendering of Lenin's theoretical writing 'he was cutting,
manipulating or mangling' any passages 'which might have embarrassed
Trotskyist propaganda'.

Trotsky to Serge (in French)

Coyoacan, March 5, 1937

Dear friend,
   You know as well as I do what the press of the Comintern is like.
Each time one picks up and holds an issue of *L'Humanité,* it is by an
act of violence to oneself. My young friends have drawn my attention
to the article by Jacques Sadoul against you, exceptional even for this
prostituted sheet. It took more than a week, I have to admit, before I
was able to force myself to read its two short columns. What a base
epoch we live in! And with what base men! Jacques Sadoul judges and
excommunicates you in the name of the revolution, awarding favours
and disfavours as an authorised participant of the civil war in Russia.
He places himself between you and Lenin as the latter's trusted confidant.
   I am impelled to express my sympathy and solidarity with you, and
at the same time to tell the workers of France: *Jacques Sadoul is a liar!*
Each line of his article is a lie, substantially or subjectively.
   Jacques Sadoul who, over his whole life, has been a cowardly parasite
on the working-class movement, states that you are lacking in moral
courage. One reads it and doesn't believe one's own eyes. Moral
courage and Jacques Sadoul!... When this personage arrived in Russia,
he was a confirmed French patriot. But he preferred to serve his beloved
country as a legitimised deserter rather than on the battlefield.[245]
   In the course of the Russian Revolution he acted as an observer on
the make, a careerist won over to the Bolsheviks to the degree that the
Bolsheviks had proved their success. Jacques Sadoul's first concern was
to avoid burning his bridges with his Embassy, with his Military Mission,
that is with the circles to whom he was incomparably closer than to
the workers and peasants of Russia.
   Lenin viewed Sadoul with a contemptuous irony. I can vouch for
this because more than once it fell to me to defend Sadoul in front of
Lenin. Through the necessities of my post, I used Sadoul's services, his

connections and information-gathering, and so took an interest in him. I have to confess, my indulgence in him was excessive!

Lenin used to say about him, 'He's just a little Jean Longuet!' I answered Lenin with a joke: 'Even Longuet can sometimes be useful.' As circumstances would have it, Sadoul was present at the First Congress of the Communist International. Not a few adventurers at that time were attracting themselves to the movement. The Soviet revolution was victorious, the war was becoming protracted, and Sadoul risked less in Moscow than he would have done in France. I remember his speech at the congress, in which he had the impudence to speak of none other than Jean Longuet as a possible ally: 'He will cross to the revolution, perhaps five minutes before its victory, perhaps five minutes after, but he will come...' I felt Lenin's ironic gaze pointed towards me: 'There's your Sadoul, one of those who will come to us five minutes before victory.'

But where this slanderer reaches the limit of vileness is in the lines where he speaks of your careerism, your concern for 'material advantages', and where *he*, Jacques Sadoul, calls *you*, Victor Serge, 'a valet of the pen'. There is nothing more repulsive than a servile philistine whose powerful bosses have told him that 'everything is permitted'. You have remained in the ranks of the Opposition without hesitating, in the midst of unprecedented repression, when those less firm than you capitulated one after another. In prison and in deportation, you have been in the cohort of those whom the butchers of Thermidor have been unable to break. You, my dear friend, have chosen a pretty rotten way to secure a 'career and material advantages' for yourself. Why didn't you follow the example of Jacques Sadoul? He tripped around the Russian Revolution until it became possible for him to get back to France.[246] There he became a correspondent for *Izvestia*. From Paris he sends despatches of insipid twaddle, dictated for him by GPU agents. What a courageous, valiant, heroic post! Certain people who had talked with Sadoul in the last few years used to tell me, 'Sadoul has sympathy with you, but...' I would reply to them with the Russian proverb: out of such sympathy 'you can't make a decent fur-lining'. The sympathy of these gentlemen only ever assumes a material shape five minutes after the victory. They are all the same, Cachin, Duclos,[247] Vaillant-Couturier,[248] Thorez[249] and their sort, valets of the pen, valets in every way. Moscow gives them the hint, and they rush to the Moscow trial as eager false witnesses. They listen intently to the speeches of the inquisitors and the victims without understanding a word of Russian. What use would it be to them anyway to know the language? The character of their testimony is known well in advance: 'We have heard with our own ears...', they swear on oath. As if those donkey's ears of theirs were any instrument for the truth to penetrate.

Dear Victor Serge! Like you, we know the proper contempt for these people. We shall teach this contempt to the young revolutionary generation. A single article by Sadoul is enough to enable a sure diagnosis: *Stalinism is the syphilis of the working-class movement.* The Comintern is doomed to ruin. The Sadouls of this world will abandon the sinking ship like rats. They will betray the Soviet Union five minutes before its mortal danger. So, let's teach the younger generation how to despise this fungus on humanity. A few more years will go by, and the vanguard of the proletariat will pass over the bodies not only of the valets but of their masters as well. You will be among those whose name will be forever linked with the renaissance of the working class's struggle for liberation.

Leon Trotsky

Letter 36: Serge to Trotsky (in Russian)

9 Verbrugge, 38 av. des Hortensias,
Schaerbeek,
Belgium, Brussels
March 20, 1937

Dear Lev Davidovich,

I waited impatiently for your reply to my letter of January 10, which I sent to Diego Rivera,[250] c/o one of his friends Ignacio Millau, whose address I got from the counsellor at the Mexican Embassy here. And now that letter has come back to me. They did not get the addressee at home three times! I am sending my belated letter to you now. I have this to add. The Stalinists have launched a really fierce denunciation against me, stopping short of literally no slander. My former 'friend' Sadoul, who is bound up with the Soviet Embassy by pecuniary relations, has played the foremost and quite disgusting role in this campaign. There is nothing surprising about it, of course. In the first days of April I'll be moving to Paris. I must say that I've initiated a considerable and undoubtedly fruitful activity around the Moscow trial. I'll intensify it in Paris and also turn towards the literary work of novel-writing, so as to consolidate my hold on the place (also to have some rest emotionally, and ultimately, to fight with this, in my view, excellent weapon – literary work). You probably received my books *Déstin* and

De Lenine à Staline: if some parts of these works provoked your critical judgement, please let me know of it in a few lines. My pamphlet *Seize fusillés*[251] is being printed now. I am translating your new book.[252] I was very pleased with the page on the flood of lies ... after all, this is a system, and a monstrous one. I experienced its implementation in different circumstances: I was lying in bed in the Orenburg surgical hospital. There were about fifteen hungry, constantly hungry, workers and peasants lying in the same ward. They became literally ill from constant hunger. All of them got abscesses, furuncolosis and so on, as a result of emaciation. Whereas the radio all day long transmitted floods of lies about the happy-life: speeches and ovations from the collective farms' congress in Moscow. It is difficult to describe how horrible it was.

In order to avoid misprints, which occurred in *The Rev[olution] Betrayed*, I asked Lev Lvovich to go over the final proofs with me.

The day before yesterday, at a friend's house, I learnt, by chance, the words of 'a member of the Central Committee(?)' of the Spanish party, who had been in the same house an hour before me – 'We'll have to shoot about 5,000 POUM'ists in the near future, then everything will be all right.' They are carrying on quite serious preparations for it. The Spanish Stalinists are looking for their own Noske and pursuing the policy of Noske. A comrade from the POUM told me that Azana had ironically said about the Spanish Communists: 'These people discredit us. After all, one should at least promise something!' I had many personal contacts with the Spaniards. I am convinced that the POUM is the only healthy, thinking mass organisation there and believe that despite its many mistakes it behaves splendidly on the whole. I consider the line taken by comrades-sectarians deeply equivocal. They believe that small groups of foreigners, who possess a 'pure orthodox ideology' can implant this ideology from outside, and that they must carry on factional activites inside the POUM and direct their attention towards the creation of a separate party.[253] It seems to me that we have to start from Spanish reality, develop and use what is there. The factional attitudes led to the deepening of the gulf between the leadership and the so-called ortho-doxies from the Fourth. Now all this has eased off a little, but did not vanish. The POUM is certainly not a Bolshevik-Leninist party; there are no Bolshevik-Leninists in Spain in general. I think that the Bolshevik-Leninists must learn to work with other Marxist revolutionaries, to influence them, collaborate with them, in order to become an influ-ential current themselves they must abandon the imposition of their hegemony... A great change of attitudes is required. It is getting possible (and necessary) with the revival of the working-class movement.

In the previous letter I wrote to you about the necessity to undertake persistent work for the support and rescue of our comrades in Stalin's prisons. In Paris I'll devote myself to this work with every effort. If the New York Committee supports the Paris one we shall achieve something. We must start by compiling a detailed card-index of biographical data, out of which we can later extract material for a book, pamphlets, etc. We must intensively publicise a number of names. We must achieve the recognition of some Red Cross organisation in order to be able to receive information and render material aid. We must enlist the aid of Peshkova[254] and of the International Red Cross (in Geneva) and create an international fund and a new permanent committee out of the public sympathetic to our cause. It is patently clear that *there is no deportation any more*. Everyone is locked up. (Even if there is still some sort of exile for the Trotskyites, it is only to such wretched places as Turukhansk,[255] for instance). It is also clear that desperate struggles, hunger-strikes and every kind of torture are taking place in concentration camps and isolators. It is clear that there has never *never* been such a horror in Russian prisons! We must raise this question, together with the question of the trials, tirelessly and widely. If you have in your archive the photos of the imprisoned comrades (MM Yoffe,[256] Kossior,[257] Eltsin and others), please make copies of them and send them to me for publicity purposes. It hardly needs saying that I work day and night. My wife is in a very bad condition. My son grows up very well, he is very active. My little daughter (in Paris) too. Materially we are holding out.

Most heartfelt greetings to both of you and, *salud a los compañeros de Mexico!*

Victor Serge

Letter 37: Serge to Trotsky (in Russian)

February 18, 1938[258]

Dear Leon Davidovich and Natalia Ivanovna,

Once again you are struck by an infinite and incredible misfortune.[259]

The departure of Lev Lvovich is irreparable to all of us. I want to tell you that in these black days I and numerous other comrades, known and unknown to you, who have considerable and yet secondary disagreements with you, all of us deeply and whole-heartedly share your grief.

We'll have to fill the place of the departed comrade in the struggle as best we can with our disjointed efforts. If I can be of any help to you in these circumstances, you must know that I'll be happy to do it.

I was told that some comrade-Oppositionist has come out – was exiled? from the USSR. He is still stuck somewhere on his way to Paris.

With warm greetings,
Victor Serge

Place Severine Apt. 179,
Pre St. Gervais,
Seine

Letter 38: Trotsky to Serge (in Russian)

April 15, 1938

Dear Victor Lvovich,

NI and I received your letter about the death of our son and read your warm article about him[260] with much gratitude.

In your letter you touched upon our disageements and called them 'secondary'. Unfortunately I cannot agree with this at all. If the disagreements between Bolshevism and Menshevism are secondary, then what is meant by the word primary? *Révolution Prolétarienne* is an utterly reactionary organ which only distracts a number of people from the working-class movement. If your disagreements with us are secondary, why do you contribute not to our publications, but to the publications which are mortally hostile to us through the very nature of their programme? In dozens of articles I argued that the policy of the POUM is at best the policy of Martov.[261] You never replied to any of my arguments. Instead, at the critical moment you publicly expressed your solidarity with the POUM and assumed responsibility for its policy.[262] One can act in this way only if one is consciously moving towards a *complete rupture* and *implacable struggle*. How can you in these circumstances talk of 'secondary' disagreements?

The bankrupts of anarchism, united with the bourgeoisie and the Stalinists against the workers, found nothing better to cover their bankruptcy with than by raising a campaign on the issue of... Kronstadt. Instead of stamping on the traitors of the revolution and falsifiers of history, you immediately spoke in their defence. Your excuse and extenuations make things no better, only worse. Our enemies get the opportunity to say, 'Even Victor Serge, who's only got secondary disagreements with Trotsky, recognises that...', and so on. In other words, you took up a position not merely on the right wing of the Fourth International, but on the left wing of its implacable adversaries. In perspective, all those organisations like the POUM are just the surface of history's current. The only really revolutionary factor in the near future will be the Fourth International.

I am very sorry that you did not put your excellent talents at the service of this really progressive movement of ours. On my part, I am still ready to do everything to create conditions for collaboration. 'Secondary' disagreements, really *secondary*, are inevitable and could not hinder such collaboration. But only on one condition: if you yourself decide that you belong to the camp of the Fourth International and not to the camp of its adversaries.

Sincere greetings from NI.

A comradely handshake and best wishes.

Leon Trotsky

Letter 39: Serge to Trotsky (in Russian)

Paris, March 18, 1939[263]

Dear Leon Davidovich,

There were many reasons why I haven't answered the letter you wrote to me a long time ago. I kept postponing my reply (I am living in extremely difficult circumstances), then I decided I couldn't entrust to paper the description of the Fourth International movement, which I should have given you. Paper can always get into the hands of a third party.

I've decided not to react at all to the article in the *Bulletin*.[264] You are too inaccurate, too unjust and unnecessarily offensive. I don't know who keeps you informed and how, but sadly, believe me, there exists a whole nest of intrigues here (which has played its part in the death of Lev Lvovich and, before that, in the death of Reiss,[265] as well as in the failure of the whole Fourth International movement in France). I can assure you personally that I took no part in any groupings 'opposed to the Fourth'. Of course I feel closer to comrade-heretics, because I believe they are right: it's time to follow a new road, not to stick to the well–trodden paths of the late Comintern (and this applies equally to the day-to-day running of the organisation). Nevertheless, not only did I not participate in any 'factional activities', but tried whenever I could to soften the inevitable split. You will hardly find another person in existing groups as alien to any kind of 'intrigue' as myself. But enough about that. The same thing all over again: one cannot say honestly, calmly and with dignity, 'Yes, we have serious disagreements' – one must always discredit or even slightly slander the other side.

Our disagreements are very great indeed. I pointed them out to you immediately upon my arrival in Belgium. Then I 'accused you of sectarianism', as you put it. Since then, my arguments against your line, which I presented to you before I expressed them to anyone else, have considerably deepened. I am convinced that one cannot build an International while there are no *parties*... One should not play with the words 'party' and 'international'. But there are no parties here. It is a dead end. Only small groups manage to hold out somehow in this deadlock, but they have no dynamism, no influence, nor even a common language with the working-class movement. One cannot build an international organisation on intolerance and the Bolshevik-Leninist doctrine, for in the whole world there are no more than two hundred people (except the surviving inmates of Stalin, perhaps) who understand, who are in a position to understand, what Bolshevism-Leninism is. One cannot build a single-headed international organisation and run it from a long way off. For the time being, no one in the Fourth International thinks except through your head.

What should be done?

The solution, I believe, lies in an alliance with all the left-wing currents of the workers' movement (its platform: the class struggle and internationalism); in free, comradely discussion of every issue, without abuse and mutual recriminations; in the creation of an International Bureau of committees and similar bodies – such a Bureau to be composed of the representatives of local movements and to work towards concrete goals; one must abandon the idea of Bolshevist-Leninist hegemony in the left-wing workers' movement and create an international alliance, which would reflect the real ideological tendencies of the most advanced sections of the working class (I am convinced that in such an alliance the Bolshevik-Leninists would have a greater influence than in their own high and mighty International.)

Apart from this, we have disagreements on the history of the revolution. I might publish a long article on the subject in the near future. To tell the truth, I have no real wish to enter into polemics with you. I value your activity too much, in spite of all these disagreements. Nevertheless, after you attacked me in the Belgian journal (*Lutte ouvrière*),[266] I had to reply in the most convincing manner.[267]

Two more words on other questions:

1. I think we must establish a complete and accurate list of our comrades, members of the Opposition of the years 1923–1929, who are imprisoned or have been imprisoned by Stalin, and loudly raise the question of their fate: *What has happened to them?* I believe that at the same time we must speak out in defence of the anarchists and Socialists, locked in the same prisons. I have repeatedly raised this question in the Committee for Investigation into the Moscow Trial here, but without result.

2. As a result of my comradely relations with all currents of the working-class movement, I had to break with the Paris group of Bolshevik-Leninists. It would be more accurate to say, perhaps, that they have broken off with me and by so doing displayed a complete lack of elementary camaraderie. I'll write about it in a PS.

My most heartfelt greetings to you and NI. I want you to remember that I remain on duty and will be happy at any time, regardless of all our arguments, to be of service to you.

                                                                   Victor Serge

PS. My rupture with the Bolshevik-Leninists occurred in the following way. A comrade, who doesn't belong to the group, expressed to me the serious suspicions which he had about L Ya. Ginsberg.[268] They seemed to me to be so worthy of attention that I confided them to the three most reliable comrades (Rosmer, Wullens, Elsa Reiss)[269] with the intention of starting an enquiry. Elsa told the group about it. (The whole group consists of no more than 4 or 5 comrades, and Ginsberg plays a paramount role in it. One shouldn't have taken the risk of causing her offence, if she were, as she seems to be, a truly dedicated comrade, but neither should the possibility of getting to the root of the matter be neglected.) The group refused to look into *the substance* of the affair, or so I was informed through Comrade Etienne.[270] Instead – it 'brought an action' against me.[271] This put an end to any further talk on the matter.

BI Nicolaevsky[272] told me many times that he vouches for L Ya. Ginsberg. I was satisfied with that, and all the more willingly because L Ya. has always made an excellent impression on me. I very much regret that indirectly and involuntarily I offended her (with my suspicion) but it happened solely through the tactlessness of certain members of the group. I also regret that the matter couldn't be properly investigated. I still think that there is 'foul play' around the group. It all happened about six months ago.

                                                                           VS

Letter 40: Trotsky to Serge (in French)

Coyoacan, DF, May 6 1939

Dear comrade,

Your letter, while very friendly in a personal sense, demonstrates to me again that you are passing through a prolonged ideological crisis,[273] and that you are turning your dissatisfaction with yourself into a dissatisfaction with others. You write about intrigues, false information, etc. I don't know anything about these, I know only your writings and your actions. Against the Fourth International you support everything that is 'supportable'. This proves that, politically, your solidarity with us is much weaker than your antagonism. After the foreseeable reverses to your politics, which for my part I term individualistic and even, if you will forgive the word, adventuristic, you will just have to change your way of going about things. I have not lost the hope of seeing you return to the path of the Fourth International. But, at present, you are its adversary, and a hostile one at that, who nevertheless tries to insist on being treated as a political friend.

With my best regards,
L Trotsky

Letter 41: Serge to Trotsky (in Russian)

August 9, 1939

Dear Leon Davidovich,

The *Bulletin of the Opposition* no. 77–78 of February?[274] has only now reached me. You subject me to a harsh criticism in it, ascribing to me the article [*prière d'insérer* to '*Leur Morale*'][275] which I have not written, nor edited, nor do I know its author![276]

I should like to add that while I have translated your book with utmost care, I have not inserted a single line into it. I should also add that all the 'arguments' which you ascribe to me are at great variance with everything which I have written on the civil war and Socialist ethics in my books and articles. There are only ten lines (on the CHEKA) in the whole of your article which really pertain to our disagreements.

You have absolutely no grounds, no right, to accuse me in such an uncivil manner of what you yourself describe as 'laying an egg' in 'someone else's nest'.

You could easily enquire about the real author of the *prière d'insérer* from the publisher, from Rosenthal,[277] or from me.

I hope you will take it to be necessary to publish this letter of mine in the next issue of the *Bulletin of the Opposition*. I have every moral right to this satisfaction.[278]

with Socialist greetings,
Victor Serge

3 Serge, Trotsky and the Spanish Revolution

Introduction by D.J. Cotterill

In July 1936, the sense of tension that had filled the years between the Great War of 1914–18 and the beginning of the Second World War in September 1939 sharpened with the outbreak of the Spanish Civil War. From its beginnings, signalled by the military uprising in Spanish North Africa against the Popular Front-inspired government, it served as a focus for the major political groupings of the crisis-torn interwar years, becoming a rallying point for their competing aspirations.

Not surprisingly then, the war raised differing hopes in these discordant factions. The far right and military looked for a strong state and authoritarian government; the Republicans, allied as in France with the Socialists and Communists in a 'Popular Front', hoped for a liberal bourgeois democracy; while others, like Trotsky and Serge, anticipated the renewal of social revolution. For them, Spain represented the 'highest stage of proletarian revolt achieved since the revolutionary wave of 1917–1919'.[1]

As can be seen from the correspondence in Chapter 2 above, Serge and Trotsky had radically differing viewpoints on the efficacy of a Popular Front, and on the attitude which the Fourth International should adopt towards it, in both Spain and France. Central to these issues where Spain was concerned, was the role played by the POUM and its leader Andrès Nin: first in supporting the Popular Front's programme during the Cortes elections and the front's subsequent entry into the Catalan government; and second in the failure of initiative during the crucial events of May 1937, which saw Stalin extend the tactics of political repression from Russia to Spain in an effort to purge genuinely revolutionary elements from the conflict. As this chapter will attempt to show how these events impacted upon Serge's relations with Leon Trotsky, it will be necessary first to provide an overall context, by following events in the Spanish Republic from 1936 until its defeat at the hands of the Nationalists in 1939.[2]

In Spain, the creation of a Popular Front had been as problematic as in France, and the role of the Comintern was crucial to its resolution. The decision of the Seventh Comintern Congress to sanction the tiny Spanish Communist Party's cooperation with the Socialist and Republican parties allowed the PCE 'its first opportunity to enter effectively the troubled arena of Spanish politics'.[3] Its subsequent ability to broker an agreement between the left and right wings of the fractious Socialist Party, led respectively by Largo Caballero and Indaleco Prieto, and to achieve cooperation with the Republicans of Manuel Azaña, won for it a prominence in Spanish affairs previously denied it. As the war unfolded, this significance became far greater than the relative size of its membership.

Agreement was finally reached on the formation of an electoral pact, as opposed to a formal arrangement to govern, between the left Republicans, the Socialists and the Communists of the PCE on the 15 January 1936. While the anarchists, the other prominent element of the left, maintained a traditional distance from electoral politics, their militants did support the Front in the elections on the 16 February and so contributed to its victory, although this was won by only a narrow margin of the popular vote. The new government's programme was modest to say the least. Although it called for the release of political prisoners and the rehabilitation of those persecuted following the October uprising of 1934 (and, after all, it could do no less), it was, despite the demands of the Socialist left, lacking any economic or social policies of reform. The programme was thus, as E.H. Carr points out, a 'mild and anodyne document, evidently designed to rally a wide coalition of divergent interests and sectors of opinion, united only in their commitment to the republic and to some form of democratic government'.[4] As such it fitted perfectly Stalin's desire to hold the forces of social revolution in check and maintain the coalition with the bourgeoisie against the Fascist threat, for his own political ends rather than those of the Spanish people.

Despite this apparent show of moderation from the Republican government, the parties of the right and their military allies viewed the growing militancy of the working classes as a provocation to social revolution, and perceived that the inherent instability of the Popular Front coalition could not long deny the workers' expectant mood. Moreover, the right concluded that it had little to gain from electoral politics as then constituted in Spain, despite the narrowness of the popular vote against it, and determined on armed rebellion against the Republic as the only hope of a return to power.

Following much plotting and prevarication the rising began on the night of 17/18 July 1936, the date having been brought forward after the plot was discovered in the Spanish colony of Morocco. On the mainland, the rebels' initial objectives were to seize control of the major cities, with the possible exception of Madrid and Barcelona, and eventually force the Republican government to surrender. However, events did not go as the rebels had hoped; amid much confusion, even bordering on farce, sides were taken for or against the government – and were changed again according to developments in each area. The military's failure to achieve its objectives by taking the government by surprise should have spelled disaster for the rebels, with the navy and small airforce remaining loyal to the Republic. But General Francisco Franco, who had joined the plot at the last moment from his virtual exile in the Canary Isles, appealed directly to Nazi Germany for help in airlifting the stranded Foreign Legion from Morocco to the mainland. Hitler's enthusiastic response in providing Franco with the necessary aircraft prevented the collapse of the rebellion on the mainland, projected Franco into the *de facto* leadership of the Nationalist cause and set the pattern for the foreign intervention that came to characterise the conflict.

The confused picture at the beginning of the rebellion now quickly stabilised, with the Nationalists controlling the west and northwest of Spain, with the exception of the Basque country, and the Republicans in control of the east and northeast, including the capital Madrid and the all-important industrial area of Catalonia and its capital Barcelona. This stand-off could lead to nothing other than a protracted and bloody civil war, which was a direct consequence of the Republic's failure to crush the rising within the first 48 hours, compounded by Prime Minister Quiroga's refusal to countenance the arming of the workers. The unions, fearful of government inaction and the possibility of its total collapse, responded by calling strikes, commandeering transportation and factories and mobilising into militias. On the morning of the 19 July Quiroga resigned and President Azana called upon Martinez Barrio to form a government, which, in the event comprised only Republicans. Barrio's first act was to attempt a negotiated settlement with the rebels, which was turned down flat by General Mola. With its seeming sole purpose defeated, the government immediately fell. Azaña now turned for his next prime minister to José Giral, whose more purposeful stance saw him decree the dissolution of the army and order the arming of workers' organisations.

Giral's government could never hope to obtain the full support of all the elements within the Republican coalition now that a system of dual power had effectively been created. It became increasingly clear to Republicans and Socialists alike that only the left Socialist Largo Caballero could maintain the link with the revolutionary committees that had been established. The resignation of Giral's government on 4 September paved the way for Caballero's premiership. Once in power Caballero's first task was to set about creating a broader-based administration, including members of the PCE, which would attempt to assert central control over these local committees. The anarchists were offered places within Caballero's government and refused, but through a tacit acceptance of the need for a change in the conduct of the war they accepted the concept of central control. Thus at the end of September in the strategically important region of Catalonia, the Anti-Fascist Militia Committee was eventually subsumed within the Catalan 'Generalidad', with the CNT joining the Catalan government.

Undoubtedly Largo Caballero's prestige was instrumental in cementing the political agreements thought necessary for a successful prosecution of a conventional war against the Nationalist rebels. However, neither the political changes nor the courage of the Spanish people in resisting the military could hope to prevail, in the face of sustained German and Italian help for the rebels. By the autumn of 1936 a series of military reverses for the Republic put the Nationalists within striking distance of Madrid, eventually forcing the government in November to abandon the capital for the relative safety of Valencia. Although the fall of Madrid would not have spelled total disaster for the Republic, its symbolic significance as the heart of Spain could have tipped the balance dangerously in favour of the rebels. The heroic but desperate defence of the city seemed to serve only to underline the critical situation faced by the Caballero administration.

Morally, any legitimate government facing an equivalent threat could have expected the aid and assistance of the other major democracies. However the response from the European powers, especially Britain, to the Republic's request for material help was an attempt to contain the conflict and, ostensibly, prevent the flow of munitions to the peninsula. France, guided by the Conservative British government, had been persuaded to propose an internationally binding agreement to this effect. This was eventually signed by all the leading powers, including Germany and Italy, and supervised by a Non-Intervention Committee whose members were drawn from among the signatories.

This so-called non-intervention policy was, as E.H. Carr points out, 'tainted with hypocrisy', for 'Nobody believed that it would be observed.'[5] The continued supply of arms to the Nationalists from both the Italians and the Germans attested to this fact. Internationally, the policy had less to do with containment than with Britain's attempts to come to terms with Hitler and, it could be cynically argued, to protect its financial interests in Spain. To that end the British government was at best ambivalent to the requests of a Republican government whose principal allies were Mexico and the Soviet Union. The situation for Léon Blum in France was considerably more problematic, for while he had no desire for France to appear divided from Britain, especially in the face of Hitler's bellicose rhetoric, his government had come to power that spring on a coalition platform similar to that in Spain, and the policy of non-intervention was seen, in French terms anyhow, as one Popular Front 'failing to help another'.[6] This was a blow from which Blum's prestige never recovered, and with his administration stumbling thereafter he fell from power as the crisis in Spain reached a critical peak in 1937. The USSR, another of the signatories to the agreement, came under pressure from within the Comintern as the ceaseless flow of German and Italian munitions tipped the scales of war away from the Republic. By the autumn of 1936 the number of Soviet advisers and personnel in Spain had increased, however, reflecting the emerging importance of the Spanish PCE, and a trickle of supplies began to break the agreement. In all its essentials non-intervention had now become a fiction which the Soviet Union could no longer sustain, or even wish to:

> On October 7, at a particularly heated meeting of the non-intervention committee, the Soviet delegate read a declaration that the Soviet government 'cannot agree to turn the non-intervention argument into a screen to cover military aid to the insurgents from some participants in the agreement', and that, 'unless violations of the non-intervention agreement are stopped at once, it will consider itself free from the obligations flowing from the agreement'.[7]

With the mask of non-intervention finally removed, the Soviet Union stepped up its rate of supply to the beleaguered Republic.

For the Republicans the consequence of this help was Stalin's increased influence over the affairs of the government and the conduct of the war, mediated through the Comintern and the PCE. Stalin's policy in Spain, tied as inevitably as it was to his larger political aims, presented him with as many dilemmas as advantages. While Soviet help to Republican Spain elevated his standing in the eyes of many, and while he could not, as Deutscher claims, 'but wish Franco's defeat', it was also true that:

The civil war, on the other hand, was fraught with revolutionary com-
plications. The working-classes, armed for the defence of the republican
Government, were tempted to establish a proletarian dictatorship,
Communist or Anarcho-Communist. The landless peasants, in a
country feudal as old Russia, pressed for agrarian revolution.[8]

This was a scenario that could have seen the end of the delicate balance
of power ranging Russia with Britain and France against Germany, and
could have wrested the control of world revolutionary leadership from
Stalin's grasp. The prospect of this led Stalin to 'conduct from the Kremlin
a civil war within the Spanish civil war'[9] to hold back the forces of social
revolution. This policy effectively brought the PCE, the Republicans
and the Socialist right to oppose the left of the Socialist Party and, more
devastatingly still, the anarchists, syndicalists and independent Marxists
of the POUM. It was conducted by effectively stifling the spontaneous
military and industrial organisation that had arisen at the start of the war.

This policy, though applied across the whole of Republican Spain,
had its clearest effects in the POUM stronghold of Catalonia, where
the newly formed PSUC engaged in a vigorous power struggle against
the POUM and other revolutionaries, using innuendo, threats and
physical intimidation, including suggestions that the POUM was a
Trotskyist organisation in the pay of Franco, Hitler and Mussolini. Serge,
who had publicly stated his support for the POUM at the outbreak of
the war, chronicled the course of this coercion in the pages of *La
Révolution prolétarienne*, with his article 'Crimes in Russia, Intrigues in
Spain',[10] drawing a parallel with the recent trials in Russia and the tactics
now being adopted by the Stalinist-inspired forces in Spain. Later, as
the provocation intensified, Serge informed his comrades in the POUM,
through the pages of its paper *La Batalla*, not to be 'under any illusions',
as the 'campaign that has started against you is not going to end. In the
present state of affairs the Stalinist bureaucracy is utterly unable to
tolerate any political formations which are outside its influence and which
know it too well.' For, as Serge continued:

> The plan of the Stalinists can only be: to quarantine Red Catalonia,
> forming against it a bloc of the liberal bourgeoisie, the petty bour-
> geoisie and the reformist and official Communist section of the
> working class, and to subdue Barcelona by force. As a beginning, to
> destroy the POUM, neutralising the anarcho-syndicalists; then to
> destroy the CNT. The eventual aim: to institute a parliamentary
> democracy where they will enjoy a concealed hegemony.[11]

This pattern of provocation against the CNT – FAI led inevitably to an explosive and tragic final confrontation between the Communist-inspired government and the POUM and anarchists. In May 1937, the PSUC seized the opportunity presented by a string of military defeats that spring, to move against the POUM and the anarchists. More will be said later about the exact nature of the repression faced by the POUM; but here it is necessary to record that the PSUC's attempts to exert total control by seizing strategic points in Barcelona held and controlled by the CNT – FAI led to several days of fighting in Catalonia which ended with the outlawing of the POUM, the arrest of its leaders and the murder by agents of the Soviet Union of its most prominent member, Nin. None of this did anything to enhance the position of Largo Caballero, who in resisting attempts by the Stalinists to act against the POUM had aroused the wrath of his Communist sponsors. Caballero, referred to as the 'Spanish Lenin' when he had risen to power in September, was now replaced as Prime Minister by the more amenable Negrin.[12]

The success of Stalin's policy in conflating the POUM with 'Trotskyism' and therefore, as in the show trials in Russia itself, presenting it as an agent of Hitler and Mussolini, now left the Stalinists masters of the scene in Spain. Despite this, the military defeats continued to multiply, more especially as Soviet military aid to the Republicans proved in the end to be neither of the quantity or latterly of the quality of that supplied by the Axis powers of Germany and Italy. The Nationalists now made steady progress at the expense of Republican Spain, despite heroic acts of defence, especially on the Ebro. Continued dissensions within the Republican coalition, however, made worse by the trial of the POUM leadership, had a devastating effect upon morale. In the spring of 1939 the Republic was close to collapse. The end came with the surrender of Madrid on 29 March, but Stalin by then had abandoned the Republic to its fate and was secretly negotiating a non-aggression pact with Hitler.

The events outlined here had a twofold effect on Serge and Trotsky's relations. The first was, a broadening of their organisational differences over the Popular Front, as Serge continued to support the POUM and Nin. The second was the controversy that arose in anarchist circles, comparing the tactics of the Stalinists in Spain to those of the Bolsheviks in Russia, and centring upon the Kronstadt rising of 1921. This was a theme that Serge enlarged upon, bringing his disagreements with Trotsky on to a public level and angering his former friend. Their relationship never recovered from this.

Trotsky and Serge had known Nin since the early days of the Communist International in the Soviet Union, which Nin had attended as a Spanish delegate. Nin, as one of the founding members of Spanish Communism, worked for the Comintern as secretary of the trade union organisation. He became close to both Serge and Trotsky, whom he supported in his struggle with Stalin in the 1920s, sharing with them the persecution that flowed from the defeat of the Trotskyist Opposition. It came as a surprise therefore when Nin was released from the Soviet Union and allowed to return home after the fall of the Spanish monarchy in 1930.

After his release Nin corresponded extensively with Trotsky as events in Spain unfolded.[13] Their relationship became strained, however, over Nin's refusal to support Trotsky's tactic of entry into the French Socialist Party and Nin's role in the creation of the POUM and its subsequent support for the Popular Front at the elections in February 1936. Nin now saw Trotsky as a sectarian, and for his part Trotsky considered Nin a class collaborationist;[14] thus by the time Serge arrived in the West in April 1936 Trotsky's relations with Nin had broken down completely.

As the situation in Spain moved inexorably towards civil war, Trotsky was, as Greeman says, hopeful that: 'Nin would finally break with the Popular Front politicians and lead the armed masses to push forward the social revolution through the instrumentality of the militias, factory committees, juntas, and other organs of popular power.'[15] This is reflected in his letter to Serge on 5 June 1936, when he wrote that despite not being hopeful of 'converting Nin into a revolutionary', the signs for a rapprochement looked favourable. He proposed that Serge should use his good offices with Nin to 'try to influence him back', but for this to happen Nin 'must openly unfurl the banner of the Fourth International in Spain'.[16] Indeed throughout that summer Serge was keen to offer his proposals to Trotsky as to how the Fourth International should react to the events in Spain, suggesting that:

> the conference [of the Fourth International] and the French organ-
> isation should immediately elect substantial delegations to leave
> immediately for Spain [...who should] conduct broad propaganda
> aimed at the rank and file and the newspapers, and if possible [place]
> a band of (?) 10 or 20 comrades at the disposal of the workers' front
> in Spain.[17]

Later Serge proposed that the Fourth International should fight alongside the partisans of the CNT – FAI to assure the freedom of opinion for all the tendencies within Spain:

to prevent the bureaucrats of every stripe from turning the revolution into a Stalinist-type prison for the workers [...For] We consider you, the anarchists and syndicalists, to be our class comrades and dedicated revolutionaries. We offer you our fullest cooperation along with uncompromising criticism and ideological struggle, carried out in a fraternal atmosphere.[18]

It is clear from Trotsky's letter of 19 August 1936 that, despite certain tensions generally expressed between the two men over the Popular Front, a large measure of agreement existed over Spain:

What you write about Spanish, or rather Catalonian anarchists is absolutely true and I am extremely glad about our unity of opinion on this principal question of the present moment. Unfortunately we are only observers... The most important thing now would be to find organic forms of collaboration between the POUM and the unions in Catalonia (juntas, soviets, Committees of Action?), *even at the expense of considerable concessions in organisational matters*. [emphasis added.][19]

The hopeful sentiments expressed by Trotsky in his exchanges with Serge during that first summer of the war did not survive the political changes of the autumn,[20] engendered by the elevation of Caballero to Prime Minister and Minister of War, which saw the POUM enter the Generalidad with its leader Nin accepting a post as Minister of Justice. With Trotsky by now interned in Norway awaiting a visa for Mexico, the first effects of these developments were evident in the increased rhetoric of the Fourth International, accusing the POUM of class collaboration in joining the Generalidad, and in the POUM's response by expelling from the party the few Trotskyists who had been members. By the time Trotsky was safely in Mexico, Serge was already indicating how far the situation had deteriorated, telling Trotsky of the considerable differences that had arisen between himself and other comrades in the Fourth International 'over Spanish affairs and the POUM',[21] which effectively precipitated the first split between Serge and Trotsky's followers.

This split occurred following Serge's attendance at the Fourth International conference, held, according to Vereeken's recollection, on 12–13 January 1937. There Serge and the comrades he was closest to, Vereeken and Sneevliet, opposed the policy of the Fourth International in Spain, proposing a motion of solidarity with the POUM which was defeated and which had them, according to Vereeken again:

singled out and accused of denigrating and dishonouring the 'heroic work' carried out by the 'Bolshevik-Leninists' who, in agreement with the IS, were trying to form a new revolutionary leadership to take the place of the 'treacherous leadership' of the POUM.[22]

Serge, bitterly dismayed by the failure of his attempts to re-establish comradely relations between the Fourth International and the POUM, and in equal measure devastated by the machinations of the Fourth over Spain and other questions, now began to distance himself from its groups and activities, as he recalled in his *Carnets* some years later: 'from 1937 onwards I removed myself completely from this "movement"'.[23]

From his letter to the POUM Executive Committee of 18 January 1937 through to his 'Notes on the Spanish Drama' written in the immediate aftermath of the tragic events of Barcelona that May, Serge, while consistently warning of the dangers it faced, publicly reiterated his support for the POUM and the line it had taken.[24] In his letter to Trotsky on 20 March 1937 Serge justified this position with his conviction that the 'POUM is the only healthy, thinking mass organisation there and [I] believe that despite its many mistakes it behaves splendidly on the whole'. And once again he took issue with the Trotskyists whose 'factional attitudes led to the deepening of the gulf between the leadership [of the POUM] and the so-called orthodoxies from the Fourth'. Furthermore, Serge in stating that it was necessary to 'start from Spanish reality', and 'develop and use what is there', echoed the discussions over the Popular Front of the previous summer. He believed that while the 'POUM is certainly not a Bolshevik-Leninst party', the 'Bolshevik-Leninists must learn to work with other Marxist revolutionaries, to influence them, collaborate with them, in order to become an influential current themselves they must abandon the imposition of their hegemony'.[25]

During this period Trotsky made no direct reply to Serge, other than the open letter defending him against the attacks of the Communist press in France.[26] However, it was the mistakes of the POUM which actively occupied Trotsky at this juncture rather than the wholesome nature of the organisation itself. Trotsky's attitude to the situation in Spain, and to the POUM and Nin, can be gleaned from his public pronouncements at the time and from his published correspondence with other comrades. To the French News Agency Havas, in his first public interview after arriving in Mexico, he expressed himself happy to accept that the POUM was not a Trotskyist party and went on to say that despite having 'warm sympathy for the heroism with which the members of

the party, above all the youth, struggle at the front', he had had to criticise
its policies often, for 'The POUM has committed the error of participating in the electoral combination of the "Popular Front".' And in
his opinion it had then committed the 'second error of entering the
Catalan coalition government'.[27]

In a letter to a comrade only a few days later, Trotsky further criticised
the policy of the POUM leadership, effectively Nin, as being one of
'adaptation, expectation, hesitation, that is to say, the most dangerous
of all policies during a civil war, which is uncompromising', damning
it as the policy of 'Martov, not of Lenin. And for victory, the policy of
Lenin is needed.'[28] A little later Nin was again personally condemned
by Trotsky for making nothing other than six years of mistakes in
impeding the creation of a genuinely revolutionary party in Spain.[29]
We are a long way here from the promising signs of the summer of
1936 and Serge's hoped-for understanding between the Fourth International and the POUM. There was little to suggest that Trotsky would
use his influence to swing the Fourth International behind the organisation; rather, there was a strengthening of the earlier rhetoric against
Nin and the POUM.

Throughout this period the situation on the ground in Spain continued
to deteriorate dramatically. Then in the summer of 1937 a series of military
reverses precipitated the Stalinists' first direct moves against the revolutionaries in Catalonia and preparations for the ousting of Caballero,
whom they now perceived as an obstacle. Following the steadily
increasing rise in provocative incidents the PSUC attempted to take
control of strategic points in Barcelona held by the CNT – FAI. This
was met with a spontaneous move to the barricades by the workers, a
move which the POUM supported despite the pessimism of its leadership
as to what could be achieved.[30] It was this pessimism, not communi-
cated in any direct way to the workers, that effectivly prevented the
POUM leadership from taking the initiative at this decisive phase, for
they believed themselves 'too weak to lead the workers to power'.[31]
Moreover a deep sense of loyalty to the anarchist leaders in Catalonia
led them to fall in behind the anarchist leadership when 'The CNT-
anarchist ministers of the Valencia government proceeded to endorse
a meaningless paper "compromise" and then called the workers to lay
down their arms and return to work.'[32] For the POUM this was a most
fatal error. The repression of the organisation began immediately, with
the disarming and rounding up of its militants, the arrest of its leadership
and the disappearance of Nin to certain death at the hands of Stalinist
agents. On 28 May 1937 the POUM journal was banned, and on

16 June the organisation itself was outlawed by decree.[33] Sadly the group's comrades in the CNT – FAI stood aside and did nothing to prevent these arrests; it was an ignoble end and, as Greeman says, 'If the POUM failed to rise to its historic mission, the behaviour of the CNT – FAI leaders was nothing short of a betrayal.'[34]

As we have already noted, this left the Stalinists in control of the situation, but their repression had finally killed off the Spanish Revolution as effectively as Franco could have wished or done himself. The Spanish proletariat and peasantry, now doubly betrayed, stumbled to defeat with Stalin clinging to the coat-tails of Hitler.

The pressure of these events, as we have seen, drove Serge away from activity within the mainstream of the Trotskyist movement in Europe. It did not, however, force an immediate rupture between himself and Trotsky, despite the difficulties Serge was having with the Fourth International. This can be attested by the spirited defence of Serge that Trotsky offered when his comrade was attacked by the Communist press in France following the success of his book *De Lenine à Staline*. It was rather the aftermath of the May events and the inevitable post-mortem, forcing their disagreements into an open forum, that give rise to the estrangement.

Trotsky, in response to the questions of a German journalist likening the tactics of the Stalinists in Spain to those of the Bolsheviks in Russia during the civil war,[35] especially towards the anarchists and in particular with regard to the suppression of the Kronstadt uprising of 1921, gave answers that Serge felt were unsatisfactory. He therefore published an article on Kronstadt in *La Révolution prolétarienne*,[36] 'Fiction and Fact. Kronstadt', which sought to open what he considered to be in the light of recent events an educative and informative discussion; in Serge's view this was a healthy exercise for revolutionaries to indulge in. Trotsky was less than pleased with Serge's decision to extend this debate, to which others now added their views, embroiling Trotsky in what he considered to be unnecessary arguments at this delicate political juncture. The course of this controversy is detailed in Chapter 4 below and thus lies outside the scope of this section, but its immediate consequence was, as we have seen from Chapter 2 above, a falling off of the correspondence between Serge and Trotsky.

Following Serge's letter of 20 March 1937 it was nearly a year to their next exchange, when Serge wrote to offer condolences for the premature death of Trotsky's son Leon Sedov.[37] Trotsky was moved to reply, but only to resume their polemic, to offer his criticism of Serge's assertion that their disagreements were only secondary: 'In your letter you touched upon our disagreements and called them "secondary". Unfortunately I cannot agree with this at all. If the disagreements between Bolshevism and Menshevism are secondary, then what is meant by the word primary?' Trotsky further castigated Serge for joining in the Kronstadt controversy: 'Instead of stamping on the traitors of the revolution and falsifiers of history, you immediately spoke in their defence.'[38] With the atmosphere between the two men now so poisoned it became easy for the provocateur at the heart of the Fourth International to complete the rift by exploiting the publicity insertion to Serge's translation of Trotsky's *Their Morals and Ours*.[39]

It seems fairly clear from the evidence that the opposing positions that Serge and Trotsky adopted on the events in Spain could only have led to a split. Moreover, given the nature of the defeat of the POUM in circumstances that Trotsky clearly outlined in advance, it seems that Serge's support of the POUM was politically naive. It could likewise be argued that Serge's stance was as much a product of the stridency of the Fourth International against the POUM and that this led Serge to adopt, despite his own warnings, a less than critical approach both to the POUM as an organisation and to Nin as its leader. Equally, had the Fourth International gone any way towards adopting Serge's suggestions how different might events have been? The accuracy of Trotsky's earlier comment to Serge, that they were 'only observers',[40] is striking when set against the machinations of the Fourth International against the POUM and the totality of the war itself, whose most decisive juncture must surely have been the effective abandonment of the Republic to the fiction and hypocrisy of non-intervention. But with Trotsky's followers visibly divided and exerting little authority over the Spanish proletariat, and with Serge an increasingly isolated figure, it is difficult to see how they could have influenced events and prevented the revolution's eventual ruin.

THE DOCUMENTS

Victor Serge. Letter to Andrès Nin[41]

Brussels, August 7, 1936

Dear Andrès,

My old friend, I'm very anxious about you and happier even more to know at last that you are inside the great upheaval, using to the full all the hours that you have. (I have had the most disquieting news about

Joaquin [Maurin]; don't delay in giving me any better news if he is safe, don't delay a minute.) I hesitated before writing to you, having a strong sense of the emptiness of words and of anything one can feel or think or say from a distance in moments when action is all that counts. I know that you probably can't write back. But send some sort of acknowledgement and your own publications. Perhaps they will bring me a bit of the tonic air of a revolution in which I still believe after nearly twenty years. I believe in it because I have enough knowledge of the workers of Spain and the general situation you are in, and because ever since 1917 it has seemed to me that an exceptional responsibility would come into your grasp in this sick world of the West. This sickness of the West, this debility of the old system on which the Fascisms feed is basically the debility of the working class. Nowhere, except in Russia for a few years, has it risen to the height of its task; it has let slip the best opportunities to free itself and put an end to chaos, it has let itself be led by charlatans, innocents and cowards, and its revolutionary bankruptcy has made a historical fortune for the Mussolinis and the Hitlers. But that debility could be explained by the blood-letting imposed on it by the war. What would the physical shape be of Europe today if France, Germany, Austria, Italy had five or six million more proletarians, who now would be men in their forties, matured by the experience of work and struggle? But the Spanish working class never underwent that frightful bleeding, it kept all its vital forces intact. Its numerical and moral superiority (the moral strength resulting from the integrity of its forces, as with the inner equilibrium of a healthy man) is such, therefore, that I find it incontestably the class which is destined to triumph. All the various Rights united against it are still a minority, educated it is true and with generals at its call for everything, but less capable of fighting properly even on the scale of numbers: what the generals mainly know is how to send other people to be killed. It would need in your party senseless divisions, errors, retreats, I don't know what failings in judgement for them to be able to beat you. Or else perhaps some man of genius, a Bonaparte born specially to kill his own country, might be found among the military and perform wonders. I think that such men are not produced by history against the masses, and mention this hypothesis only to state the problem fully.

On the contrary, you must count on events to give *you* new men, to forge in the crucible a true party of revolution destined to assume all its responsibilities. Men from all parties, all tendencies (and none) will form it without a great process of brainwork, just giving themselves in daily action. Everywhere, at every instant there is room for revolutionary initiative, devotion, courage and intelligence: when each one does his own best, you will see the real stalwarts of the proletariat forming just about everywhere. As I see it, it is these new militants that your propaganda must address mainly, without placing too much importance on the particular backgrounds they come from, in a fraternal spirit concerned to diminish all that divides and strengthen all that unites.

I ask myself just how the problem of power is getting posed in your ranks. A lot of people would like to drown in the Republic's defence: but which Republic? The one which has been maintaining an army now at work murdering the country? Because, basically, it is the Republic which has been feeding those generals of yours in Melilla,[42] right to the present time! The cause which is really at stake is that of the working class and of Socialism. There has to be some good cause to set against the waste, some service to balance the blood spilled by so many comrades. Only a fool or a deceiver could still have any illusions about the 'sensible' democratic formalisms which have got you to where you are. If the generals fail in their coup they can be of immense service to you in wrenching off the masks, annihilating certain illusions, obliging the proletariat at last to take decisive strides towards an entirely different Republic where democracy will mean liberty and the power of the workers, instead of being a compromise with the counter-revolution that lies in ambush behind laws it holds in contempt. After such a lesson, I should think there will no longer be any question of your returning to the point of departure, a point which will be understood by the genuinely Republican elements of the petty bourgeoisie and even those bourgeois who are intelligent enough to spare themselves a civil war of even more atrocious proportions. It is only the working class that can fight Fascism: it alone can create a republic worthy of the name, a democracy which will not be another ambush. It has the right to govern: it can and must begin to heal the wounds and overcome the miseries, to transform society. To vacillate now on this point means compromising everything since the workers cannot be asked to get themselves killed with nothing more serious to defend than the Republic of Señores Alcala Zomora[43] and Azaña. I have observed with satisfaction how the very necessities of the struggle have forced the arming of the proletariat, and then measures of nationalisation and workers' control in various domains. You yourself may remember how I sent you several years ago, from a Leningrad where I was virtually a prisoner, a sort of message intended as a preface to a little book of mine that you wanted to publish: *Lenine 1917*.[44] At that time I quoted to you from Lenin's first letters, written at Zurich in the very first days of the Russian Revolution. I called these letters 'the art of commencing a revolution'. In March 1917 Lenin wrote: armament of the workers, formation of workers' militias, there is no other salvation! That much has been done. Now it is a matter of holding on to your weapons, recalling the experience of 1848 and of all time: first the people fight on the barricades, and then the politicians wheedle the power away from them and ensure that the revolutionary *avant-gardes* are massacred. That, as a rule, is how the bourgeois republics are founded. Be suspicious, my friends, it is not only the generals that you have to fear. There are certain advocates more skilful and better disguised than they, who tomorrow will ask you to surrender your rifles and not proceed too quickly too far, and to keep out of the strong rooms and safes... After getting past the risk of being killed, you will run that of being conned.

But we can have a limitless confidence in you, comrades. Your safety lies in your own hands, and depends on the firmness and the vision that you possess. There is no authority more legitimate than that of a people in arms and in a state of legitimate defence. Among you what workers' institutions will fill the functions that were performed by soviets in the Russian Revolution? The Alianzas Obreras?[45] The revolutionary committees? The unions? From this distance the possibilities open to you are far from clear, but there is one certainty, and it is that, under pain of being finally defeated – even if it is initially victorious – the working class must control everything through its own organisations. It has only itself to rely on. The Popular Front will be useful only to the extent that it is controlled by the working class. Workers' control of government, workers' control of production, workers' control of the armed forces! This last point is indisputably the most important one.

I read that Ascaso is dead, and was overwhelmed by the news even though all I knew about him was his legend as a militant. After that there were newspaper reports of serious incidents provoked by other anarchists. I thought back to the Russian Revolution: we had our Ascasos then, like Justin Zhuk who upon his release from the Schlus-selburg prison seized the city there for Soviet power and was killed in the civil war; or like Zhelezniakov who chased the speech-makers out of the Constituent Assembly and was later killed in the Ukraine by the Whites. But these could not salvage the Russian anarchist movement from its collapse nor give the Russian Revolution all that their capacities would be permitted, because of the bunglers, the gut-anarchos, the reckless, the uncontrollable committed blunders (and worse) one after another. This tragic history must not be allowed to repeat itself in Spain. If the comrades of the FAI and the CNT can impose a discipline of

free souls in the midst of revolution, their influence will be a precious
antidote against the statist and bureaucratic tendencies of the working-
class movement: their collaboration will bring life to the liberty of the
workers.

I am thinking of all this with a terrible tension running through my
whole being. The common peril, the common will for victory and world
transformation, the community of spilt blood and felt hopes (since, for
both tendencies, 'the emancipation of the working class will be the task
of the workers themselves'): is there not in all this some basis for the
reconciliation, in and through action and by emulation in the service
of the revolution, of the anarchists and the Marxists?

Affectionate memories to your wife and your daughters (who must
be quite big now). A warm fraternal salute to Andrade, Gorkin[46] and
all our friends. I shake your hand in friendship.

Victor Serge

Victor Serge. Letter to La Batalla[47]

Brussels, October 5, 1936

Esteemed comrades of La Batalla,

For some days now I have been receiving your daily. Thank you.
Allow me, as an old militant and as an old journalist, to congratulate
you on the excellent presentation you have succeeded in making of it.
It brings me here the living voice of the Spanish Revolution which is
reaching its full height at the moment when the Russian working class,
weary with twenty years of sufferings and sacrifices and in a suffocat-
ing isolation, has withdrawn to a secondary place under the pressure of
bureaucratic thinking. It is you who are picking up the torch and
continuing the work. And I assure you that, in the depths of the prisons
and the Siberias all Oppositionists of the USSR, Socialists, syndicalists,
anarchists and Trotskyists, are with you with all their hearts. It is just a
year ago that I and my friends deported to the Urals, left Communists
and anarchists, lived through agonising days as we deciphered the
events from the Asturias in the newspapers. If the Soviet government
would agree to permit the enrolment in your militias of those revolutionaries whom it is depriving of liberty, many of October's warriors
would very soon be with you. I have not seen these men for some months
but I know their ideas and their wishes, and fulfil a duty by sending
you this message in their name. We believe that only the working class
can today bring salvation to the world, by fulfilling its mission wholly

and unyieldingly. That class has the right to everything, since in conquering everything it liberates all humanity. Good luck and fraternal greetings from your,

Victor Serge

Victor Serge. 'Crimes in Russia, Intrigues in Spain'. From *La Révolution prolétarienne*.[48]

With each resounding crime perpetrated by those contemptible rulers of totalitarian states the human spirit of our times falls a little lower and the next crime is made just that bit easier. After the sixteen shot in Moscow, what is the value of the life of Edgar André?[49] The Nazi executioner's axe strikes. What now is the value of the life of the fighters of October who have been swallowed up in Stalin's jails?

At the end of November, just when there appeared in the *Cahiers des Droits de l'Homme* in Paris the strange report by Mr Rosenmark to the effect that the murder of Lenin's comrades had been carried out with sufficient respect to the process of law, there unfolds the alarming trial of Novosibirsk where the falsity of the confessions is so brazen that the reader has to rub his eyes in disbelief. Such is their criminal cynicism that you would have to go back a long way to find its equal. Nine unfortunate wretches, one of whom was a German, all engineers and technicians at the mine where a terrible accident cost the life of fourteen workers, appeared before the court and confessed unstintingly. Stickling, the German, admitted to being an agent of the Gestapo. The engineers declared that they had the accident on the orders of Trotskyists in order to harm 'our great People's Commissar Ordjionikidze'[50] and in order to prepare the road for the coming of Fascism to the USSR! This is at the same time both scandalous and idiotic. During the proceedings, one of the accused admitted to having taken part near Moscow, in 1927 – nineteen-twenty-seven! – in a meeting at which Trotsky sealed his alliance with the Nazis. I'm not exaggerating; it's the honest truth. Of course, neither was there, nor could there have been a single Trotskyist in the dock. There were only some unfortunate wretches, tortured, terrorised and compliant, deprived of shame and bereft of reason, torn between the certainty of being shot if they resisted and the slender hope of survival even at that price...

Like a refrain, the name of Muralov[51] keeps coming up, a genuine Left Oppositionist since 1927, who took Moscow in February 1917 and retook it in October 1917, a tireless soldier of two revolutions. He has disappeared. Piatakov,[52] the most defeatist of defeatists, who abandoned us in 1928 to become the faithful servant of Stalinism, has also disappeared. A friend who knows him well and I were wondering why and could only think of two explanations: Get rid of the witnesses! And again: Piatakov drank. Perhaps he shot his mouth off while drunk, and said things that he still felt deep down.

The nine accused were inevitably condemned to death. The German was reprieved, naturally, and as a result saved the life of two of the Russians: only six executions took place. And they are preparing new trials.

And they are preparing other things, too, because everything is linked, because the workers' revolution is one and the same worldwide; everything that rots it, bloodies it, betrays it in one place affects painfully and dangerously all others.

Let's lance the wound. Why keep silent about these matters? Of course we can understand the eloquent silences of Vendredi... These are the facts. In Spain there is a major workers' opposition party, that is to say one that is resolutely opposed to the Stalinist concept of Socialism, to the totalitarian state, to the bureaucratic system, called the Partido de Unification Marxista – The Workers Party of Marxist Unity – abbreviated to the POUM.

One of its founding members, Joaquin Maurin, was shot by the rebels. The head of its first motorised column, Etchebehere, a pure proletarian hero, was killed in Madrid many long weeks ago... And Germinal Vidal and José Oliver and Pedro Villarosa... the dead of this party can no longer be numbered.

At the same time when the Junta to defend Madrid was being set up, the only party committee that had not left the capital was the POUM's; and though the influence of this party was measurably as great as the Stalinists', the POUM found itself excluded from the Junta.

Socialist militants, syndicalists and anarchists wanted to collaborate with the POUM and informed our friends Andrade and Gorkin accordingly. The anarchist Minister Juan Lopez (CNT) went on record to this effect in an interview with delegates from the POUM which was reported in the press of Valencia.

Here we learn that it was pressure of ultimatums from the Stalinist party and the Soviet legation in Madrid which forced the exclusion of the POUM from the Junta of Defence. *Batalla* (27 Nov) commented on this unbelievable event saying (note the moderation of its tone):

'It is intolerable that those who provide us with a certain amount of aid should expect to impose on us their preconceived political norms, their vetos and their de facto control of Spanish political life.'

From that time onwards, there followed certain other acts of aggression against Spanish revolutionaries: the sacking of the offices of the Communist Youth (question: Jeunesses Communistes; is this the youth organisation of the CP of Spain or is it a united front formation of left-wing youth??) of Madrid by a gang of Stalinists and the banning of the Madrid paper of the POUM, the first blow against freedom of opinion struck under the revolutionary democracy.

Batalla adds that 'The Soviet consulate in Barcelona is orchestrating a campaign of insults and slander against us.'

Even worse, there are threats: the Spanish Stalinists have also felt free to talk about 'using the iron fist'(sic). We'll have to see about that. But this tone and style of speaking should not be forgotten.

On 28th November, the Soviet consulate issued a venomous statement to the press officially accusing the press of the POUM of being 'in the pay of international Fascism'. *Treball*, the organ of the Stalinist party in Barcelona (the PSUC) categorically denounces the comrades from the POUM as 'agents of Franco-Hitler-Mussolini' and daily adds that, anyway, they are Trotskyists and consequently agents of the Gestapo, 'as has been proved at the Moscow trial'. So you can see how all these infamies are linked and how far they can stretch!

It is in order to make the strangling of revolutionaries in Spain more effective that the old revolutionaries are being murdered in Russia!

Of course it goes without saying that Soviet influence is equally great over the petit-bourgeois press of Catalonia where many politicians would dearly love to be rid one day of the most intransigent revolutionary proletarians. *La Humanidad* faithfully repeats all these vile lies.

Batalla answers on the 29th, in a very firm but moderate note, recalling the number of its dead, its tradition of loyalty to the principles of Communism and that it defended the USSR in periods when many of its present adulators were proffering insults.

Then there occurred a curious underhand intervention, particularly curious since the POUM is a member of the Government of the Generality(?) of Catalonia, and in which my old friend Nin is in charge of the Justice Department. The censors intervened to prevent the re-publication of the statement by the POUM in other journals like *Batalla*.

And we also learn, at the same time, that dark plots are being hatched to exclude the POUM from the Government of the Generality.

If the Stalinist manoeuvres succeed (and for this to happen the comrades of the CNT and the FAI would have to allow themselves to be conned – something that they would dearly pay for in the future), the ensuing phases of the operation would be obvious: the Soviet consulate in Barcelona would endeavour to obtain the banning of *Batalla*, that is to say impose the rule of the gag on the Catalan workers' movement, and to complete the seizure of this movement, judicial comedies *à la* Moscow and Novosibirsk would be organised against Spanish revolutionaries, trials about 'plots with Hitler-Franco-Mussolini...'

By denouncing their political opponents as 'agents of international Fascism', to a people, often illiterate, fighting for its very life and homes, the official representatives of the USSR and the Spanish Stalinists are committing a genuine crime against the common cause and opening the way for many others. This type of calumny is a poisonous weapon that cannot be lightly used. Within the embattled camp of the Spanish Revolution, the agents of Fascism must be shot or, if they are unwitting agents, rendered harmless. The revolutionaries at whose face this kind of filth is being thrown and who feel themselves herded towards some ambush should themselves put their slanderers in the dock. The comrades of the POUM have demonstrated their strength and cool-headedness often enough to merit our trust. May the international workers' opinion stand by with vigilance.

Victor Serge

Victor Serge. Letter to the Executive Committee of the POUM in La Batalla[53]

January 18, 1937

Dear comrades,

I am seizing an outstanding opportunity to send you this letter without its passing through the censorship in the post, where the Stalinists have certainly not omitted to place their agents... I want to draw your attention very rapidly to a number of important questions.

1. Don't be under any illusions, the campaign that has started against you is not going to end. In the present state of affairs the Stalinist bureaucracy is utterly unable to tolerate any political formations which are outside its influence and which know it too well. Prepare yourselves for a long and extremely dangerous struggle, for these people stop at nothing. Above all, avoid the unpardonable mistake of believing that you can do any kind of deal with them; or of imagining that moderation and loyalty on your side will hold your enemies to a minimum of honesty. In Russia we spent more than ten years trying to come to an understanding with the bureaucrats, to show ourselves as faithful and disciplined, to prove our revolutionary virtues before men who were actually leading us to

physical extermination – for that solution is a political necessity for the class of climbers who in that country have wrested the power from the working class.

2. There must be some way, surely, of preparing short little leaflets in Russian, drafted in basic terms, aimed at the Russian seaman visiting Spain. On subjects such as: What Is the POUM?, Why We Are Slandered, Towards Socialism or Back to the Bourgeoisie, etc. They could easily be printed in Paris. The Russian reader must be told that the mere possession of such a leaflet on Soviet territory or aboard a Soviet ship will cost him years of imprisonment. For this reason the leaflets will not be taken readily by the Russian sailors – who never go out alone but only in pairs, one of them a Stalinist to spy on the other; besides, the crews who sail abroad are selected very specially. So you must find ways of distributing them or sticking them up on the quayside, etc.

3. The plan of the Stalinists can only be: to quarantine Red Catalonia, forming against it a bloc of the liberal bourgeoisie, the petty bourgeoisie and the reformist and official Communist section of the working class, and to subdue Barcelona by force. As a beginning, to destroy the POUM, neutralising the anarcho-syndicalists; then to destroy the CNT. The eventual aim: to institute a parliamentary democracy where they will enjoy a concealed hegemony.

4. On your general political line I am completely in agreement with you. In respect to perspectives, bear with me as I offer the following variation for your attention. Of course there is no solution except in a planned economy for the benefit of the workers, ie in the *practical* transition to Socialism. However, you are menaced by two Fascist powers, and the working class in the democratic countries is still in no position effectively to counter the activity of the bourgeoisies who, fundamentally, would rather have Franco than a proletarian regime. Circumstances compel you to take account of this situation by some half-measures. In 1920–21, in order to foil a Japanese intervention in the Far East, the Russian Bolsheviks established a Far Eastern Democratic Republic at Chita and Vladivostok: this had a parliament and left a certain freedom, rather theoretical it is true, for bourgeois property. (In fact the army was Sovietised and the parliament at Chita had a strong revolutionary-proletarian majority.) This republic was founded, on the instructions of Lenin and the CC, by Ivan Smirnov[54] who was shot last July in Moscow, and the anarchist, Shatov, was its war minister. The main point is to ensure effective control of production and the armed forces and the effective hegemony of the revolutionary workers' organ-

isations in the bodies of authority. The names of the institutions, the officials, the titles and even the constitutional forms are quite secondary.

5. Concerning Trotskyism. A Trotskyist sectarianism unfortunately exists, the result of a decade's resistance to persecution. Even though my closest comrades have been the Trotskyists of Russia I find it legitimate for the POUM to want to safeguard its proper character as a mass party. The Spanish Revolution has to be Spanish and Lenin employed these very terms to indicate that any movement in a given country must have its own character and follow its own development. Nevertheless, within your mass party there must be room for the Trotskyist Communists of the left, even doctrinaire ones, provided that they accept its fraternal discipline: and, on the Russian question, I must hope that, at an appropriate time, you will express the sharpest possible condemnation of the bureaucratic oppression there and give full credit to the Oppositionists who over ten years have been paying with their lives for upholding the thought and will of revolutionary Marxism.

6. On the Russian question I suggest there must be some way of commencing a serious joint initiative with the CNT on behalf of the revolutionaries imprisoned there and for the principles of free opinion in the revolution – in defending this principle against the Stalinist bureaucracy you will be posing the question in its true political context and on the strongest possible grounds.

Here is what I propose might be done:

The workers' organisations in Catalonia should publicly offer asylum and the right to work to all revolutionaries deprived of liberty in the Soviet Union, without any distinction of tendency. Principle for this offer: the Spanish revolution believes in freedom of speech within the working class and resolutely undertakes its defence. All this can be put in very moderate terms... And the Catalan workers' organisations should use diplomatic channels to ask the Soviet government for the release, with the right to travel to Spain, of a number of representative militants. They should invite the Soviet Union's consulates to make sure that all the revolutionaries deported and imprisoned there know that they have been offered asylum... A whole series of official and public approaches would have to be started with the working-class bodies and then with the Soviet representatives. The following list of representative personalities might be considered for the demand (the dates of their imprisonment are entered in brackets):

Socialists: Tsederbaum (1921), Cherevanin (1931), Eva Broido (1928), Vladimir Skazin (1934).

Anarchists: Aron Baron (1919), Vladimir Barmash (1927), Sandomirski, Novomirski (1934), Otello Gaggi (1934).

Old Socialists: Barzov and Ryzanov (1931).

Trotskyists: Boris and Victor Eltsin, Fedor Dinglestadt, Groigori Yakovin, Socrate Gevorkian, Maria Yoffe, Dora Zak, Vassili Pankratov, Vassili Chernykh, Chanaan Pevsner, Lado Dumbadze. All in prison since 1928. Alexandra Bronstein (1935).

Foreign Communists: Voya Vujovic, Luigi Calligaris, Stenka Dragic, Stefan Haeberling.

Foreign anarchists: Zeinl Muhsam, Gustave Bouley.

Left Social Revolutionaries: Maria Spiridonova, Trutovsky, Kamov (1919).

It should be added that in actual fact all the members of all these tendencies have been imprisoned.

I end now, dear comrades. At the end of the week I shall be sending some articles for *La Batalla*. The comrade who will give this letter to you will also give you, among others, news about myself. I hope to see you soon and while I am here will do everything I can to be useful to you. I believe that the POUM can show the international workers' movement a really fine example by its unity and its spirit of free criticism, and that at the present time it is the natural rallying point for all those in the world who sincerely want the Socialist revolution. Fraternally yours.

[copy unsigned]

Victor Serge. 'Notes on the Spanish Drama'. From *Les Humbles*[55]

It is necessary to say what nobody is saying: to break the web of voluntary and involuntary complicities. A peculiar silence surrounds certain features of the Spanish drama: those features in particular which relate it to the drama going on in the USSR. The technology of modern news–diffusion works superbly in its propagation of lies for vested interests. Nonetheless, serious things are happening, and we ought to be forewarned of the surprises of tomorrow and the next day. For those who can find security by closing their eyes, history has its own surprises in store – very unpleasant ones.

Three great ideological tendencies have dominated the Spanish Revolution.

First Position: That of Stalinist Communism and the liberal right of the bourgeoisie. (It should be realised that the Stalinists have a strong influence over the much-infiltrated Socialists, especially over the Republican government at Valencia which is totally dependent on

Soviet support.) 'Spain is in the midst of its bourgeois revolution: the task is now to open the path to capitalist development. Spain is engaged in a war against the fascist powers for the cause of the democracies (ie, bourgeois democracies). The Sacred Union; the strong state; the regular army; and respect for property. Whoever speaks of Socialism or the Socialist revolution is playing the game of the enemy, is an agent of the enemy. We must stay within the ground of the Republican constitution and carry on the fight against Fascism: after that we shall see.'

Second Position: That of the radical bourgeoisie and of the centrist and reformist Socialists who are attached to the Socialist ideal and accustomed to the defence of piecemeal working-class interests (Azaña, Companys, Prieto). 'It is impossible to go back to the Republic which existed before the military rising. Profound structural reforms must be undertaken for the benefit of the workers. All the same, the tiger of popular revolt must be kept well caged. Large-scale reforms, certainly: but no discussion of a Socialist system, so that we don't frighten off the middle classes or set the capitalist world against us.'

Third Position: The revolutionary one, that of the FAI, the CNT and the POUM (Partido Obrero de Unificacion Marxista). It is impossible to separate the war from the revolution since it is impossible to win without giving the workers solid reasons for shedding their blood. The real choice before us is: Socialism or Fascism. We are not going to fight for the Republic which put Franco, Quiepo[56] and Mola in charge of its army; which in past years massacred the anarchists at Casas Viejas and the Socialists at Oviedo. We want a different republic. Agrarian reform; workers' control of production; nationalisation of the main industries and of transport; workers' control of the armed forces. For the tasks of reconstruction, note particularly that there must be rationing and the institution of a planned economy; an economy planned, that is, for the benefit of the nation of those who labour, not for the profit of the capitalists when they return from their bolt-holes abroad. 'A workers' and peasants' government' is what the POUM proclaims. The anarchists, on this key question of power, continue to say *nothing*.

Since the Socialists of Spain confine themselves in practice to the vaguest possible professions of anti-Fascism, the main political battle is delivered between the Stalinists – who are formidably active, and dominated by Russian specialists – and the revolutionary tendency of the anarchist (FAI, CNT) or Marxist POUM persuasion. The main stages of this battle can now be summarised:

1. After the formation of the Junta of Defence in Madrid, the POUM (the only party whose committee refused to leave the capital) is evicted

from the Junta, even though its militias are fighting everywhere on the front, and although the Socialists and anarchists rely firmly on its collaboration. There has been an explicit veto on the POUM from the ambassador of the USSR, and the need for Soviet military aid must take priority...

2. Before July 1936, there was hardly any Stalinist presence in Catalonia, where the POUM, founded by Joaquin Maurin (shot by Fascists), was the only popular Marxist party. So a Stalinist party is founded through the fusion of a number of small groups of a Socialist tendency. This party immediately acquires material resources of an almost inexhaustible scale; it enjoys the support of Antonov-Ovseyenko, Consul-General of the USSR (Antonov-Ovseyenko is highly compromised in the Soviet Union through his friendship with Piatakov, Rakovsky and various others either shot or imprisoned in the Moscow trials; he is more or less a doomed man, but this fact only intensifies his zeal as a policy-implementer). The new party, the PSUC, demands the elimination of the POUM from the Generalitat government, thereby provoking a crisis in the coalition. The CNT and the radical Esquerra would have liked to resist but they are cornered: the USSR will not provide arms for a government which includes a party labelled as 'Trotskyist' because of its resolute hostility to the Stalinist bureaucracy. The CNT and Esquerra capitulates: anything to get hold of those munitions. *Izvestia* writes that 'the POUM has been ignominiously expelled from the Catalan government'(sic).

3. The arms bought and paid in gold by the Generalitat are still kept back from Catalonia by the Soviet Union: the Stalinists at first use the very real danger to Madrid as an excuse to divert the consignment in question to the threatened capital; then they refer to the torpedoing of the supply ship *Komsomol*, which was (apparently) on its way to Catalonia with an arms cargo. The outcome is that the weapons which were used as leverage in all this political blackmail have still not arrived...

4. Through parallel procedures, the POUM is expelled from the defence Juntas of the Asturias (where José Oliver has just fallen in battle) and of Aragon (where it has lost Germinal Vidal, Pedro Villarosa and many others, and gained the victories of Monte Aragon and Estrecho Quinto).

5. Catalonia remains too Red in the calculations of the Stalinists, who exert over the Valencia government a hidden influence which (despite the presence of five anarchist ministers) is often preponderant. Valencia now refuses the credits necessary for the Catalan state's developing war industry; to the Catalan militias it refuses to supply armaments. The

Stalinist press ostentatiously declares that Barcelona is packed with men who won't fight; why (their newspapers ask) is no offensive being launched in Aragon? *Solidaridad Obrera* (CNT) and *La Batalla* reply: because you have failed to send us the cartridges! The *Journal de Barcelone*, an organ of idealistic, cosy moderation published in Paris by the Generalitat, writes on March 18, 1937 that in regard to armaments, Catalonia has been 'boycotted and pushed aside'.

6. Equally scandalous: the crisis of grain supply in Barcelona, though it would be quite easy to purchase grain from abroad. What forces refuse or dispute the credits necessary for this, and why? The revolutionary militants know the answer pretty well and do not conceal it.

7. Meanwhile in Madrid the Stalinists, masters of the situation there thanks to the International Brigade, attempt to outlaw the CNT (the Yague incident)[57] and succeed in depriving the POUM of all its propaganda, radio and press media. Largo Caballero refuses to take responsibility for these measures and promises an enquiry, but visibly can do nothing... The censors in Madrid suppress any critical newspaper references to the Soviet Union; they ban a passage of the *Communist Manifesto* and any usage of the word 'revolution'.

8. Against the POUM and (with a degree of deceptive moderation) against the anarchists as well, a campaign of slanders is launched, limitless in violence. Mikhail Koltsov, the *Izvestia* correspondent (a tragic occupation nowadays), writes, in an article reproduced by *L'Humanité*, the Brussels *Voix du peuple* and countless similar sheets, that the POUM is a formation of Franco-Hitler-Mussolini agents who are organising treason in the front line and Trotskyist-terrorist assassinations in the rearguard (statements repeated verbatim). At the moment of this crazy article's publication, Jésus Blanco, the leader of the POUM youth, has been killed in Madrid while commanding the attack on an enemy position: aged twenty-one. In Catalonia all political organisations, with the exception of the PSUC and the Stalinist-led UGT, engage in a solemn pact to abstain from insult and slander in their polemics. *Treball, Mundo Obrero* and *Ahora* prove assiduously, by reference to the Moscow trials, that the POUM is in Franco's service...

9. The same sources accuse the anarchists of various assassination attempts. Much publicity was given to the alleged attemps against Yague in Madrid and Comorera[58] in Barcelona: actually, in neither case did any attempted killing take place. On the other hand, the hero of the FAI *Durruti*[59] *was* killed, behind the lines in suspicious circumstances, through a bullet in the back. The anarchists, through their scruples over unity, made no accusations against anyone. In February six anarchists

were murdered in a neighbourhood not far from Madrid. At Alicante the founders of a new section of the POUM were arrested by some Stalinists and taken to a cemetery to be shot, but were saved by a Socialist militant. Out of concern for anti-Fascist unity, the incident has not been publicised.

10. The Stalinists in Barcelona demand the suppression of the control-patrols which were the institutions of a workers' policing. They either obtain or impose the Generalitat's re-establishment of a Security Corps formed from elements of the old police. It is the start of the disarming of the workers and the rearming of those forces which traditionally fought against the working class (end of February).

11. They also advocate organising a regular and disciplined army, totally outside the control of the workers' organisations and in fact to be commanded by the former officers and Soviet advisers. But how could the militants of the CNT and the POUM agree to do battle, constrained by the military code, under the orders of commanders who do not hide their desire to crush them by force, ie to shoot them?

12. The fall of Malaga to Franco, an impregnable workers' city surrendered without a battle, through treason, resulted in the resignation of the head of the general staff, Colonel Asensio, and produced a number of important revelations. This suppressed scandal put an end to the design of exploiting a lamentable defeat in order to institute an internal state of siege, directed against the language of revolution. At Malaga, as in the general staff, it was the Stalinist influence which prevailed. It became apparent that the criticism of revolutionaries is less dangerous than certain states of mind among governing quarters.

Here are incidents from recent days in Barcelona: On March 8, officers of the Karl Marx Division (which a fortnight ago refused to give covering fire to the CNT and the POUM militias then under attack in Aragon) get ten tanks delivered to them from a depot. Scarcely have the tanks been driven off when it is discovered that the requisitioning order for them was forged. The tanks are in the Voroshilov barracks, whose commanding colonel at first denies the fact. In the end, they are sent back to the depot. Matters are now warming up. It seems clear from this incident that the PSUC has been planning to start a forcible coup. *Solidaridad Obrera* and *La Batalla* demand an enquiry and appropriate punishment, for the deed is atrocious. The Generalitat pleads with them not to insist so much, for fear of aggravating dissensions... And on March 11 it is *La Batalla*, the organ of the POUM, which is suspended for five days for failing to respect the censorship! (An inexplicable decision, made public on the 16th.)

Izvestia writes on February 24: 'Soon it will be understood in Barcelona, as it has already been in Madrid, that any serious struggle against Fascism has to commence with the extermination of the Fascist-Trotskyist provocation on the home front...' I come out of a friend's house here where a Spanish Stalinist passing through Brussels on some mission has made a statement whose words are repeated back to me: 'We've already liquidated fifteen hundred POUM types, and we have still to shoot another five thousand in Barcelona.' On these perspectives, the anarchists would be taken care of in the next batch...

It is not so long ago that an experiment in this kind of politics was conducted in Germany, where Noske cheerfully had the Spartakists shot, in the name of democracy. Today it has become very obvious for whom Noske was preparing the way. (Mid-March.)

Since these notes were committed to paper, the situation has continually worsened. The facts may be left to speak. At the beginning of March the Anti-Fascist Committee of Llerca, near Gerona (Catalonia), which had been formed by seasoned POUM militants, is imprisoned, and only after some sharp interventions by workers' organisations are released. At Villanueva de Alcardate, in the Madrid region, fifteen CNT members and a Republican who happens to be with them are massacred with grenades by 'people from a certain party', as the anarchist press delicately puts it. Meanwhile in Valencia, Maroto and 208 anarchists are arrested – and they are still in prison at the beginning of May. On this affair the opinions of ministers who represent the CNT in the Caballero cabinet are unknown... Maroto is a civil war fighter comparable to Durruti in valour. In Euzkadi (the Basque republic) the organ of the CNT is suppressed by a police force headed by a Stalinist official. At the end of March comes an obscure announcement by President Companys on a governmental crisis in Catalonia: he speaks of the necessity for a government which governs, and hints that the formation of a 'presidential cabinet' may be necessary. What is going on? Simplifying a little: the PSUC, a party of the Stalinists, demands the strengthening of the police and of authority (its own) and the disarming of the revolutionary control-patrols; it wishes to impose a tough general, Pozas, of its own choice, nominated by Valencia, as a commander of the militias on the Aragon front. But, since it is impossible in reality to create a Catalan government against the CNT, the FAI and the POUM, the crisis is prolonged...

On April 27, Roland Cortada, a Stalinist militant of the UGT, is assassinated by unknown persons in the outskirts of Barcelona. A few days previously, an obscure syndicalist killed by the Generalitat's new police had been buried without public demonstrations; the anarchists had refused to make capital out of this 'regrettable incident'. In contrast, the Stalinists seem determined to exploit Cortada's death to the full. Andrade writes in *La Batalla* that 'a veritable pogrom atmosphere is being created against the revolutionary organisations'. April 28: The anarchist Antonio Martin, who had a huge moral authority in the Puigcerda region, is killed near Bellver by 'peasants'... In Barcelona the atmosphere is electric. *La Batalla* states on April 30, 'The machine-guns which are in short supply at the front are being put on show in Barcelona as a reply to revolutionary hopes... A plan is being implemented which reminds us of what happened in Russia after the assassination of Kirov... In our own midst, the role of Noske's Social Democracy is being played by Stalinism.' The CNT and POUM newspapers raise, in moderate terms, the question of the Valencia government's responsibility for the front at Euzkadi (Guernica destroyed, Bilbão endangered, Euzkadi without air support). And recall how, for reasons of domestic politics, the Aragon front is without supplies. The new Generalitat cabinet is so unpopular that on the 29th unruly crowds have prevented it from continuing its deliberations. It issues a communiqué saying that 'it has decided to restore public order'. The POUM newspaper promptly asks *what* order is being talked about. On May 3 Señores Companys and Tarradellas order their police to disarm the militants of the CNT, FAI and the POUM, formerly members of the control-patrols that were abolished through the Stalinist party's pressures. (Have they forgotten that the Paris Commune began when another Republican señor, Thiers, attempted to disarm the National Guard?) However, it turns out to be the militants who disarm the Generalitat's police. On May 4, fighting is evident in Barcelona and the workers appear to be winning. On the 5th, Companys announces a 'new solution' to the problem of power and authority: a solution which needed more than a hundred dead in the streets before these political experts could discover it. Yes, it needed the best workers' blood spilled on the stones before they could understand – and have they yet understood? That in these days to seek to disarm the Catalan proletariat and impose on it a strong government against its will is nothing less than to stab the entire working class of Spain in the back. Order and authority are possible and necessary in Catalonia, but *with* the working class, not against it. Otherwise an enormous massacre has to be begun. Some, it is true, have agreed in advance to such a course. Without hesitation, *L'Humanité* has classed the Ascasos and Durrutis who fought on May 4 as 'agents of Hitler and Mussolini'.

Latest News

The disquieting silence over Barcelona persists. Yesterday I was told that most of the POUM leadership has been arrested: Andreu Nin, according to rumour, will be shot, or else has already been killed. I do not believe it. It is not easy to decapitate a strong workers' party of 40 to 50 thousand members with several thousand in its militias at the front. But it is certain that the whole weight of the Stalinist reaction is being brought to bear on this party, whose dissolution it has been demanding. The POUM's cohesion and ideological strength present a particularly formidable front to Stalinism; and since the POUM is far weaker than the CNT and the FAI, its strangulation offers the most convenient prelude to the throttling of the workers' movement.

La Batalla of May 4 prints the POUM's slogans: 'The United Front of Revolutionaries'. In sharp but guarded terms it reports the beginning of the Stalinist *coup de force*. It was on the orders of the Public Order Commissar Rodriguez Salas, a PSUC representative, that the CNT and UGT militants charged with guarding the Central Telephone Exchange were violently assaulted by the forces of the police. This aggression was clearly premeditated: it is now understandable why in March the PSUC tried to steal ten of the Generalitat's tanks. It is the PSUC which, for its purpose of assailing the revolution, has unleashed civil war within the Civil War... On the same day at 9 pm. police officers and members of the PSUC arrested Camillo Berneri,[60] one of contemporary anarchism's finest intellects, and another Italian comrade: on the following day their bodies were found, riddled with bullets...

VS

Leon Trotsky. 'The Murder of Andrès Nin by Agents of the GPU'. August 8, 1937[61]

When Andrès Nin, the leader of the POUM, was arrested in Barcelona, there could not be the slightest doubt that agents of the GPU would not let him out alive. The intentions of Stalin were revealed with exceptional clarity when the GPU, which holds the Spanish police in its clutches, published an announcement accusing Nin and the whole leadership of the POUM of being 'agents' of Franco.

The absurdity of this accusation is clear to anyone who is acquainted with even the simplest of facts about the Spanish revolution. The members of the POUM fought heroically against the fascists on all fronts in Spain. Nin is an old and incorruptible revolutionary. He defended the interests of the Spanish and Catalan peoples against the agents of the Soviet bureaucracy. That was why the GPU got rid of him by means of a well prepared raid on the Barcelona jail. What role in this matter was played by the official Spanish authorities remains a matter for speculation.

The newspaper dispatch inspired by the GPU calls Nin a 'Trotskyist'. The dead revolutionary often protested against this appellation, and with complete justification. Both under the leadership of Maurin and under that of Nin, the POUM remained hostile to the Fourth International. It is true that during the years 1931–1933, Nin, who was not then a member of the POUM, kept up a friendly correspondence with me. But as early as the beginning of 1933, differences of opinion on questions of principle led to a complete break between us. In the course of the last four years, we have exchanged only polemical articles. The POUM excluded Trotskyists from its ranks. The GPU calls everyone who is in opposition to the Soviet bureaucracy a Trotskyist. This makes their bloody vengeance easy.

Quite apart from the differences of opinion that separate me from the POUM, I must acknowledge that in the struggle that Nin led against the Soviet bureaucracy, it was Nin who was right. He tried to defend the independence of the Spanish proletariat from the diplomatic machinations and intrigues of the clique that holds power in Moscow. He did not want the POUM to become a tool in the hands of Stalin. He refused to co-operate with the GPU against the interests of the Spanish people. This was his only crime. And for this crime he paid with his life.

Victor Serge. 'A Goodbye to Andreu Nin'. From *La Révolution prolétarienne* [62]

1921, Moscow. The echoes of the cannonades at Kronstadt still weigh on our souls. People are still not used to eating the first white bread produced by the NEP. This great and battered Commune seems to be entering its convalescence. The two of us are walking in the lovely summer evenings amid the murmur of the crowd on the boulevards. The trees surround us with a sombre freshness. There is no illumination, since the lighting is still off. My companion has come from Barcelona and will go back there via Cairo. He is a delegate of the CNT to the Communist International: young and slender, with a mass of curly hair, eyes happy within the gold-rimmed spectacles, and a well-modulated voice that holds laughter and, already, a certain resolve. Andreu Nin explains to me that he is not at all an anarchist, but strictly a syndicalist. His thinking has no utopian element, his sole concern is to conquer and organise production...

We meet again at the Congress, in the Hall of Columns of the House of Trade Unions in the Kremlin. There is his white blouse, unbuttoned at the collar, his strongly defined profile, his personal warmth. We meet once again in the evening in Joaquin Maurin's room at the Hotel Lux, to talk about art, the Red Army, the Red Terror, and organisation, and toss around all the great problems that there are. That is where we are, at the heart of the great problems: it is not words that we discuss, but human lives, above all our own.

1923. We are sitting at a café table on the Ring, in Vienna. Andreu, after being imprisoned in Germany, had taken refuge in Moscow; there he is Secretary to the Red International of Trade Unions. He is passing through Vienna on a mission, and brings me black tidings. Lenin is weakening: Lenin is perhaps dying: Lenin knows that he is finished. In Lenin's eyes there is a terrible sadness. He is afraid of what will be done when he goes. Bukharin goes out to see him in the gardens out at Gorky, hiding behind bushes to avoid upsetting the invalid. When Bukharin returns, with a disturbed expression in his eyes, he says, 'He is suffering unbelievably, he has full consciousness...' Sometimes Lenin asks for a newspaper by making signs, and spells out the headline with little movements of his lips... Once Lenin has gone the crisis will break out; we know the sickness of the revolution only too well; on the horizon we can see immense shadows gather...

1927, Moscow. Andreu has committed himself to the cause of the Opposition. He is with those who are demanding freedom of thought and speech in the Bolshevik Party and thorough reform of the regime, with the aim of returning to a workers' democracy. Outside of this there is no salvation, that is what we all feel. We will be expelled from the party, sacked, this much we anticipate. Shall we be deported like our companions? He is going to lose his wife, his daughters, his books, his work table, his life as an indefatigable producer, tomorrow, when, under GPU escort, he is due to depart for Kazakhstan. He does not leave, much to his own surprise: his renown abroad has prevented it.

1931. At last the revolution is calling crowds out in Madrid. Andreu rushes to see me in Leningrad, and we take counsel. He laughs like a child: 'Just imagine, the coppers in Madrid have capes with a red lining on the inside; on the third day they are wearing them with the red on the outside. They are trailing behind events, that's clear... Listen to this, old chum. Thousands have been seen queuing up outside the offices of Primo de Rivera's party: they've come to resign from it as a matter of urgency, you get it... An Archbishop sent his resignation in by telegram; a prudent, anxious man, His Grace...' Andreu has a clear sense of the comedy in all the drama. Tomorrow he will send the Central Committee a demand couched in such terms that they will have immediately either to clap him in jail or let him leave Russia. If prison is to be his destiny I will raise hell in whatever small way that I can. If it is to be liberation for him, he will work to help release me from my own semi-captivity. I have a sharp recollection of something he said: 'In any case, back in Spain I have to prepare myself to take quite a lot as far as prison goes... It's going to be awfully complicated, this Spanish revolution...'. Soon after this I get a postcard from him postmarked Riga...

1932. His wife Olga sends me a short message from Barcelona, agony in its lines. After the anarchist rebellions, reaction seems to be on top. Andreu has been arrested and sent from there to Africa. I warn some friends in France but they never receive my letter. And I hear nothing more about Andreu. I, at the other end of Europe, am myself locked away: and will be for years more.

1936, Brussels. At last I am getting letters from him, rushed, untidy, brimming with facts and with force. He is at the head of a workers' party of the far left, formed by old Oppositional Communists, resolutely hostile to Stalinist totalitarianism. He has a rough ride ahead of him, surrounded by the anarchists who won't 'have anything to do with politics' but often engage in bad politics, with the most superb bravery, by the indecisive, basically bourgeois Republicans, and by the gathering intrigue of the Stalinists... Following his lengthy experience of Russia, his vision of things is dangerously clear. During the first months, while Counsellor for Justice in the Catalan government, he brings the judicial side of the revolution under the rule of law, with sweeping simplification of procedures and the creation of Popular Tribunals. The Stalinists demand his removal from the government and, since they have rather persuasive arguments (in the shape of the armaments they control), they are successful...

June 1937. On the 17th, horrible news reaches us. Andreu Nin has been arrested on the previous day in Barcelona and taken to an unknown destination by the Stalinist police. It is said that he was shortly afterwards murdered. The government at Valencia knows nothing, the one in Barcelona can do nothing. Friends of his, Socialists and trade unionists from Britain and France, take the train and get to the scene. Señor Irujo, the Minister of Justice, offers them reassurance. Nin is alive, everybody is fully aware of the enormity of the slanderous accusations mounted against him; but he is in Madrid in a special prison belonging to the

Communist Party, from which it is going to be necessary to see to his release.

And that is the end. There was no way for anyone to get his release. Nobody knows what has become of him, what has become of one of the most ardent tribunes of the Spanish proletariat. Whether he was put on a ship bound for Russia or murdered in a back street, as the rumours have it – it is the end. Goodbye, my friend. Your great, brave life remains with us, with its seed of writing and action. Your terrible death also remains with us. It is to the very end, just as you did, that we have to fight so that Socialism may be free.

Victor Serge

Leon Trotsky. 'The Capture of Power Was Possible in May'[63]

At a distance of some thousands of miles, without having the information that one could find solely at the place of action, one was still able to ask in the month of May whether the conquest of power was not materially possible. But since then documents, reports, innumerable articles have appeared in the press of all tendencies. All the facts, all the data, all the testimony lead to the same conclusion: the conquest of power was possible, was assured, as much as the issue of the struggle can be assured in general. The most important evidence comes from the anarchists. Since the May insurrection, *Solidaridad Obrera* has not ceased to repeat the same plaintive melody: 'We are accused of having been the instigator of the May rebellion. But we were completely opposed to it. The proof? Our adversaries know it as well as we: If we had wished to take power, we could have accomplished it in May with certainty. But we are against dictatorship, etc, etc.'

The misfortune is precisely that the CNT did not want power. The misfortune is that the leadership of the POUM was passively adapting itself to the leadership of the CNT. The misfortune (of a most modest size) is that Vereeken, Sneevliet, and Victor Serge are passively adapting themselves to the attitude of the POUM. Worse yet, at the decisive moment when we attempted to shake the fatal self-sufficiency of the POUM ('their own building, their own radio station, their own printing press, their own militia'), when we attempted to make comprehensible to the leaders of the POUM that the revolution has its pitiless logic, which does not tolerate half measures (that is, moreover, precisely why the Stalinists have superseded the socialists and the anarchists), it is at this critical moment that the Vereekens, the Sneevliets, the Victor Serges have placed their cudgels between the spokes.

They have found it advantageous to support the leadership of the POUM against us, that is, to support their hesitations, their inconsistencies, their opportunism. The latest events have brought their pitiless verification. Since the so-called July days, the POUM, far from being strengthened, has been virtually crushed. The CNT, of which the POUM was a shadow, is now losing its positions one after another. We do not know if the Spanish revolution can yet be saved by a new eruption from below. But the CNT and the POUM have done just about everything to assure the victory of the Stalinists, that is, of the counter revolution. And Vereeken, Sneevliet, and Victor Serge have done everything to support the POUM on the road to ruin.

Leon Trotsky. 'Role of the POUM'[64]

The record of the POUM is not much better. In point of theory, it tried, to be sure, to base itself on the formula of the permanent revolution (that is why the Stalinists called the POUMists Trotskyists). But the revolution is not satisfied with theoretical avowals. Instead of mobilizing the masses against the reformist leaders, including the anarchists, the POUM tried to convince these gentlemen of the superiorities of socialism over capitalism. This tuning fork gave pitch to all the articles and speeches of the POUM leaders. In order not to quarrel with the anarchist leaders, they did not form their own nuclei inside the CNT, and in general did not conduct any kind of work there. To avoid sharp conflicts, they did not carry on revolutionary work in the republican army. They built instead 'their own' trade unions and 'their own' militia, which guarded 'their own' institutions or occupied 'their own' section of the front.

By isolating the revolutionary vanguard from the class, the POUM rendered the vanguard impotent and left the class without leadership. Politically the POUM remained throughout far closer to the Popular Front, for whose left-wing it provided the cover, than to Bolshevism. That the POUM nevertheless fell victim to bloody and base repressions was due to the failure of the Popular Front to fulfil its mission, namely to stifle the socialist revolution – except by cutting off, piece by piece, its own left flank.

Contrary to its own intentions, the POUM proved to be, in the final analysis, the chief obstacle on the road to the creation of a revolutionary party. The platonic or diplomatic partisans of the Fourth International like Sneevliet, the leader of the Dutch Revolutionary Socialist Workers' Party, who demonstratively supported the POUM in its halfway measures, its indecisiveness and evasiveness, in short, in its centrism, took upon themselves the greatest responsibility. Revolution abhors centrism. Revolution exposes and annihilates centrism. In passing, the revolution discredits the friends and attorneys of centrism. That is one of the most important lessons of the Spanish revolution.

4   Kronstadt and the Fourth International

Introduction by Susan Weissman

When Victor Serge first arrived in Mexico in September 1941 – a small miracle in itself – he gravitated to Avenida Viena, where the Old Man had lived and been killed. Serge had last seen Trotsky in 1927; though they corresponded while they were both in exile in Europe, their paths never crossed again. Despite the terribly difficult relationship between these two Left Oppositionists, Serge lived most of his adult political life 'in the tail of Trotsky's comet'.[1] He was perhaps the best known 'Trotskyist' in the West, despite his later treatment by Trotsky and the Trotskyists. Walking along Rio Churubusco towards Trotsky's compound on Avenida Viena, Vlady recalled, 'my father saw the wall around Trotsky's house, where the Old Man was killed. He began to weep, and then broke into sobs'.[2]

Surely one of the greatest tragedies of the years 1936–40, from the time Serge was expelled to the West till the time Trotsky died, was that their relationship was so filled with acrimony. The role of the GPU in this was great, though real political differences also emerged, clouded by slander, misunderstandings and sectarian debates.

Stalin had erred in expelling Trotsky: outside the USSR Trotsky mounted a sustained fight against him, exposing his crimes to the world. Now Stalin had let another Oppositionist slip through to join Trotsky, another member of the revolutionary generation of Bolsheviks, whose voice was equally eloquent. That these two anti-Stalinist Bolsheviks had survived at all was serendipitous; that they now had the chance to work together in the West was astonishing. Serge had stood with Trotsky's Left Opposition since 1923, whether in the open, in clandestinity, or through prison and deportation.

How then did their relationship unravel? This chapter presents the documents relating to their differences, from Kronstadt to the Fourth International, to *Their Morals and Ours*, where the hand of the GPU is all too obvious.

The Left Opposition in exile was in constant, real danger of physical liquidation and its members worked in a milieu of suspicion, demoralization and despair. The role of the NKVD cannot be overlooked in this regard, though it would be equally incorrect to overstate its influence, since real political differences did exist, in an atmosphere that was not always conducive to the free expression of critical thought, especially unorthodox thought.

This was particularly discouraging to Serge, who was wrestling with the contradictions he had begun to consider inherent in 'guided organizations'. He often quoted Rosa Luxemburg's dictum that 'liberty is the liberty of the man who thinks otherwise', a principle more easily expressed than practised on the far left, with 'the best-disposed men, professing in principle respect for free thought, [... who] in reality do not know how to tolerate thought which is different from their own'.[3] From Paris to Mexico, Serge continually associated with refugee revolutionaries who embodied intolerance, with all the concomitant consequences of inquisitions and expulsions. More than simply discouraged, Serge sought to understand the problem which surely undermined their effectiveness. He also noted that back in the USSR the bureaucracy knew how to mobilise these feelings against the Opposition, and yet the Opposition itself exhibited the same qualities.

The problem, according to Serge, lay in the inability to reconcile intransigence, a necessary quality, with respect for others. In Russia, Serge wrote, politics failed because Socialists treated Marxism as a 'faith, then a regime, a double intolerance in consequence'.[4] Serge thought the dilemma could be solved by 'fighting intransigence,' and 'by an absolute rule of respect for others, [...] for the enemy even'.[5] These are noble sentiments, but in practice they challenged even Serge. In the final year of his life, he remarked to Hryhory Kostiuk[6] that he remained 'intransigently socialist'.[7] Earlier Serge had observed, 'Respect for the enemy, the Totalitarians make it difficult, if not impossible.'[8]

Although Serge himself fell victim to the dirty divisive work of agents, he was conscious that political differences and organisational practices were also responsible for straining his relations with Trotsky.

By mid-1937, Serge and Trotsky began to have serious disagreements. In 1938 Serge entered into a polemic over Kronstadt which was splashed across the pages of *The New International*, *La Lutte ouvrière*, *La Révolution prolétarienne*, and the *Bulletin of the Opposition*. The Kronstadt debate came in the wake of the Spanish Civil War and had everything to do with the role of the anarchists and the POUM. Despite assurances from Trotsky that the Fourth International would pledge itself to struggle in sympathy with the POUM,[9] it never did; in fact 'the Trotskyists were directing all their fire at the POUM',[10] which Sedov dismissed as 'destined to stab the Revolution in the heart'.[11] Serge nonetheless took part in the Fourth International, including its founding conference, and worked with its members in what he felt was a stifling internal atmosphere, where it was difficult to 'detect the hope of the Left Opposition in Russia for a renewal of the ideology, morals and institutions of Socialism'. In the Forth, Serge found a crude caricature of Trotsky's intransigence, here translated into simple inflexibility. Its shallow dogmatic and sectarian thinking was all very discouraging to Serge. He was certain that:

> no fresh thinking could emerge [from it]. The life of these groups was maintained by nothing but the prestige of the Old Man and his great, unceasing efforts; and both his prestige and the quality of his efforts deteriorated in the process.[12]

Serge's attitude to the POUM, the French Popular Front and the Fourth International were based on his concern that the revolutionary Marxists should not be cut off from the political arena that held the attention of the working class. Although Serge was perhaps overly enthusiastic about what could be achieved with the Popular Front[13] and the POUM, he also understood that the Trotskyists would be seen as sectarian and that this would result in their isolation, depriving an important struggle of their revolutionary influence. Furthermore, the behaviour of the Fourth International in relation to the Spanish events was disturbing: Serge wrote to Sedov that its attitude and actions would lead only to schisms and the discrediting of the Fourth.[14] Serge's disdain for their tactics in Spain and his insistence on solidarity with the POUM was seen by the Trotskyists as a capitulation to reformism, and Serge was indelibly labelled a centrist.

The stamp 'moralist' came from Serge's renewal of the debate on Kronstadt. This debate took place in late 1937 and throughout 1938, in journals in Europe and America. In 'dredging up' this ignominious chapter in Bolshevik history, Serge had not changed his position of siding with the party, but he wanted the party to understand how it came to be in the position of executing workers. The libertarians and anarchists in Europe were quick to point to the similarities between the Moscow trials and the suppression of the Kronstadt rebellion. While the anarchists and POUMists were being betrayed by the Communists in Spain, the Kronstadt debate served as a foil for the larger argument that Stalinism was the natural outgrowth of Leninism. Serge did not share this view, nor was its construction his purpose in intervening in the debate about Kronstadt.

Serge insisted that it was not only healthy to look back at what had happened, and how it could have been avoided, but that this was essential to draw the lessons of history. Trotsky agreed that it was 'necessary to learn and think' but said that advice was very easy to give after the event.[15] Trotsky aimed his fire at 'moralists', such as Souvarine and Ciliga, who were interested in the question of his personal responsibility for this event. Serge entered the fray in order to defend the ideals of October from those, like Ciliga, who 'judged [the revolution] in the light of Stalinism alone' and who directed personal attacks 'against Trotsky out of bad faith, ignorance and sectarian spirit'.[16] Serge took on Anton Ciliga's ahistorical critique, stating:

> A little direct contact with the people was enough to get an idea of the drama which, in the revolution, separated the communist party (and with it the dust of the other revolutionary groups) from the masses. At no time did the revolutionary workers form more than a trifling percentage of the masses themselves. In 1920–21, all that was energetic, militant, ever-so-little socialistic in the labor population and among the advanced elements of the countryside had already been drained by the communist party, which did not, for four years of civil war, stop its constant mobilization of the willing – down to the most vacillating [...] Eloquence of chronology: it is the non-party workers of this epoch, joining the party to the number of 2,000,000 in 1924, upon the death of Lenin, who assure the victory of its bureaucracy. I assure you, Ciliga, that these people never thought of the Third International. Many of the insurgents of Kronstadt did think of it; but they constituted an undeniable elite and, duped by their own passion, they opened in spite of themselves the doors to a frightful counter-revolution. The firmness of the Bolshevik party, on the other hand, sick as it was, delayed Thermidor by five to ten years.[17]

Clearly Serge and Trotsky had much in common here. Furthermore, it was Trotsky, not Serge, who brought up the Kronstadt debate, in the course of defending himself against the calumny of the Moscow trials. Serge took the opportunity to raise some issues he thought were worthy of reflection because they had an educational value for the left in the West.

Trotsky's tone, in all of his replies, was one of exasperation. He seemed most angry by the debates Serge raised. On 2 December 1938 Trotsky wrote a short piece that was published in the *Bulletin of the Opposition* in January 1939, entitled 'Victor Serge and the Fourth International', stating that Serge, now a member of the centrist POUM, was an opponent of the Fourth.[18] When Serge published in *Partisan Review* an article called 'Marxism in Our Time',[19] Trotsky replied though there is no evidence that he had read Serge's piece. Trotsky's disagreements with Serge here turned into a simple *ad hominem* attack:

> the ranks of the disillusioned include not only Stalinists but also the temporary fellow travellers of Bolshevism. Victor Serge [...] has recently announced that Bolshevism is passing through a crisis which presages in turn the 'crisis of Marxism.' In his theoretical innocence, Serge imagines himself the first to have made this discovery [...] That the old Bolshevik Party has spent itself, has degenerated and perished – that much is beyond controversy [...] this does not at all invalidate Marxism, which is the algebra of revolution. That Victor Serge himself is passing through a 'crisis', i.e. has become hopelessly confused like thousands of other intellectuals – is clear enough. But Victor Serge in crisis is not the crisis of Marxism.[20]

Serge wrote to Trotsky on 18 March 1939:

> I've decided not to react at all to the article in the *Bulletin*. You are too inaccurate, too unjust and unnecessarily offensive. I don't know who keeps you informed and how, but sadly, believe me, there exists a whole nest of intrigues here.[21]

In a postscript to this letter, Serge told Trotsky that his rupture with the French Bolshevik-Leninists occurred because he had been told by a 'comrade' that there were serious suspicions about Lola Ya. Ginsburg.[22] Serge thought this should be investigated and confided in Rosmer, Wullens and Elsa Reiss. Elsa told the group, who 'refused to look into *the substance* of the affair, or so I was informed through comrade Etienne. Instead – it "brought an action" against me.' While it appears that Lilia Ginsberg, known personally as Lola and politically as Paulsen or Yakovlev, was not the NKVD agent, she protected and vouched for the reliability of Etienne/Zborowski – the real agent. Zborowski was apparently successful in turning Serge into a political pariah for the group. Trotsky followed this line, and subjected Serge to a horrendous offensive of vitriolic prose.

In a fragment found among Trotsky's papers in Mexico, written sometime in 1939, he reached perhaps the peak of his animosity:

Victor Serge claims that his enunciations, statements, and corrections, always revolving around his own personality, must without exception be printed by the workers' publications. Why? On what basis? What does Victor Serge represent today in the workers' movement? An ulcer of his own doubts, of his own confusion and nothing more [...] What do people of the Victor Serge type represent? Our conclusion is simple: these verbose, coquettish moralists, capable of bringing only trouble and decay, must be kept out of the revolutionary organisation, even by cannon fire if necessary.[23]

Clearly Trotsky was reaching beyond viciousness to deadliness. It was as if all his frustrations at being physically prevented from playing a leading role in the struggle in the USSR and Europe were vented in his literary tantrums against comrades like Serge. His own son, Lev Lvovich Sedov, a frequent subject of Trotsky's anger, recognised the deleterious effects of this kind of outburst:

I think that all Dad's deficiencies have not diminished as he has grown older, but under the influence of his isolation, very difficult, unprecedentedly difficult, got worse. His lack of tolerance, hot temper, inconsistency, even rudeness, his desire to humiliate, offend and even destroy have increased. It is not 'personal,' it is a method and hardly good in organisation of work.[24]

Serge's translation of Trotsky's polemic on means and ends, *Their Morals and Ours* (February 1938), brought more unwarranted controversy to their relationship. Unfortunately the controversy was not over the content of the book, which Serge thought contained 'many fine pages at the end'.

The book was subtitled 'Marxist vs. Liberal Views on Morality' and provoked a debate between Trotsky and John Dewey, among others. Trotsky was at his polemical best in this book, utilising colourful and truculent language to depict his opponents. He set out to distinguish revolutionary morality, which is rooted in concrete historical circumstances, from the abstract and timeless morality argued by liberals, social democrats and others whom Trotsky labelled in vintage descriptive terms. The 'fine pages at the end' contain a discussion of the 'Dialectic Interdependence of End and Means'. Here Trotsky insisted that base means lead to base ends, that 'organically the means are subordinated to the end'; in other words, the product could only be as pure as the process.[25]

The dispute with Trotsky was not over Serge's translation, or any unspoken disagreements about the ideas Trotsky expressed, but over the promotional prospectus in the French edition, which crudely attacked Trotsky. Without checking with the publisher, Trotsky assumed Serge had written this invective:

> For Trotsky, there is no such thing as morality *per se*, no ideal or eternal morality. Morals are relative to each society, to each epoch, relative especially to the interests of social classes [...] True morality must defend the interests of humanity itself, represented by the proletariat. Trotsky thinks that his party, once in power, today in the opposition always represented the real proletariat; and he himself, the real morality. From this he concludes, [...] that shooting hostages takes on different meanings depending on whether the order is given by Stalin or by Trotsky or by the bourgeoisie [...] Trotsky, basing himself on Lenin, declares that *the end justifies the means* (on condition that the means are effective: for example, individual terrorism is generally ineffective). There is no cynicism in this attitude, declares the author, merely a statement of the facts. And it is to these facts that Trotsky says he owes his acute conscience, which constitutes his *moral sense*.[26]

It is inconceivable that Serge could have penned or inspired these thoughts, which were so out of character with the body of his published work. Instead of verifying the facts with Serge or Les Editions du Sagittaire, Trotsky lifted his pen and wrote a furious addendum to *Their Morals and Ours* on 9 June 1939, an essay entitled 'The Moralists and Sycophants against Marxism: Peddlers of Indulgences and Their Socialist Allies, or the Cuckoo in a Strange Nest'. He wrote:

> some 'friend', [...] contrived to slip into a strange nest and deposit there his little egg – oh! it is of course a very tiny egg, an almost virginal egg. Who is the author of this prospectus? Victor Serge, who is at the same time its severest critic, can easily supply the information. I should not be surprised if it turned out that the prospectus was written [...] naturally not by Victor Serge but by one of his disciples who imitates both his master's ideas and his style. But, maybe after all, it is the master himself, that is, Victor Serge in his capacity of 'friend' of the author?[27]

The piece exudes Trotsky's vexation with the 'independents' loosely associated with the Left Opposition. One can detect his obvious frustration at being an ocean away from the discussion, an ocean away from reining in the dissidents. The essay is devoted to a scathing attack against Victor Serge (the moralist) and Boris Souvarine (the sycophant) in language that is memorable for its viciousness. Trotsky sustained some seven pages of tirade, accusing Serge of 'Hottentot Morality,' of publicly becoming a member of the POUM, of being a 'petty-bourgeois moralist' who 'thinks episodically, in fragments, in clumps', of wanting 'to purge human history of civil war'. Further, Trotsky berated Serge for dating the degeneration of the revolution from the moment the CHEKA began the secret trials. Trotsky wrote: 'Serge plays with the concept of revolution, writes poems about it, but is incapable of understanding it as it is.' Apparently one of Serge's worst attributes was that he wrote lyrically, even poetically, about revolution; Trotsky returned to this issue in several articles.[28] More to the point, Trotsky went to the heart of his animosity to Serge:

> when we evaluate from the Marxian standpoint the vacillations of a disillusioned petty-bourgeois intellectual, that seems to him an assault upon his individuality. He then enters into an alliance with all the confusionists for a crusade against our despotism and our sectarianism [...] On the other hand, Victor Serge has systematically helped centrist organizations drive from their ranks the partisans of the Fourth International.[29]

He ended his diatribe with: 'the moralism of V. Serge and his compeers is a bridge from revolution to reaction'.[30] The essay sought to lump Serge with other anti-Bolsheviks and anti-Leninists, those who saw Stalin as the heir to Lenin. It is remarkable for its obvious ignorance of Serge's writings, from his *Year One*, to his *Lenin*, his civil war writings, his *From Lenin to Stalin*, his novels, not to mention his articles.

Serge was disheartened by what this vicious onslaught represented. In the *Memoirs* he lamented:

> Deplorably misinformed by his acolytes, he wrote a long polemical essay against me – imputing to me an article of which I was not the author and which was totally at variance with my frequently expressed opinions. The Trotskyist journals refused to publish my corrections. In the hearts of the persecuted I encountered the same attitudes as in their persecutors [...] Trotskyism was displaying symptoms of an outlook in harmony with that of the very Stalinism against which it had taken its stand, and by which it was being ground into powder [...] I was heartbroken by it all, because it is my firm belief that the tenacity and will-power of some men can, despite all odds, break with the traditions that suffocate, and withstand the contagions that bring death. It is painful, it is difficult, but it *must* be possible. I abstained from any counter-polemic.[31]

Although denied access to Trotskyist journals, Serge nonetheless attempted internally to refute the charges, to clear the air and his name. Publicly he refused to dissociate himself from Trotsky. He wrote to Dwight MacDonald:[32]

> In his recent attacks on me, Leon Davidovich has so abused me that I'm almost glad I no longer have the means to answer him. He began by criticising me without having read what I wrote, and continues to attribute to me an article that I did not write in a journal with which I have no association. His entire article entitled 'Moralists and Sycophants' is thus entirely falsely based, since he ascribes ideas and arguments to me that were never mine. However, I have written a great deal in the last twenty years on these subjects and he should know this! He would also do well to find out who wrote the article he attributes to me without so much as a care. All this is terribly sad. I sent *NI* and LD himself some corrections, the fate of which are unknown. In Europe the publications that attacked me in this way never published my replies. So I stopped replying. I am adamant.[33]

Serge then penned a reply to Trotsky which he did not publish. It was discovered among Serge's papers by Peter Sedgwick, who translated and published the essay in *Peace News*, 27 December 1963, under the title 'Secrecy and Revolution – A Reply to Trotsky'. In a letter Serge wrote to Angelica Balabanova[34] on 23 October 1941, he explained why he refrained from a public debate with the Old Man, who was engaged in a resolute fight against Stalinism and whose ideas Serge still deeply respected:

> in all this painful argument with the Old Man, I kept such esteem and affection for him that, even though he wrote a long polemical attack accusing me of writing an article which was never mine and of advocating ideas which were never mine, I first sent a powerful rebuttal to the printers of *La Révolution prolétarienne* (Paris) and then took it back from them, preferring to suffer this unjust attack in silence. And I still think I was quite right: truth can work its way out in different ways than by offensive polemics.[35]

Serge also wrote to Trotsky on 9 August 1939, denying any connection with the odious prospectus. Trotsky replied on 7 September, in *Bulletin of the Opposition*, 'Another Refutation by Victor Serge',[36] that he 'willingly accept[ed] his declaration', and then proceeded to attack Serge for having 'a confused mood of uncertainty, disillusionment, dissatisfaction, and repulsion from Marxism and proletarian revolution'. As to the authorship of the prospectus, Trotsky wrote:

> if not he personally, then one of his disciples or co-thinkers. The supposition that the prospectus was written by Victor Serge occurred to various comrades, independently of one another. And not by chance: the blurb constitutes a simple resumé of Victor Serge's latest sermonisings.[37]

Which comrades? Etienne? Pierre Frank?[38] Whether or not Etienne directly raised the issue with Trotsky, or incited others to do so, he could be justly proud of accomplishing his objective of dividing the two surviving Left Oppositionists and occupying them with incessant internal intrigue. Yet Trotsky seemed to dismiss the possibility of the involvement of the NKVD. In a letter to Serge on 6 May 1939 Trotsky wrote:

> you are passing through a protracted ideological crisis, and [...] you are turning your dissatisfaction with yourself into dissatisfaction with others. You write about intrigues, false information, etc. I don't know anything about these [...] I have not lost the hope of seeing you return to the path of the Fourth International. But, at present you are its adversary, and a hostile one at that, who nonetheless tries to insist on being treated as a political friend.[39]

Serge was adamant that he

> never published a single line concerning that work [*Their Morals and Ours*] of his, in any publication or in any shape or form [...] I am not the author of this prospectus: I have had no part, direct or indirect, in composing it: I have no idea who its author is: and I do not care either. Is that clear enough?[40]

The real author of the prospectus is still unknown. Serge's son, Vlady, believes Zborowski wrote it,[41] and I put that question to him several times, without ever being graced with a reply. Pierre Broue believes an editor wrote it,[42] which could have been done under Zborowski's guidance.

The rupture over the prospectus was really the culmination of disagreements over larger issues: Serge's support of the POUM and his attitude to the Fourth International. Trotsky was offended by this 'defection' and the excessive tone of his polemic reflected his anger.

Defection notwithstanding, Serge still functioned in the orbit of Trotskyism and held the Old Man in great esteem; and he was considered a 'Trotskyist' by the larger political public. He later wrote in his diary:

I went on translating the Old Man's books, [...] and to defend him. I remained in the eyes of the general public the best-known 'Trotskyist' writer – while the 'B[olshevik]-L[eninists]' disparaged me as far as they could. I had become for them a 'petit-bourgeois intellectual' of whom they had to 'make use of the influence' and the 'questionable sympathy'. – The sense of possession of the truth, the intolerance and the aggressiveness devoid of critical sense of *Leur Morale* [sic] made me furious although there are fine, worthwhile pages at the end of this essay. I said so to some Trotskyists who wrote and told the Old Man and that at once brought fresh attacks upon me. The saddest thing was that they were always insulting and always based on inaccurate data. It would have been so simple to state: We're at considerable variance on such and such a point, – but the Old Man and his followers had become completely incapable of holding such a straightforward dialogue. The frightening atmosphere of persecution in which they lived – like me – made them inclined to a persecution complex and to the practice of persecution.[43]

The rupture between Serge and Trotsky was never really completed; it had the character of a quarrel with room for conciliation. Even as Trotsky spewed out the worst venom, some of which is quoted above, he always left the door open for cooperation, provided of course that Serge were to work within the Fourth International. For Serge's part, the pain of Trotsky's vitriol was great, but it did not deflect from his essential appreciation of the 'greatness' of Trotsky, whose 'traits were those of several generations, developed to a very high degree of individual perfection'.[44]

With this appreciation in mind, Serge replied to Trotsky's invective against him:

Whether Trotsky wills it or not, no limit has been set to the analysis of the Russian revolution, which he has served so outstandingly, so tremendously – despite the measure of responsibility that must be laid to his name for certain tragic errors. And no amount of ponderous irony, no broadsides of discredit, directed against men who dare to think and sometimes to pronounce according to their conscience, will render him free to substitute mischievous polemic for the necessary debate to which, with a little less pretension to infallibility, he could bring the most precious contributions of all.[45]

All the more tragic, then, that Serge and Trotsky were not able to work together in those dark years, that Serge's generous, comradely and dignified attitude to Trotsky was not reciprocated.

Worse, for Serge, was the destructive behaviour of the Trotskyists. It is clear that Serge did not think Trotsky a Trotskyist in this sense. Trotsky's inflexibility could be understood, wrote Serge, because he was 'the last survivor of a generation of giants'. For the present generation and the future, however, Serge was convinced that:

Socialism too had to renew itself in the world of today, and that this must take place through the jettisoning of the authoritarian, intolerant tradition of turn-of-the-century Russian Marxism. I recalled, for use against Trotsky himself, a sentence of astounding vision which he had written in 1914 I think: 'Bolshevism may very well be an excellent instrument for the conquest of power, but after that it will reveal its counter-revolutionary aspects'.

In the same essay, which Serge wrote in memory of Trotsky, he described his former comrade as:

a doer, but one who brought to everything he did a lyrical touch [...] His absolute conviction that he knew the truth made him impervious to argument toward the end and detracted from his scientific spirit. He was authoritarian, because in our time of barbaric struggles thought turned into action must of necessity become authoritarian. When power was within his reach in 1924 and 1925, he refused to seize it because he felt that a socialist regime could not be run by decree.[46]

Further, Serge attested:

Our Oppositional movement in Russia had not been Trotskyist, since we had no intention of attaching it to a personality, rebels as we ourselves were against the cult of the Leader. We regarded the Old Man only as one of our greatest comrades, an elder member of the family over whose ideas we argued freely [...] I came to the conclusion that our Opposition had simultaneously contained two opposing lines of significance. For the great majority [...] it meant resistance to totalitarianism in the name of the democratic ideals expressed at the beginning of the Revolution; for a number of our Old Bolshevik leaders it meant, on the contrary, the defence of doctrinal orthodoxy which, while not excluding a certain tendency towards democracy, was authoritarian through and through. These two mingled strains had, between 1923 and 1928, surrounded Trotsky's vigorous personality with a tremendous aura. If, in his exile from the USSR, he had made himself the ideologist of a renewed Socialism, critical in outlook and fearing diversity less than dogmatism, perhaps he would have attained a new greatness. But he was the prisoner of his own orthodoxy, the more so since his lapses into unorthodoxy were being denounced as treason. He saw his role as that of one carrying into the world at large a movement which was not only Russian but extinct in Russia itself, killed twice over, both by the bullets of its executioners and by changes in human mentality.[47]

THE DOCUMENTS

Leon Trotsky. Extract from letter to Wendelin Thomas, 6 July 1937[48]

Your evaluation of the Kronstadt uprising of 1921 is basically incorrect. The best, most self-sacrificing of the sailors were completely withdrawn from Kronstadt and played an important role at the fronts and in the local Soviets throughout the country. What remained was the grey mass with big pretensions ('We are from Kronstadt'), but without political education and unprepared for revolutionary sacrifice. The country was starving. The Kronstadters demanded privileges. The uprising was dictated by a desire to get privileged food rations. The sailors had cannon and battleships. All the reactionary elements, both in Russia and abroad, immediately seized upon this uprising. The White emigrés demanded aid for the insurrectionists. The victory of this uprising could bring nothing but the victory of the counter-revolution, entirely independent of the ideas the sailors had in their heads. But the ideas themselves were deeply reactionary. They reflected the hostility of the backward peasantry toward the worker, the self-importance of the soldier or sailor in relation to 'civilian' Petrograd, the hatred of the petty bourgeois for revolutionary discipline. The movement therefore had a counter-revolutionary character, and since the insurgents took possession of the arms in the forts they could be crushed only with the aid of arms.

No less erroneous is your estimate of Makhno.[49] In himself he was a mixture of fanatic and adventurer. He became the concentration of the very tendencies which brought about the Kronstadt uprising. The cavalry in general is the most reactionary part of the army. The equestrian despises the pedestrian. Makhno created a cavalry of peasants who supplied their own horses. These were not the downtrodden village poor whom the October revolution first awakened, but the strong and well-fed peasants who were afraid of losing what they had. The anarchist ideas of Makhno (ignoring of the state, nonrecognition of the central power) correspond to the spirit of this Kulak cavalry as nothing else could. I should add that the hatred for the city and the city worker on the part of followers of Makhno was complemented by a militant anti-semitism. At the very time when we were carrying on a life and death struggle against Denikin[50] and Wrangel, the Makhanovists attempted to carry out an independent policy. Straining at the bit, the petty bourgeois (Kulak) thought he could dictate his contradictory views to the capitalists on the one hand and to the workers on the other. This Kulak was armed; we had to disarm him. This is precisely what we did.

Victor Serge. Extract from 'Fiction and Fact. Kronstadt'[51]

Kronstadt
In reply to a German journalist[52] who was questioning him on these matters, Leon Davidovich Trotsky has published, in the Russian-language Bolshevik-Leninist *Bulletin of the Opposition* (issue of July 1937),[53] an excessively brief letter where he discusses the Kronstadt rising of 1921 and Makhno. Ida Mett[54] has responded to him in these pages with some new and very telling questions. Trotsky more than any other person could one day give us the great historical work on the harshest and most memorable years of the revolution, the work which all of us need for an initial balance sheet of this immense experience. There are very many of us that await it, and trust that to some small degree it may be conceived in a spirit of criticism, or rather of self-criticism... And that is why these few lines published in the *Bulletin of the Opposition* seem to me today to be in various respects insufficient and inaccurate.

Trotsky writes: 'What remained (at Kronstadt) was the grey mass with big pretensions ... unprepared for revolutionary sacrifice. The country was starving. The Kronstadters demanded privileges ... The movement therefore had a counter-revolutionary character and since the insurgents took possession of the arms in the forts they could be crushed only with the aid of arms...'.

I was in Petrograd at that very time, a collaborator of Zinoviev; I followed the events closely; later I gave an attentive reading to the collected issues of *Izvestia* published by the Soviet of insurgent Kronstadt. It is true to say that the country was starving: it would be true even to say that the country was at the end of its strength, that all of it was literally dying from starvation. It is untrue that the sailors of Kronstadt demanded privileges; they demanded, for the cities generally, the abolition of the militia's barricades which stopped the population from looking for provisions in the countryside on their own initiative. Later, when they found themselves engaged in mortal combat, they formulated a demand which was, politically, extremely dangerous at that moment but which was of general interest, disinterested and sincerely revolutionary: 'Freely elected soviets'.

It would have been easy to forestall the uprising by listening to Kronstadt's grievances, by discussing them, even by giving satisfaction to the sailors (we shall have the proof of this assertion in a moment). The Central Committee committed the enormous mistake of sending Kalinin[55] there, who already had the comportment of an incompetent, hardfaced bureaucrat; all he knew was to threaten, and he got himself booed. Even when the fighting had started, it would have been easy to avoid the worst: it was only necessary to accept the mediation offered by the anarchists (notably Emma Goldman and Alexander Berkman)[56] who had contact with the insurgents. For reasons of prestige and through an excess of authoritarianism, the Central Committee refused this course. In all this the responsibility of Zinoviev, the President of the Petrograd Soviet, was particularly great: he had just misled the whole party organisation and the entire proletariat of the city by announcing to us that 'the White general Kozlovsky had seized Kronstadt by treason'. It would have been easy and humane, and more politic and more Socialist, not to resort to massacre after the militiary victory won over the Kronstadters by Voroshilov, Dybenko and Tukhachevsky.[57] The massacre that ensued was outrageous.

The economic programme of Kronstadt was so legitimate, so far in reality from being counter-revolutionary, and so easy to grant, that in the very hours when the last of the mutineers were being shot, Lenin implemented these same demands by getting the 'New Economic Policy', or NEP, adopted. The NEP was imposed on him by the risings at Kronstadt, Tambov and other places. For it must be said plainly: for months Lenin and the Central Committee had been under terrible misconceptions of what was possible; the CC was unwilling to see what the whole country sensed and knew: that War Communism had become a blind alley in which it was impossible for people to live.

Trotsky had recognised this a year previously. In February 1920 he proposed to the Central Committee a list of measures ending the requisitioning of grain and founding a new economic policy. Lenin had the proposal rejected, to his own cost. His error was at the price of heavy bloodshed and suffering for the Russian people. Why not say so? We have no need of the fraudulent legend of an infallible Lenin.

Once armed conflict between Red Kronstadt and the Bolshevik government had begun, the question became posed in these terms: which of the two contending forces better represented the higher interest of the toilers? Actually it was the clash of two infatuations. The instigators of the uprising, the anarchists and the left Social Revolutionaries, hoped for a 'third revolution' against the dictatorship of the party. They would not see what was clearly the case, that an exhausted nation, whose revolutionary vanguard was already decimated, no longer possessed either the moral or the material resources, either the men or the ideas, for a new and more Socialist revolution. They wanted to release the elements of a purifing tempest, but all they could actually have done was to open the way to a counter-revolution, supported by peasants at the outset, which would have been promptly exploited by the Whites and the foreign intervention. (Pilsudski was getting his armies ready to launch on the Ukraine.) Insurgent Kronstadt was not counter-revolutionary, but its victory would have led – without any shadow of a doubt – to the counter-revolution. In spite of its faults and its abuses, the Bolshevik Party is at this juncture the great organised, intelligent and reliable force which, despite everything, deserves our confidence. The revolution has no other mainstay and is no longer capable of a radical internal renewal. This is what we concluded, we Communists of the rank and file, who could hear so unmistakably the crack of the timbers in the whole building...

Victor Serge

Victor Serge. 'Ideas and Facts; Kronstadt 1921 – Against the Sectarian Spirit – Bolshevism and Anarchism' [58]

Kronstadt 1921
In making its contribution to the discussion of Leon Trotsky's letter on this topic (which I took up in the RP dated September 10 last), *La Lutte ouvrière* [59] presents the issue in so one-sided a manner that it manages to brush everything away. So cavalier a treatment of history would reduce the labour of analysis and reflection, which is incumbent on all of us, to an apologia completely removed from any Marxist approach – assuming, that is, that we have to take its commentary as more than a hasty note drafted, as it were, at the printer's deadline... The LO actually writes: 'The only question which calls for an answer is this: given a revolution triumphant but menaced by the social and economic con-

tradictions of the Civil War ... was it right for it to crush movements whose growth would mean the opening of the path leading to capitalist democracy?'

Quite clearly this is *not* the only question, for the whole history of Bolshevism and the soviets has to be grasped: and it is virtually the exact opposite of the question which revolutionaries have been asking themselves, with the most legitimate of anxieties, in relation to Kronstadt. Which is: Given the dictatorship of the proletariat, exercised by the Communist Party, was it right for it to use forcible repression against the protests, demands, propositions and demonstrations of workers stricken by famine? We should remember that before Kronstadt there had been Astrakhan. Was it right to repress movements whose underlying origins were in a working-class democracy? My own inclination is to believe that quite early on there was an abuse of 'firmness', that is of administrative and military measures in relation to the masses and the dissidents of the revolution. Experience has shown that this facilitiated the installation of bureaucratic despotism. Here there is a profound lesson to be drawn for us to return to an honest idea of the dictatorship of the proletariat (against the dispossessed owners), as a broad and genuine democracy of the workers.

La Lutte ouvrière 'in addition takes the opportunity of scotching the legend according to which Kronstadt 1921 was an immense massacre. The truth is quite different.' Is the truth different, comrades? If so, tell it: give details and indicate your sources... A massacre does not have to be 'immense' to be outrageous and by definition anti-Socialist. By hundreds, if not by thousands, the Kronstadt sailors were shot on the spot. Three months later they were still being taken out by night from the prisons of Petrograd, in small batches, to be executed in the cellars or the exercise yard. Three months later – when the NEP which they had demanded was proclaimed, when their deaths – kept secret – could not even serve as a deterrent! And they were not in any way connected with the Whites...

This sombre page of history seems to foretell a future whose dark depths we scutinise today, when it has become the present. The LO recalls that the Tenth Party Congress, at Lenin's instigation, despatched a large number of its delegates for the assault on Kronstadt. But it does not tell everything on the subject. The Tenth Congress had just uttered a solemn condemnation of the *Workers' Opposition* which even then was attacking the encroachments of the bureaucracy and demanding more democracy for the workers. For the first time an opposition – one which (as Lenin and Trotsky were to perceive two years later) was largely right on several points – was tagged with a label at odds with its actual doctrine (the Congress resolution accused these Bolsheviks of anarcho-syndicalism), threatened with expulsion and broken by the sending of its delegates to the Kronstadt front. Dybenko, notably, who was being made out to be an anarchist sympathiser, went to fight Kronstadt.

Give another reading to the platform of the 1920-1 Workers' Opposition and recall how, eighteen months later, Lenin (then at the limit of his strength) proposed to Trotsky a pact of battle against the party bureaucracy, which was becoming increasingly insolent; recall how, two years later, the Left Opposition (Trotsky, Preobrazhensky, Sere-bryakov,[60] Piatakov and Rakovsky) will open its first battle and suffer defeat: by then it was too late.

Two of the authors of the Workers' Opposition platform, veteran militants from a quarter of a century of revolution who have for years been in jail, are perhaps still alive in some central prison: Shlyapnikov and Medvedev. Alexandra Kollontai survives in a diplomatic career...

Against Sectarian Spirit

These are still red-hot topics. Is that the reason for refusing to touch them? On the contrary: twenty years after the first victorious Socialist revolution, we all feel ourselves to be vanquished. Out of a magnifi-cent workers' victory we have seen the rise, on the basis of the Socialist ownership of the means of production, of an inhuman regime, profoundly anti-Socialist in the way it treats human beings. In the face of such results, are not disputes between the sects bound to occur? Have not our common adversaries won the contest, apparently? It is easy (and idiotioc) to draw conclusions on the bankruptcy of revolutions, of Marxism, etc; easy for the reformists to say 'Ah, if only they had followed the roads of democracy!' (As if these roads had not been followed, alas with fatal results in Italy, Germany and Austria!) And it is easy for the libertari-ans to exclaim: 'Ah if only they had let the Russian anarchists alone!' This at the very time when the Spanish Revolution is going from defeat to defeat under our very eyes, despite the dominance of the anarchists in the labour movement there – and despite their sincerity and admirable courage, which nobody will contest. Let me say a few personal words on this point. The anarchists have often reproached me for not having exerted myself sufficiently in the USSR, in Lenin's time, against the repression of anarchism. This repression I always considered to be an error, and in every circumstance I consistently did all that I could to get it stopped or diminished; but I could not achieve a great deal. Now, in the light of events in Spain, one can have a better appreciation of this sort of situation. At the Extraordinary Soviet Congress of last year, the delegates from the CNT did nothing, and could do nothing, for their persecuted Russian comrades. The CNT has not been able to prevent the strangulation of the POUM, and has not even given large publicity to Nin's murder. We have seen its own members imprisoned in their hundreds while the CNT was in the government! Of course I am not unaware that there was a mass of interventions within the corridors of power. If the CNT could not stop the persecution of the anarchists in Spain, what could be done on that score in the Russian Revolution by an isolated militant?

Before this colossal experience of two decades and more, I can see only one attitude that is productive: that of critical analysis and the disarming of the sectarian spirit. To keep calling one another 'petty bourgeois', instead of coolly studying the events of 1921, for example, in all their complexity, will get us nowhere. Rather let us bring our sanest faculties to bear upon reality. The precious lessons which the Russian Revolution could bring us are obscured, muddied and compromised by the bureaucratic counter-revolution which has got hold of the old banners; we shall only retrieve those banners by liberating our minds from exhausted formulas, discredited clichés, the resentments of sects or individuals, and above all from the insupportable claim to have a monopoly of the truth.

Bolshevism and Anarchism

In a remarkable article by Trotsky on the relationship, or rather the total antagonism, between Bolshevism and Stalinism (*Bulletin of the Opposition*, no. 58–9, October) there is this extraordinary passage: 'The author of these lines discussed with Lenin more than once the possibility of allotting to the anarchists certain parts of the territory for the carrying out, with the consent of the population, of their stateless experiment. But civil war, blockade and hunger left too little time for such plans…'.

Leon Trotsky. Extract from 'The Hue and Cry over Kronstadt'[61]

The NEP and the Kronstadt Uprising

Victor Serge, who, it would seem, is trying to manufacture a sort of synthesis of anarchism, POUMism and Marxism, has intervened very unfortunately in the polemic about Kronstadt. In his opinion, the introduction of the NEP one year earlier could have averted the Kronstadt uprising. Let us admit that. But advice like this is very easy to give after the event. It is true, as Victor Serge remembers, that I had already proposed the transition to the NEP in 1920. But I was not at all sure in advance of its success. It was no secret to me that the remedy could prove to be more dangerous than the malady itself. When I met opposition from the leaders of the party, I did not appeal to the ranks, in order to avoid mobilising the petty bourgeoisie against the workers. The experience of the ensuing twelve months was required to convince the party of the need for the new course. But the remarkable thing is that it was precisely the anarchists all over the world who looked upon the NEP as... a betrayal of communism. But now the advocates of the anarchists denounce us for not having introduced the NEP a year earlier.

In 1921 Lenin more than once openly acknowledged that the party's obstinate defence of the methods of military communism had become a great mistake. But does this change matters? Whatever the immediate or remote causes of the Kronstadt rebellion, it was in its very essence a mortal danger to the dictatorship of the proletariat. Simply because it had been guilty of a political error, should the proletarian revolution really have commited suicide to punish itself?

Or perhaps it would have been sufficient to inform the Kronstadt sailors of the NEP decrees to pacify them? Illusion! The insurgents did not have a conscious programme and they could not have had one because of the very nature of the petty bourgeosie. They themselves did not clearly understand that what their fathers and brothers needed first of all was free trade. They were discontented and confused but they saw no way out. The more conscious, ie the rightist, elements, acting behind the scenes, wanted the restoration of the bourgeois regime. But they did not say so out loud. The 'left' wing wanted the liquidation of discipline, 'free Soviets', and better rations. The regime of the NEP could only gradually pacify the peasant, and, after him, the discontented sections of the army and the fleet. But for this time and experience were needed.

Most puerile of all is the argument that there was no uprising, that the sailors had made no threats, that they 'only' seized the fortress and the battleships. It would seem that the Bolsheviks marched with bared chests across the ice against the fortress only because of their evil characters, their inclination to provoke conflicts artificially, their hatred of the Kronstadt sailors, or their hatred of the anarchist doctrine (about which absolutely no one, we may say in passing, bothered in those days). Is this not childish prattle? Bound neither to time nor place, the dilettante critics try (17 years later!) to suggest that everything would have ended in general satisfaction if only the Revolution had left the insurgent sailors alone. Unfortunately, the world counter-revolution would in no case have left them alone. The logic of the struggle would have given predominance in the fortress to the extremists, that is, to the most counter-revolutionary elements. The need for supplies would have made the fortress directly dependent upon the foreign bourgeoisie and their agents, the White emigrés. All the necessary preparations toward this end were already being made. Under similar circumstances only people like the Spanish anarchists or POUMists would have waited passively, hoping for a happy outcome. The Bolsheviks, fortunately, belonged to a different school. They considered it their duty to extinguish the fire as soon as it started, thereby reducing to a minimum the number of victims.

Victor Serge. Extract from 'Once More: Kronstadt'[62]

I receive your review with great pleasure. It is obviously the best revolutionary Marxian organ today. Believe me that all my sympathies are with you and that if it is possible for me to be of service to you, it will be most willingly rendered.

I shall some day reply to the articles of Wright[63] and LD Trotsky on Kronstadt. This great subject merits being taken up again thoroughly and the two studies that you have published are far, very far, from exhausting it. In the very first place, I am surprised to see our comrades Wright and LD Trotsky employ a reasoning which, it seems to me, we ought to beware of and refrain from. They record that the drama of Kronstadt, 1921, is evoking commentaries at once from the Social Revolutionists, the Mensheviks, the anarchists and others; and from this fact, natural in an epoch of ideological confusion, of the revisions of values, of the battles of sects, they deduce a sort of amalgam. Let us be distrustful of amalgams and of such mechanical reasoning. They have been too greatly abused in the Russian revolution and we see where it leads. Bourgeois liberals, Mensheviks, anarchists, revolutionary Marxists consider the drama of Kronstadt from different standpoints and for different reasons, which it is well and necessary to bear in mind, instead of lumping all the critical minds under a single heading and imputing to all of them the same hostility towards Bolshevism.

The problem is, in truth, much vaster than the event of Kronstadt, which was only an episode. Wright and LD Trotsky support a highly simple thesis: that the Kronstadt uprising was objectivly counter-revolutionary and that the policy of Lenin's and Trotsky's Central Committee at that time was correct before, during and after. Correct this policy was, on an historic and moreover grandiose scale, which permitted it to be tragically and dangerously false, erroneous, in various specific circumstances. That is what it would be useful and courageous to recognise today instead of affirming the infallibility of a general line of 1917–1923. There remains broadly the fact that the uprisings of Kronstadt and other localities signified to the party the absolute impossibility of persevering on the road of War Communism. The country was dying of bitter-end statification. Who then was right? The Central Committee which clung to a road without issue or the masses driven to extremities by famine? It seems to me undeniable that Lenin at that time committed the greatest mistake of his life. Need we recall that a few weeks before the establishment of the NEP, Bukharin published a work on economics showing that the system in operation was indeed the first phase of socialism? For having advocated, in his letters to Lenin, measures of reconciliation with the peasants, the historian Rozhkov[64] had just been deported to Pskov. Once Kronstadt rebelled, it had to be subdued, no doubt. But what was done to forestall the insurrection? Why was the mediation of the Petrograd anarchists rejected? Can one, finally, justify the insensate and, I repeat, abominable massacre of the vanquished of Kronstadt who were still being shot in batches in the Petrograd prison three months after the end of the uprising? They were men of the Russian people, backward perhaps, but who belonged to the masses of the revolution itself.

LD Trotsky emphasises that the sailors and soldiers of the Kronstadt of 1921 were no longer the same, with regard to revolutionary consciousness, as those of 1918. That is true. But the party of 1921 – was it the same as that of 1918? Was it not already suffering from a bureaucratic befoulment which often detached itself from the masses and rendered it inhuman towards them? It would be well to reread in this connection the criticisms against the bureaucratic regime formulated long ago by the Workers' Opposition; and also to remember the evil practices that made their appearance during the discussion on the trade unions in 1920. For my part, I was outraged to see the manoeuvres which the majority employed in Petrograd to stifle the voice of the Trotskyists and the Workers' Opposition (who defended diametrically opposed theses).

The question which dominates today the whole discussion is, in substance, this: When and how did Bolshevism begin to degenerate?

When and how did it begin to employ towards the toiling masses, whose energy and highest consciousness it expressed, non-socialist methods which must be condemned because they ended by assuring the victory of the bureaucracy over the proletariat?

This question posed, it can be seen that the first symptoms of the evil date far back. In 1920, the Menshivik social-democrats were falsly accused, in a communiqué of the CHEKA, of intelligence with the enemy, of sabotage, etc. This communiqué, monstrously false, served to outlaw them. In the same year, the anarchists were arrested throughout Russia, after a formal promise to legalise the movement and after the treaty of peace signed with Makhno had been deliberately torn up by the Central Committee which no longer needed the Black Army. The revolutionary correctness of the totality of a policy cannot justify, in my eyes, these baneful practises. And the facts that I cite are unfortunately far from being the only ones.

Let us go back still further. Has not the moment come to declare that the day of the glorious year of 1918 when the Central Committee of the party decided to permit the Extraordinary Commissions to apply the death penalty *on the basis of secret procedure, without hearing the accused who could not defend themselves*, is a black day? That day the Central Committee was in a position to restore or not restore an inquisitional procedure forgotten by European civilisation. In any case, it committed a mistake. It did not necessarily behoove a victorious socialist party to commit that mistake. The revolution could have defended itself better without that.

We would indeed be wrong to conceal from ourselves today that the whole historical acquisition of the Russian revolution is being called into question. Out of the vast experience of Bolshevism, the revolutionary Marxists will save what is essential, durable, only by taking up all the problems again from the bottom, with a genuine freedom of mind, without party vanity, without irreducible hostility (above all in the field of historical investigation) towards the other tendencies of the labour movement. On the contrary, by not recognising old errors, whose gravity history has not ceased to bring out in relief, the risk is run of compromising the whole acquisition of Bolshevism. The Kronstadt episode simultaneously poses the questions of the relations between the party of the proletariat and the masses, of the internal regime of the party (the Workers' Opposition was smashed), of socialist ethics (all Petrograd was deceived by the announcement of a *White* movement in Kronstadt), of humaneness in the class struggle and above all in the struggle within our classes. Finally it puts us today to the test as to our self-critical capacity.

Unable to reply more thoroughly for the moment to comrades Wright and LD Trotsky, I hope you will be good enough to submit this letter to the readers of *The New International*. It will perhaps contribute towards priming a discussion which we ought to know how to bring to a successful issue in a spirit of healthy revolutionary comradeship.

Paris, April 28, 1938
Victor Serge

Leon Trotsky. Extract from 'More on the Suppression of Kronstadt'[65]

In my recent article on 'Kronstadt' I tried to pose the question on a political plane. But many are interested in the problem of personal 'responsibility'. Souvarine, who from a sluggish Marxist became an exalted sycophant, asserts in his book on Stalin that in my autobiography I kept consciously silent on the Kronstadt rebellion; there are exploits – he says ironically – of which one does not boast. Ciliga in his book *In the Country of the Big Lie*[66] recounts that in the suppression of Kronstadt 'more than ten thousand seamen' were shot by me (I doubt whether the whole Baltic fleet at that time had that many). Other critics express themselves in this manner: yes. Objectively the rebellion had a counter-revolutionary character but why did Trotsky use such merciless repressions in the pacification [and – ?) subsequently?

I have never touched on this question. Not because I had anything to conceal but, on the contrary, precisely because I had nothing to say. The truth of the matter is that *I personally did not participate in the least in the suppression of the Kronstadt rebellion, nor in the repressions following the suppression*. In my eyes this very fact is of no political significance. I was a member of the government, I considered the quelling of the rebellion necessary and therefore bear responsibility for the suppression. Only within these limits have I replied to criticism up to now. But when moralists begin to annoy me personally, accusing me of exceeding cruelty not called forth by circumstance, I consider that I have a right to say: 'Messrs. moralists, you are lying a bit'.

The rebellion broke out during my stay in the Urals. From the Urals I came directly to Moscow for the 10th Congress of the party. The decision to suppress the rebellion by military force, *if the fortress could not be induced to surrender, first by peace negotiations, then through an ultimatum* – this general decision was adopted with my direct participation. But after the decision was taken, I continued to remain in Moscow and took no part, direct or indirect, in the military operations. Concerning the subsequent repressions, they were completely the affair of the CHEKA.

How did it happen that I did not go personally to Kronstadt? The reason was of a political nature. The rebellion broke out during the discussion on the so called 'trade union' question. The political work in Kronstadt was wholly in the hands of the Petrograd committee, at the head of which stood Zinoviev. The same Zinoviev was the chief, most untiring and passionate leader in the struggle against me in the discussion. Before my departure for the Urals I was in Petrograd and spoke at a meeting of seamen – communists. The general spirit of the meeting made an extremely unfavourable impression upon me. Dandified and well-fed sailors, communists in name only, produced the impression of parasites in comparison with the workers and Red Army men of that time. On the part of the Petrograd committee the campaign was carried on in an extremely demagogic manner. The commanding personnel of the fleet was isolated and terrified. Zinoviev's resolution received, probably, 90% of the votes. I recall having said to Zinoviev on this occasion: 'Everything is very good here, until it becomes very bad.' Subsequent to this Zinoviev was with me in the Urals where he received an urgent message that in Kronstadt things were getting 'very bad'. The overwhelming majority of the sailor 'communists' who supported Zinoviev's resolution took part in the rebellion. I considered, and the Political Bureau made no objections, that negotiations with the sailors, and in case of necessity, their pacification, should be placed with those leaders who only yesterday enjoyed the political confidence of the sailors. Otherwise, the Kronstadters would consider the matter as though I had come to take 'revenge' upon them for their voting against me during the party discussion.

Whether correct or not, in any case it was precisely these considerations which determined my attitude. *I stepped aside completely and demonstratively from this affair.* Concerning the repressions, as far as I remember, Dzerzhinsky had personal charge of them and Dzerzhinsky could not tolerate anyone's interference with his functions (and properly so).

Whether there were any needless victims I do not know. On this score I trust Dzerzhinsky more than his belated critics. For lack of data I cannot undertake to decide now, *a posteriori*, who should have been punished and how. Victor Serge's conclusions on this score – from third hand – have no value in my eyes. But I am ready to recognise that civil war is no school of humanism. Idealists and pacifists always accused the revolution of 'excesses'. But the main point is that 'excesses' flow from the very nature of revolution which in itself is but an 'excess' of history. Whoever so desires may on this basis reject (in little articles) revolution in general. I do not reject it. In this sense I carry full and complete responsibility for the suppression of the Kronstadt rebellion.

Coyocan, July 6, 1938   L Trotsky

Victor Serge. 'Reply to Trotsky' Extract from 'A Letter and Some Notes' [67]

By a note published in America at the end of July, Leon Trotsky finally specified his responsibilities in the episode of Kronstadt. The political responsibilities, as he has always declared, are those of the Central Committee of the Russian Communist Party which took the decision to 'suppress the rebellion by military force if the fortress could not be induced to surrender first by peace negotiations and then through an ultimatum'. Trotsky adds: 'I have never touched on this question. Not because I had anything to conceal but, on the contrary, precisely because I had nothing to say ... *I personally did not participate in the suppression of the rebellion nor in the repression following the suppression ...'.*

Trotsky recalls the differences which separated him at the time from Zinoviev, chairman of the Petrograd Soviet. '*I stepped aside'*, he writes, '*completely and demonstratively from this affair'*.

It will be well to remember this after certain personal attacks directed against Trotsky out of bad faith, ignorance and sectarian spirit. For there is room, after all, in history for distinguishing between the general political responsibilities and the immediate personal responsibilities.

'Whether there were any needless victims', continues Trotsky, 'I do not know. On this score I trust Dzerzhinsky more than his belated critics ... Victor Serge's conclusions on this score – from third hand – have no value in my eyes ...'. Dzerzhinsky's conclusions however, are from seventh or ninth hand, for the head of the CHEKA did not come to Petrograd at that time and was himself informed only by a hierarchical path on which a lot could be said (and Trotsky knows it better than anybody). As for myself, residing in Petrograd, I lived among the heads of the city. I know what the repression was from eye-witnesses. I visited anarchist comrades in the Shpalernaya prison, imprisoned moreover in defiance of all common sense, who saw the vanquished of Kronstadt leave every day for the ordnance yard. The repression, I repeat, was atrocious. According to the Soviet historians, mutinous Kronstadt had some 16,000 combatants at its disposal. Several thousand succeeded in reaching Finland over the ice. The others, by hundreds and more likely thousands, were massacred at the end of the battle or

executed afterward. Where are Dzerzhinsky's statistics – and what are
they worth if they exist? The single fact that a Trotsky, at the pinnacle
of power, did not feel the need of informing himself precisely on this
repression of an insurrectional movement of workers, the single fact
that a Trotsky did not know what all the rank and file communists knew:
that out of inhumanity *a needless crime* had just been committed against
the proletariat and the peasants – this single fact, I say, is gravely significant. It is indeed in the field of repression that the Central Committee
of the Bolshevik party committed the most serious mistakes from the
beginning of the revolution, mistakes which were to contribute most
dangerously, on the one hand, to bureaucratising the party and the state,
and on the other, to disarming the masses and more particularly the revolutionists. It is high time this was acknowledged.

Victor Serge. 'Marxism in Our Time'[68]

1

Since the Communist Manifesto was published in 1848, Marxism has
gone through many metamorphoses and suffered many attacks. Critics
still exist – and sometimes men of good will – who insist that it has
been cancelled, refuted, destroyed by history. The confused but energetic
class-consciousness of the last defenders of capitalism, however, sees in
Marxism its most dangerous spiritual and social enemy. The preventa-
tive counter-revolutions of Italy and of Germany justly proclaim
themselves 'anti-Marxist'. On the other hand, almost all workers'
movements which have won any appreciable power have been inspired
by Marxism. The CNT of Spain is almost the only exception to this
rule, and experience has shown only too well the seriousness of its ideological bankruptcy, at a moment when the consciousness of the masses
was called on to become one of the decisive factors in a revolution in
the making – a revolution perhaps aborted today precisely because of
the political incapacity of the revolutionaries.

The historic achievements of Marxism are not to be denied. The
Marxist parties of the Second International united and organised the
pre-war working class, raising it to a new dignity, shaping it demo-
cratically. In 1914 they showed themselves prisoners of the capitalism
which they fought even as they adapted themselves to it. (They adapted
themselves, in reality, a good deal more than they fought.) But it was
a Marxist party which, in the chaotic currents of the Russian Revolution,
knew how to disentangle the main lines of force, to orient itself,
constantly according to the highest interests of the workers, to make
itself, in the truest sense of the word, the midwife of a new world. Marxists

bore the brunt of the class wars of the post-war period; Spartacists in
Germany, Tiessriaki in Bulgaria, Communists everywhere. Later, at the
moment of its highest flight, the Chinese revolution was strongly
influenced by the revolutionary Marxism of the Russians – already much
deformed, incidentally, by the reaction even then arising inside the USSR.
It is true that German Marxism in its two forms – Social Democratic
and Communist – showed itself impotent before the Nazi offensive.
Along with the degeneration of Bolshevism, this is without question,
let us note in passing, the greatest defeat that Marxism has ever suffered.
Nonetheless, Marxism continues to mount the ladder of world history.
While irreconcilable oppositionists are persecuted and exterminated by
Stalinism, the Austrian Socialists carry on a struggle, desperate but
heroic, which saves them from demoralisation; the Socialist miners of
the Asturias in '34 deal a set-back to Spanish fascism.

It would be absurd to isolate Marxist thought from these social
realities. Even more than it is a scientific doctrine, Marxism is an
historic fact. If one is to understand it, one must embrace it in all its
scope. One then perceives that since the birth, the apogee and the
corruption of Christianity, there has been no more considerable event
in the life of humanity.

2

This fact goes far beyond the boundaries of the class struggle and
becomes an integral part of the consciousness of modern man – no matter
what his attitude towards Marxism. It is of secondary importance to
ask one's self if the theories of value, or of surplus value, or of the accu-
mulation of capital are still completely valid. An idle question, essentially,
and even somewhat puerile. Science is never 'finished'; rather, it is always
completing itself. Can science be anything except a process of continual
self-revision, an unceasing quest for a closer approach to truth? Can it
get along without hypothesis and error – the 'error' of tomorrow
which is the 'truth' (that is, the closest approximation of the truth) of
yesterday. It is of minor importance, also, to point out that certain predictions of Marx and Engels have not been confirmed by history and
that, on the contrary, many events have taken place which they did
not at all foresee. Marx and Engels were too great, too intelligent, to
believe themselves infallible and play the prophet. It is true – but not
important – that their followers have not always reached this level of
wisdom. It still remains true that Marxism has modified the thinking
of the man of our modern times. We are in debt to it for a renewing,
a broadening of our consciousness. In what way? Since Marx, no one

seriously denies the part played by economics in history. The relationship between economic, psychological, social and moral factors appears today, even to the adversaries of Marxism, in an altogether different light from that in which it appeared before Marx. It is the same with the role of the individual in history, and with the relationship of the individual to the masses and to society. Marxism, finally, gives us what I call 'the historical sense'; it makes us conscious that we live in a world which is in process of changing; it enlightens us as to our possible function – and our limitations – it is this continual struggle and creation; it teaches us to integrate ourselves, with all our will, all our talents, to bring about those historical processes that are, as the case may be, necessary, inevitable or desirable. And it is thus that it allows us to confer on our isolated lives a high significance, by tying them, through a consciousness which heightens and enriches the spiritual life, to that life – collective, innumerable, and permanent – of which history is only the record.

This awakening of consciousness insists on action and, furthermore, on the unity of action and thought. Here is man reconciled with himself, whatever be the burden of his destiny. He no longer feels himself the plaything of blind and measureless forces. He looks with clear eyes on the worst tragedies, and even in the midst of the greatest defeats he feels himself enlarged by his ability to understand, his will to act and to resist, the indestructible feeling of being united in all his aspirations with the mass of humanity in its progress through time.

3

One is no more able to deny the part played by economics in history than the fact that the earth is round... And even those who argue the point do not in the least deceive themselves. I should like to emphasise here an important point to which not enough attention has been paid in the past. The enemies of the working class have themselves largely assimilated the lessons of Marxism. The politicians, the industrialists and bankers, the demagogues sometimes burn the works of Marx and throw his followers into prison; but, dealing with social realities, they pay tribute to Marxist economists and political leaders. And if scholars refute the theory of surplus value, their masters do not put any less energy and stubbornness into the defence of the surplus value they appropriate as their plunder from the revenues of society. This *sub-rosa* Marxism of the enemies of socialism is in a fair way to become one of the most formidable means of defence of the privileged classes.

4

Marxism undergoes, in its own history, the conditions of development which it analyses. It is able to rise above them only in a small degree, since every gain of consciousness is an effect before it becomes a cause, and remains subordinate to pre-existing social conditions. 'Social being determines consciousness.'

The Marxism of the imperialist epoch was split. It was nationalistic and wholly reformist. Very few of its adherents – a Rosa Luxemburg, a Lenin, a Trotsky, a Hermann Gorter[69] – saw beyond the moment to horizons vaster than those of capitalist prosperity. Either this Marxism dwelt on the heights of philosophy far removed from immediate action, or it was merely reminiscent of the ancient Christian utopianism (which was, in our culture, Hebrew before it was Christian: read the Prophets!).

The Marxism of the imperialist epoch was split. It was nationalistic and counter-revolutionary in the countries where it had been reformist; it was revolutionary and internationalist in Russia, the only country in which the foundering of an *ancien régime* forced the proletariat to carry out completely its historic mission.

The Marxism of the Russian Revolution was at first ardently inter-nationalist and libertarian (the doctrine of the Communist State, the federation of Soviets); but because of the state of siege, it soon became more and more authoritarian and intolerant.

The Marxism of the decadence of Bolshevism – that is to say, that of the bureaucratic caste which has evicted the working class from power – is totalitarian, despotic, amoral, and opportunist. It ends up in the strangest and most revolting negations of itself.

What does this mean except that social consciousness even in its highest forms does not escape the effect of the realities which it expresses, which it illuminates and which it tries to surmount.

5

Marxism is so firmly based in truth that it is able to find nourishment in its own defeats. We must distinguish here between the social philosophy – scientific, to speak more accurately – and its deductions for, and applications to, action. (These are actually inseparable, and this is the case not only with Marxism but also with all those intellectual disciplines which are closely tied to human activity.) It is our business neither to force events, nor to control them, nor even to foresee them – even though we are constantly doing all these things, with varying success; our activity, being creative, boldly ventures into the uncertain; and, what we do not know generally getting the better of what we know,

our successes are rather astonishing victories. As to the Marxist line of
action, it would be enough to list the prodigious success of the Bolshevik
party in 1917 (Lenin–Trotsky), the predictions of Engels about the world
war of the future and its consequences, some lines from the resolution
adopted at the Basle Congress of the Second International (1913) – for
the Marxist line to be justified as the most rigorously, scientifically
thought-out of these times. But even when it comes to the very depths
of defeat, it is still the same. Do you wish to understand your defeat?
You will be able to only by means of the Marxist analysis of history.
Marxism showed itself impotent in Germany before the Nazi counter-
revolution; but it is the only theory that explains this victory of a party
of the declassed, paid for and supported during an insoluble economic
crisis, by the chiefs of the big bourgeoisie. This complex phase of the
class struggle, prepared by the national humiliation at Versailles and the
massacres of proletarian revolutionaries (Noske, 1918–21), is made
completely intelligible to us only by the scientific thought of the
defeated class. And this is one of the reasons which make Marxist
thought such a threat to the victors.

It is the same with the terrible degeneration of the dictatorship of
the proletariat in the USSR. There too, the punishment of the Old
Bolsheviks, exterminated by the regime which they have created, is no
more than a phenomenon of the class struggle. The proletariat, deposed
from power by a caste of parvenus entrenched in the new State, can
take an accounting of the basic reasons for its defeat and can prepare
itself for the struggles of tomorrow only by means of the Marxist
analysis.

6

The Marxism of the era of capitalist prosperity naturally lacked revolutionary ardour. It dared neither imagine nor hope for the end of the
society in which it lived. Lacking this audacity, it disavowed itself
when it became necessary. But there are times when to live is to dare.

The Marxism of the first great revolutionary crisis of the modern world,
chiefly represented by the Russians – that is to say, by men formed in
the school of despotism – has given proof of a lack of boldness of another
sort, and one quite as ruinous: it has not dared to take a libertarian position.
Or rather, it was libertarian in words and only for a short time, during
the brief period of Soviet democracy which extended from October,
1917, to the summer of 1918. Then it pulled itself together and
resolutely entered on the path of the old 'statism' – authoritarian, and
soon totalitarian. It lacked the sense of liberty.

It is easy to explain – and even to justify – this development of Bolshevik Marxism by referring to the constant mortal danger, the Civil War, the superbly energetic defence of the public safety by Lenin, Trotsky, Dzerzhinsky. Easy and just to recognise that this policy, in its early stages, made certain the victory of the workers – and a victory won in the face of difficulties that were truly without precedent. But one must realise that *later on* this policy brought about the defeat of the workers by the bureaucracy. The Bolshevik leaders of the great years lacked neither the knowledge nor intelligence nor energy. They lacked revolution-ary audacity whenever it was necessary to seek (after 1918) the solution of their problems in the freedom of the masses and not in government constraint. They built systematically not the libertarian Communist State which they announced, but a State strong in the old sense of the word, strong in its police, in its censorship, its monopolies, its all-powerful bureaus. In this respect, the contrast is striking between the Bolshevist programme of 1917 and the political structure created by Bolshevism in 1919.

After victory had been won in the Civil War, the Socialist solution of the problems of the new society should have been sought in workers' democracy, the stimulation of initiative, freedom of thought, freedom for working-class groups and not, as it was, in centralisation of power, repression of heresies, the monolithic single-party system, the narrow orthodoxy of an official school of thought. The dominance and ideology of a single party should have preshadowed the dominance and ideology of a single leader. This extreme concentration of power, this dread of liberty and of ideological variations, this conditioning to absolute authority disarmed the masses and led to the strengthening of the bureaucracy. By the time Lenin and Trotsky realised the danger and wished to retrace their steps – timidly enough, at first: the greatest reach of boldness of the Left Opposition in the Bolshevik Party was to demand the restoration of inner-Party democracy, and it never dared dispute the theory of single-party government – by this time, it was too late.

The fear of liberty, which is the fear of the masses, marks almost the entire course of the Russian Revolution. If it is possible to discover a major lesson, capable of revitalising Marxism, more threatened today than ever by the collapse of Bolshevism, one might formulate it in these terms: Socialism is essentially democratic – the word, 'democratic', being used here in its libertarian sense. One sees today in the USSR that without liberty of thought, of speech, of criticism, of initiative, Socialist production can only go from one crisis to another. Liberty is as necessary to Socialism, the spirit of liberty is as necessary to Marxism, as oxygen to living beings.

7

In the very wake of its sensational victory in the Russian Revolution, Marxism is today threatened with a great loss of prestige, and in the working-class movement, with an unspeakable demoralisation. It would be futile to pretend otherwise. We have seen, in the country of Socialist victory, the Marxist party – enjoying the greatest, the most deserved prestige – in the space of fifteen years undergo the most disconcerting degeneration. We have seen it reach the point of dishonouring and murdering its heroes of yesterday, drawing from their very loyalty, for the purposes of judicial frame-ups based on glaring forgeries, confessions which are even more sinister than they are disconcerting. We have seen the dictatorship of the proletariat transform itself insensibly into a dictatorship of bureaucrats and of police agents over the proletariat. We have seen the working class, still in the flush of its recent victories, condemned to a moral and material level decidedly below that which it had under the Czarist regime. We have seen the peasantry dispossessed and exiled by millions, agriculture ruined by forced collectivisation. We have seen science, literature, thought literally handcuffed, and Marxism reduced to formulae which are frequently manipulated for political ends and emptied of all living content. We have seen it, furthermore, falsified, crudely adapted to the interests of a regime which in its *mores*, its actions, and the new forms of exploitation of labour it has superimposed on the base of common ownership of the instruments of production. We have seen, we still see the indescribable spectacle of the black terror, permanently established in the USSR. We have seen the cult of 'the Beloved Leader', the corruption of the intellectuals and the workers' organisations abroad, the systematic lies broadcast by a huge journalistic apparatus which still calls itself 'Communist', the secret police of Moscow murdering or kidnapping its adversaries as far away as Spain and Switzerland. We have seen this gangrene spread throughout revolutionary Spain, compromising, perhaps irretrievably, the destiny of the workers. And it is not over yet. All the values which comprise the greatness of Socialism from now on are compromised, soiled, obliterated. A fatal division, between the blind and the clear-sighted, rascals and honest men, deepens in the ranks of the working class, already provoking fratricidal conflicts, rendering all moral progress impossible for the time being. For it is no longer possible to discuss with good faith and intellectual courage a single one of the theoretical and practical questions that grow out of Marxism. The social catastrophe in the USSR taints in its growth, in its very life, the consciousness of modern man.

I wrote to André Gide in May 1936, before he left for Russia: 'We make a common front against Fascism. But how can we bar its way with so many concentration camps behind our own lines? One's duty is no longer simple, and it is no longer permitted to any one to simplify it. No new orthodoxy, no sacred falsehoods can any longer dry up this running sore. In one sense only does the Soviet Union remain the greatest hope of mankind in our day; in any sense that the Soviet workers have not yet said their last word.'

Every social conflict is also a competition. If socialism is to win out over fascism, it must bring humanity social conditions which are clearly superior.

Is it necessary to emphasise again that the confused, distorted and bloody Marxism of the gunmen of Moscow – is not Marxism? That it negates, belies and paralyses itself? The masses, unfortunately, will take some time to realise this. They live not according to clear and rational thought but according to impressions which the lessons of experience slowly modify. Since all this goes on under the usurped banner of Marxism, we must expect that the masses, unable to apply Marxist analysis to this tragedy, will react against Marxism. Our enemies have it all their own way.

But scientific thought cannot regress below the Marxist level, nor can the working class do without this intellectual weapon. The European working class is still recuperating its strength, sapped by the blood-letting of the world war. A new proletariat is arising in Russia, its industrial base greatly extended. The class struggle goes on. For all the dictators' replastering, we hear the framework of the old social edifice cracking. Marxism will go through many vicissitudes of fortune, perhaps even eclipses. Its power, conditioned by the course of history, none the less appears to be inexhaustible. For its base is knowledge integrated with the necessity for revolution.

Leon Trotsky. Extract from 'Victor Serge and the Fourth International'[70]

Several friends have asked us what Victor Serge's relationship is to the Fourth International. We are obliged to reply that it is the relationship of an opponent. Ever since his appearance outside the Soviet Union Victor Serge has done nothing but change positions. There is no other way to define his political position than 'changeability'. Not on one single question has he presented clear or distinct proposals, rebuttals or arguments. He has invariably, though, supported those who have moved away from the Fourth International, whether to the right or the left. Surprising everyone, Victor Serge declared in an official letter that he was joining the POUM, without ever having attempted to reply to our criticisms of the POUM as a centrist organisation that has played a miserable role in the Spanish revolution. Victor Serge flirted with the Spanish anarcho-syndicalists in spite of their treacherous role in the Spanish revolution. Behind the scenes, he supported that ill-fated hero of 'left' trade-unionism, Sneevliet, without ever deciding to openly defend the Dutch opportunist's unprincipled politics. Simultaneously Victor Serge repeated on several occasions that his differences with us were of a 'secondary' character. To the direct question of why he did not then collaborate with the Fourth International rather than with its rabid opponents, Victor Serge never came up with an answer. All this, taken together, deprived his own 'politics' of any consistency whatsoever and turned it into a series of personal combinations, if not intrigues. If Victor Serge still speaks, even now, of his 'sympathies' for the Fourth International, it is in no other sense than Vereeken, Molinier, Sneevliet, Maslow, etc, do the same, having in mind not the real International, but a mythical one, created by their imagination in their own likeness and form, and necessary to them only as a cover for their opportunist or adventurist politics. With this nonexistent International our actually functioning International has nothing in common, and neither the Russian section nor the International as a whole takes any responsibility for the politics of Victor Serge.

December 2, 1938

Leon Trotsky. Extract from 'Intellectual ex-Radicals and World Reaction' [71]

During the last decade the older generation of the radical intelligentsia has been greatly influenced by Stalinism. Today the turn away from Stalinism in the advanced countries, at any rate, has been reaching ever wider proportions. Some are sincerely disappointed in their illusions while others are simply aware that the ship is in dangerous straits and are in a hurry to leave it. It would be naive to expect that the 'disillusioned' should turn to Marxism with which, in the nature of things, they were never acquainted. For most intellectuals their departure from Stalinism signifies a complete break with the revolution and a passive reconciliation with nationalistic democracy. These 'disillusioned' provide a culture medium *sui generis* for the bacilli of scepticism and pessimism.

They say: 'It is impossible to do anything at the present time. Europe will fall wholly under the sway of Fascism anyway, and the United States is far too powerful. The revolutionary roads lead nowhere. We must adapt ourselves to the democratic regime; we must defend it against all attacks. There is no future for the Fourth International, at all events, not for the next two or three decades...', and so forth and so on.

The ranks of the disillusioned include not only Stalinists but also the temporary fellow-travellers of Bolshevism. Victor Serge – to cite an instance – has recently announced that Bolshevism is passing through a crisis which presages in turn the 'crisis of Marxism'.[72] In his theoretical innocence, Serge imagines himself the first to have made this discovery. Yet, in every epoch of reaction, scores and hundreds of unstable revolutionists have risen to announce the 'crisis of Marxism' – the final, the crucial, the mortal crisis.

That the old Bolshevik party has spent itself, has degenerated and perished – that much is beyond controversy. But the ruin of a given historical party, which had for a certain period based itself upon the Marxian doctrine, does not at all signify the ruination of that doctrine. The defeat of an army does not invalidate the fundamental precepts of strategy. Should an artillery-man fire wide of the mark, that would by no means invalidate ballistics, that is, the algebra of artillery. If the army of the proletariat suffers a defeat, or if its party degenerates, then this does not at all invalidate Marxism, which is the algebra of revolution. That Victor Serge himself is passing through a 'crisis', ie, has become hopelessly confused like thousands of other intellectuals – is clear enough. But Victor Serge in crisis is not the crisis of Marxism.

In any case, no serious revolutionist would think of using intellectuals in confusion, Stalinists in disillusion and sceptics in dejection as a yardstick with which to measure the march of history. World reaction has unquestionably assumed monstrous proportions nowadays. But thereby it has prepared the soil for the greatest revolutionary crisis. Fascism may perhaps seize upon the whole of Europe. But it will not be able to maintain itself there not only for a 'thousand years', as Hitler dreams, but not even for a decade. The fascisisation of Europe means the monstrous aggravation of class and international contradictions.

It is absurd, unscientific, unhistorical to think that reaction will continue to unfold at the same gradual pace at which it has been accumulating hitherto. Reaction signifies this, that the social contradictions are mechanically suppressed. At a certain stage, an explosion is inevitable. World reaction will be overthrown by the greatest catastrophe in world history, or, more correctly, by a series of revolutionary catastrophes.

The coming war, which is now being awaited by everyone within the nearest future, will signify the crash of all illusions. Not only the illusions of reformism, pacifism and democratism but also the illusions of fascism. Only one beacon will rise above the blood-drenched chaos – the beacon of Marxism.

Hegel was fond of saying: all that is rational is real. This means: every idea that corresponds to objective needs of development attains triumph and victory. No intellectually honest individual can deny that the analysis and prognosis made by the Bolshevik-Leninists (Fourth Internationalists) during the past 15 years have met and still meet with confirmation in the events of our time. It is precisely in this certainty of their correctness that the basic sections of the Fourth International are strong and immutable. The catastrophes of European and world capitalism which are hovering over mankind will clear the path before the steeled cadres of the revolutionary Marxists.

Let the disillusioned ones bury their own dead. The working class is not a corpse. As hitherto, society rests upon it. It needs a new leadership. It will find this nowhere but in the Fourth International. All that is rational is real. Social democracy and Stalinocracy even today represent stupendous fictions. But the Fourth International is an impregnable reality.

Leon Trotsky. 'The Masses Have Nothing To Do With It!' Extract from 'The Moralists and Sycophants against Marxism'[73]

Victor Serge has disclosed in passing what caused the collapse of the Bolshevik Party: excessive centralism, mistrust of ideological struggle, lack of freedom-loving (*'libertaire'*, in reality anarchist) spirit. More confidence in the masses, more freedom! All this is outside time and space. But the masses are by no means identical: there are revolutionary masses, there are passive masses, there are reactionary masses. The very same masses are at different times inspired by different moods and objectives. It is just for this reason that a centralised organisation of the vanguard is indispensable. Only a party, wielding the authority it has won, is capable of overcoming the vacillation of the masses themselves. To invest the mass with traits of sanctity and to reduce one's programme to amorphous 'democracy', is to dissolve oneself in the class as it is, to turn from a vanguard into a rearguard, and by this very thing, to renounce revolutionary tasks. On the other hand, if the dictatorship of the proletariat means anything at all, then it means that the vanguard of the class is armed with the resources of the state in order to repel dangers, including those emanating from the backward layers of the proletariat itself. All this is elementary; all this has been demonstrated by the experience of Russia, and confirmed by the experience of Spain.

But the whole secret is this, that demanding freedom 'for the masses', Victor Serge in reality demands freedom for himself and for his compeers, freedom from all control, all discipline, even, if possible, from all criticism. The 'masses' have nothing to do with it. When our 'democrat' scurries from right to left, and from left to right, sowing confusion and scepticism, he imagines it to be the realisation of a salutary freedom of thought. But when we evaluate from the Marxian standpoint the vacillations of a disillusioned petty-bourgeois intellectual, that seems to him an assault upon his individuality. He then enters into an alliance with all the confusionists for a crusade against our despotism and our sectarianism.

The internal democracy of a revolutionary party is not a goal in itself. It must be supplemented and bounded by centralism. For a Marxist the question has always been democracy for what? For which program? The framework of the programme is at the same time the framework of democracy. Victor Serge demanded of the Fourth International that it give freedom of action to all confusionists, sectarians and centrists of the POUM, Vereeken, Marceau Pivert types, to conservative bureaucrats of the Sneevliet type or mere adventurers of the R Molinier type. On the other hand, Victor Serge has systematically helped centrist organisations drive from their ranks the partisans of the Fourth International. We are very well acquainted with that democratism: it is compliant, accommodating and conciliatory – *towards the right*; at the same time, it is exigent, malevolent and tricky – *towards the left*. It merely represents the regime of self-defence of petty-bourgeois centrism.

Victor Serge. 'Letter to Angelica Balabanova'[74]

23 October 1941 Mexico.

Dear Angelica,

I'm very pleased to have this short discussion with you: it would make me really happy if we could have our discussion face to face.

In all my books and articles I gave LD the enormous credit which is due to him. If I omitted to mention him in one article, I may have been wrong, but nobody should read any retraction of my judgement into this. In our era of demoralisation, people get used to misinterpreting everything, much to one's annoyance.

I know that you have for a long time been situated politically in what used to be called the Two-and-a-half International. I did think that was a mistake and that it would have been better to go back to the Second International. The CI still represented then, even with all its many defects, the energy of the Russian Revolution; the Second, with all its defects, was still the great organisation of the majority of the workers of Europe. To place oneself between the two, even with the best intentions, was to refuse to exert any influence on one or the other, and to abandon the field, in the CI's case to the bureaucratic reaction and in the other to conservative and petty-bourgeois Socialism. (I am talking of the position in 1923–25.)

You seem very unfair to me, which must be through ignorance of what I have been doing and writing in various situations. As early as 1919 the persecution of the anarchists in Russia revealed the dreadful evils there to me. It was stupid and criminal, but I couldn't find in it a sufficient reason for me to break with the party of the revolution. Around 1920 the criticisms of the Workers' Opposition struck me as accurate, but Lenin, Trotsky and Bukharin were against this opposition and I felt that a split here would not lead to any improvement. In '21, during the Kronstadt incident, Lenin was certainly wrong and Kronstadt right, but however right it was, Kronstadt was going about pushing the revolution into a fatal chaos. It was at my father-in-law's place, with my support, that the American anarchists met who offered, in vain, to act as mediators between Kronstadt and the government. Thus I am in complete agreement with you when you say that the degeneration of Bolshevism began in 1920; I would say even earlier, since at the start of 1919 I was horrified to read an article by Zinoviev (in the *Petrogradskya Kommuna*) on the monopoly of the party in power. In '23 I still found it possible to edit a publication for Zinoviev – so that I could publish in it as many of Trotsky's articles as possible, and publish *Lenine 1917* myself in France, stressing in it the libertarian character of Bolshevism in its beginnings. So you see that I am not dating the moral catastrophe of Bolshevism by reference to the day when I took up a 'position' against (?) it. I always had a position based on what I called (in *Littérature et révolution*, 1931)[75] 'the double duty': duty to the international defence of the revolution and duty to struggle internally for the recovery of the revolution. Which of these two duties takes priority depends on the particular moment of history, although they are always inseparable. Up till the present, unfortunately, no great mass movement has been able to free its activity from demogogy, defamation, etc.: we have to fight against these vile tendencies of the old society, but that does not always give us a good enough reason to break with the great movements which cannot manage to be faultless. I am very fond of clean hands, but I am prepared to sully my own hands for the revolution if it proves necessary. You seem to believe that Bolshevism always had certain inner vices (amoralism?), a position which is deeply unfair because all revolutionary parties in all epochs have had the same faults in differing degrees, without at the same time having the energy, intelligence, unselfishness and other high moral qualities of the Bolshevism of the great years (1917 – ... ?). Here is what I have written in a recent passage: 'Was the germ of Stalinism present in Bolshevism at its beginning? Certainly, just as the germs of death are present in every living organism. But Bolshevism also contained a mass of other germs, for example those of a new humanism and of a libertarian state... ' That is the real truth, and to forget it is to commit a large and serious historical injustice.

To a very large extent it was over the question of history dealing with these matters (the CHEKA, Kronstadt, the outlawing of the Mensheviks, the persecution of the anarchists) that LD and I had our split. But, in all this painful argument with the Old Man, I kept such esteem and affection for him that, even though he wrote a long polemical attack accusing me of writing an article which was never mine and of advocating ideas which were never mine, I first sent a powerful rebuttal to the printers of *La Révolution prolétarienne* (Paris) and then took it back from them, preferring to suffer this unjust attack in silence. And I still think I was quite right: truth can work its way out in different ways than by offensive polemics.

Do you read Spanish? I have had a book published here on the war in Russia, I'll send you a copy as well as one of my *Retrato de Stalin*.[76]

Yours in friendship and comradeship
[copy unsigned]

Victor Serge. Extract from 'My Break with Trotsky'[77]

End of July 1936: Muste, a delegate from the Bureau for the Fourth International formed in the United States, came to see me in Brussels and conveyed to me Leon Davidovich's proposal that I join this Bureau as a coopted member. I accepted. Muste was a former pastor, thin, dry, with greying hair, very puritanical in appearance. (Afterwards, overwhelmed by the Moscow trials, he left the movement and went back, so I was told, to his church.)

Around this time I had a correspondence with Trotsky on the matter of the Spanish anarchists whom Leon Sedov dismissed as 'destined to destroy the revolution'. I thought that they would be playing a key role in the civil war and advised Trotsky and the Fourth International to publish a declaration of sympathy with them in which the revolutionary Marxists would pledge themselves to struggle for liberty. LD said that I was right and promised that something on these lines would be done, but it never was.

In January 1937 I attended an international conference of the FI held in Amsterdam. It was held at Sneevliet's place; he lived at Overtoom and had a comfortable meeting hall under his roof. Already the Trotskyists were aiming all their fire at the POUM. I took the floor to justify the POUM's participation in the Catalan Generalitat, on the grounds of the need to control and influence the government from within and to facilitate the arming of the masses. With Vereeken and Sneevliet, I proposed a resolution of solidarity with the POUM, which ended with an appeal to the Spanish militants to preserve the unity of their party. Against this proposal Pierre Naville, Gerard Rosenthal and Rudolf Klement argued hotly: it became clear that even while addressing diplomatic compliments to the POUM, they were organising a split within it. Two British comrades who were in Amsterdam told me that the movement of the FI had less than a hundred members in their country – divided, as in France, into two rival organisations.

I returned from Amsterdam in a state of desolation, with the impression of a sectarian movement, run by manouevrings from above, afflicted by all the mental depravities against which we had fought in Russia: authoritarianism, factionalism, intrigues, manouevres, narrow-mindedness, intolerance. Sneevliet and his party had had enough of it, finding the air there unbreathable; they were honest, sober Dutch proletarians, used to fraternal norms of conduct. Vereeken, who adored the Old Man, told me 'I give you less than six months before you fall out with him. He tolerates no objection.'

Our disagreements multiplied. But the Old Man displayed great affection in his letters to me – and I had an infinite admiration for him. When he wrote, in connection with the strikes of June 1936, 'The French revolution has begun,' I wrote back to him, 'Not at all: all that has begun is the reawakening of the French working class.' I advised him against making interventions, as he did constantly, in the internal affairs of tiny groups and to stick to his great intellectual work. In the end, I wrote to him: 'One cannot build an International when there are no parties ... One cannot build parties out of rotten political behaviour and with a Russian ideological language that nobody understands ...' He replied to me, 'You are an enemy who desires to be treated as a friend ...'

The 'Bolshevik-Leninist' movement in France, with a few dozen militants and a few hundred more sympathisers, used an unintelligible jargon in its publications; it was divided between two tiny 'parties', the Parti Ouvrier Internationaliste (Rous, Naville, Rosenthal) and the Parti Communiste International (Molinier, Frank), who used their most serious energies and time in intriguing against each other and exchanging mutual denigrations at book-length. I reproached them bitterly for wasting their resouces like this when no propaganda was being launched on behalf of our imprisoned comrades in Russia. I refused to listen to any of their petty squabbles, and told Rous 'If I had joined one of your two groups, the atmosphere you have would have forced me to resign from it immediately.' (In 1940–1, under the Nazi occupation, Rous attempted, along with Jaquier of the PSOP, to form a 'national-revolutionary' party conformable to the Nazi taste; after that he was arrested.) These sordid quarrels, in which LD embroiled himself, so poisoned the atmosphere that they made impossible any serious enquiry into the death of Sedov and the murder of Klement. At Sedov's funeral ceremony, two minuscule groups came with their different banners, ostentatiously refusing all contact with one another.

From 1937 onwards I removed myself completely from this 'movement' and wrote to Sneevliet, 'This isn't a new beginning, it is an end ...' But I refrained from all controversy and endeavoured to give all the services I could to the militants and to LD. I became horrified by disgusting incidents like the attempt certain Trotskyists made to get hold of funds belonging to the POUM – an affair which was settled laboriously by a commission formed by Rosmer, Lazarevich and Hasfeld. The great and wonderful movement to which we had sacrificed so many lives in Russia thus degenerated abroad into impotence and sectarianism. I continued to translate the Old Man's books, *The Revolution Betrayed*, *The Crimes of Stalin*, *Their Morals and Ours*, and to defend him. In the eyes of the general public I was still the best-known 'Trotskyist' writer – just at the time when the 'B[olshevik]-L[eninists]' were doing their best to discredit me. For them I had become a 'petty-bourgeois intellectual' whose 'influence' and 'unreliable sympathy' had to be 'used'.

5 Victor Serge and the Left Opposition

Introduction by Philip Spencer

The struggle against Stalinism was the central focus of Serge's activity in the latter part of his political life. Although he was out of Russia working for the Comintern when Stalin first began to consolidate his position after Lenin's death, Serge kept himself fully informed of developments and had sided immediately with the Trotskyist Opposition of 1923–4.[1] Within the International, itself one of the earliest revolutionary institutions to be Stalinised,[2] Serge's position quickly became intolerable:

> The atmosphere of the International's departments was becoming impossible for me to breathe [...] I was watching it go rotten from within. And I saw that it could be saved only in Russia, by a regeneration of the Party. I had to go back.[3]

The Opposition

On his return, Serge threw himself into the work of first the Trotskyist and then the Joint Opposition to Stalin.[4] Its leaders, veterans of October, were all men he had admired from the outset, personal catalysts of his adhesion to Bolshevism. Its programme, for the revitalisation of democracy in the party and the soviets on the one hand, and of the international revolutionary endeavour on the other, spoke directly to his most central identifications with the revolution. Serge played a full role in the Opposition's heroic but ultimately doomed struggle, addressing meetings, writing leaflets, organising demonstrations to the bitter end. At times, he wrote, it seemed as if the wheel had come full circle: 'the men of the proletarian dictatorship, who had yesterday been the greatest in the land, coming back to the districts of the poor, there to seek support from man to man'.[5] Some of the episodes he was to recount later in his *Memoirs* have the most tragic poignancy about them, a last desperate attempt to reverse the course of history, to avert the disaster that, as he admitted secretly to himself, seemed increasingly inevitable. The Opposition was crushed, its programme reviled, its leaders dispersed.

Stalin's hold was now complete, the path open for his radical transformation of the Soviet Union.[6]

The fate of the Opposition was bitter indeed – veteran militants, heroes of the revolution now hounded out of the party, unable to find work, soon imprisoned and deported to the camps. Serge himself shared much of this fate for the next few years, eking out a most precarious living, losing many of his manuscripts, and in 1933 suffering deportation to the Urals.

Such repression, harsh though it was, could not break him, certainly could not force his allegiance to the regime. While others began to temporise with the regime, to vacillate, in the end to capitulate (Piatakov and Radek, for example),[7] Serge remained among the irreconcilables. (Some of these, such as Rakovsky, were of course later to capitulate too but in different, even harsher circumstances which suggested little alternative. Serge's recognition of the agony of their situation was one of his greatest achievements in both his fiction and his journalism.)

Stalinism as Counter-revolution

By the early 1930s, Serge was prepared to draw the most radical conclusions. To him, Stalinism was the absolute negation of all that the revolution had achieved and stood for. He was unable to engage in any of the equivocations or self-deceptions of others in the Opposition, let alone abroad, who willed themselves to believe that somehow some essential achievements of the revolution survived this process. For Serge the change was radical and total. As he summarised it later in his masterfully condensed account of the period, *From Lenin to Stalin*:

> Everything changed.
> The aims: from international social revolution to socialism in one country.
> The political system: from the workers' democracy of the Soviets, the goal of the revolution, to the dictatorship of the General Secretariat, the functionaries and the GPU.
> The Party: from the organisation, free in its life and thought and freely submitting to discipline, of revolutionary Marxism to the hierarchy of bureaus, to the passive obedience of careerists…
> The Third International: from a mighty organisation of propaganda and struggle to the opportunist servility of Central Committees appointed for the purpose of approving everything, without shame or nausea…

The leaders: the greatest militants of the October revolution in jail
or in exile. From Lenin to Stalin.

The ideology: Lenin said 'We shall see the progressive withering
away of the State, and the Soviet State will not be a State like others,
but a vast workers' commune… ' Stalin proclaims that we 'advance
towards the abolition of the State by way of strengthening the State'.
(sic)

The condition of the workers: the egalitarianism of Soviet society
is transformed to permit the formation of a privileged minority,
more and more privileged in comparison with the disinherited masses
who are deprived of all rights.

Morality: from the austere, sometimes implacable honesty of heroic
Bolshevism… to unspeakable deviousness and deceit.[8]

This almost laconic list is worth citing at some length because in
focusing so directly on such key elements, Serge was again highlight-
ing his own commitments. The contrasts he drew so exactly and
dramatically focused precisely on those aspects of the revolution and
Bolshevism which had won his own original loyalty, from which he
had fashioned what we have earlier called his libertarian Leninism.
They were benchmarks of a kind, crucial issues or standards by which
he would insist on measuring or defining the character of the Soviet
Union then and now. They left him in no doubt. What had occurred
in the Soviet Union under Stalin was a reaction which had destroyed
the revolution at its roots. There could be no evasions at this level. The
cause of the revolution was too serious, too sacred even, for any equivocations. 'It is impossible to write this', he said,

with a light heart. But it is equally impossible to look on in silence.
I like Charles Péguy for having written, 'He who does not cry out
the truth when he knows the truth becomes the accomplice of liars
and falsifiers'… Everything is at stake… Our foremost weapon is the
truth. That weapon cannot be spared: the wound has bled too much
[…] we have neither the right to be silent nor to close our eyes. A
sort of moral intervention becomes our duty.[9]

This emphasis on truth and morality was not merely rhetorical. Serge
came to believe that moral considerations were as, if not even more,
important in helping us to understand how and why Stalinism could
and did triumph. 'Moral criteria', he wrote,

sometimes have greater value than judgements based on political and
economic considerations. Politics and economics with their infinite

complexities permit the deceptions of statistics and slogans. Even with much knowledge, a clear insight into them is often impossible. While the indignity, the injustice, the traps set for those who only yesterday were comrades, the human degradation, the intrusion of the common police into party discussions – these things reveal the truth.

The truth was that the revolution had succumbed to 'a sort of inner counter-revolution', had been poisoned in some fatal measure from within. 'Justice is not made by iniquity, the world and men are not transformed by means of chains, loudspeakers crying out falsehoods, and vast agencies of intellectuals paid to cram people's heads with lies.'[10] The use of these means by Stalin showed more clearly than anything else the true nature of the society that was being constructed on the grave of the revolution. The terrible repression that Stalin unleashed first upon the Opposition, then upon the peasants, then upon the workers, finally upon his own supporters, was the precise instrument of counter-revolution.

The Double Duty

How could the revolution be defended? Serge's answer, his own personal programme, was to develop the notion of a 'double duty'. On the one hand one had to remain loyal to the original inspiration and achievements of the revolution, not to abandon it to those outside who had always been its enemies, always sought its destruction; on the other, one must not turn a blind eye to the revolution's own faults, the weakness of real human beings in real situations. In the deeply moving letter he wrote to those campaigning for his release from internal exile in the Soviet Union ('Everything Is Now in Question'), Serge formulated this duty explicitly:

We must not hide the fact that socialism itself contains seeds of reaction. On the soil of Russia, these seeds have brought forth a memorable harvest [...] This system is in total contradiction with everything that was said, proclaimed, willed and thought during the Revolution as properly so called, [with] the Commune-State, a broad workers' democracy, a democracy in reality and not in formulas, constituted by the system of Soviets [...] The reaction in the heart of the Revolution puts everything into question; it compromises the Revolution's own future, its principles and even its sterling past, and creates for it an internal danger much more real at present than the external ones that are harped upon – sometimes precisely in order to mask the inner dangers [...] My conviction is that socialism will only triumph, both in Russia and the world, only assert itself if it surpasses capitalism not in the building of tanks but in the organisation of social living; if it offers to humanity a better condition than capitalism does; more prosperity, more justice, more liberty, a higher dignity. Our duty is to help it do so; our duty is therefore to combat the evils which are poisoning it. This duty is a double one: defence externally and defence inwardly.[11]

The pursuit of this double duty was to occupy Serge for the rest of his political life. Expelled from the Soviet Union after a campaign by friends which succeeded (only in the nick of time) in embarrassing the Soviet government among intellectuals it was anxious to woo at the start of the Popular Front period, Serge came to the West (first Belgium, then France) determined to fulfil both duties. It was to win him few friends. His 'defence externally', loyalty to the memory of the revolution as it had actually been, marginalised him almost immediately on his arrival. By now the major division on the left appeared to be between Social Democrats who had long ago abandoned the idea of revolution altogether and Stalinists for whom the Great Leader was simply infallible. In the period of the Popular Front both sides had come to bury their differences on the subject of the Soviet Union for a mutually beneficial concentration on a crass, ultimately suicidal reformism here at home.[12] Neither had the slightest interest in allowing someone like Serge to raise the banner of revolution again, to spoil the atmosphere of unity on the left with his exposés of the Moscow trials or criticisms of the fatal shortcomings of reformism.[13]

Further left, among his ex-anarchist comrades, Serge could expect little more, despite his efforts to thread together links between anarchists and revolutionary Marxists, of the kind that he himself had spun in his journey from one to the other in the revolution itself. For most anarchists that had been the path of betrayal and his present plight perhaps a reward, certainly a consequence, of what were seen as his original illusions of Bolshevism.

Serge and Trotsky

Trotsky alone extended the hand of comradeship.[14] They were tied now by many bonds – dating back beyond Serge's membership of the Opposition inside the Soviet Union. In a sense Trotsky almost incarnated for Serge the greatness of revolutionary Marxism. A late convert to the

Bolshevik Party, Trotsky nevertheless supplied it with its real strategic vision in 1917, committing it in fact (if never explicitly in theory) to the doctrine of permanent revolution. This notion, that the working class in Russia could and would go beyond the limits imposed by the narrow, if superficially orthodox, Menshevik interpretation of Marx, had been instrumental in Serge's acceptance of Marxism in 1917. Serge's Marxism was thus from the outset thoroughly Trotskyist in character and would always remain so. Trotsky's actual part in organising the October seizure of power, as well as his remarkable defence of the revolution as leader of the Red Army, had been celebrated by Serge in many of his writings, both historical and fictional.[15] If anywhere, it may have been in some of the portrayals of Trotsky in these roles that Serge came closest to over-idealising the revolution itself. Subsequently it was Trotsky's writings of 1923–4 which focused Serge's attention on the growing crisis in the Soviet Union while he was working for the Comintern.[16] It was the Trotskyist Opposition Serge joined on his return to the USSR and Trotsky whose lead Serge followed throughout the last years and months in which legal opposition was still tolerated inside the party, even to the point of accepting, very much against his instincts, the pact with Zinoviev and Kamenev which created the Joint Opposition. (Serge's instinctive aversion was not that far off the mark. The Zinovievites' capitulation to Stalin after a rather brief period of defiance was what he had feared and predicted from the outset.) After the collapse of the Joint Opposition, the Trotskyists were left at mercy of the party machine, their leader deported and their organisation broken up. In the ensuing dark bitter days of expulsion and deportation, Serge, like other comrades, kept his spirits up by reading Trotsky's defiant criticism of the Stalinist path, his sharp and cogent critique of each new, disorientating twist and turn of the bureaucracy. For Serge, as for so many others, by the early 1930s Trotsky had become the incarnation of revolutionary resistance and survival.

Now Serge was free to join him and eagerly responded to Trotsky's urging that he collaborate in the work of the exiled Opposition. It was now that Serge produced some of his finest work – brilliant accounts of and analysis of Stalin's betrayal of the revolution; piercing exposés of the Moscow trials; the great novels on the struggle of the Opposition and the degeneration of the revolution. These works, as much as anything written to celebrate the revolution in its halcyon days, revealed the essence of Serge's political commitments. While never sentimental, they celebrated the remarkable courage and commitment of Oppositionists Serge had left behind, people who were literally prepared to sacrifice themselves to defend the revolution, the cause that was being trampled in the mud and blood of Stalinism. At the same time Serge developed a remarkable insight into the massive irrationality of Stalinism as a system, an awareness especially of the escalating paranoia at its heart.[17] No one reading these writings can doubt either the depth of Serge's commitment to the cause of revolutionary Bolshevism, or both the moral and the political basis of his opposition to its gravediggers. They are of a qualitatively different order to other, non-revolutionary anti-Stalinist writings of this or any later period, which lack any sense of who and what lost, and how and why, in those terrible years.[18]

Serge's activity as an Oppositionist was thus sustained and consistent. It was animated by the same set of convictions that had led him to Bolshevism in the first place, by a belief in the need for, possibility and actuality of a liberating revolution led by a truly vanguard party. The destruction of that revolution – its burial beneath a tide of corpses and lies, the transformation of the vanguard party into the tyranny of the one-party state, presided over by a paranoid dictator – was to be exposed and contested to the end.

Two Sources of Opposition

In all of this Serge could count on Trotsky's complete support and agreement. But Serge was not, of course, just a loyal member of the Trotskyist Opposition. His commitments were both more singular and in a sense more inclusive. The programme of the double duty was, as the dispute over Kronstadt will have already have made clear, not one that Trotsky or, *a fortiori*, any of the Old Man's fiercely loyal followers in the 1930s could really share. For them, it was vital to sustain in the face of Stalinist slander and distortion some pure model of the revolution that had, much more simply, been betrayed. Serge's insistence on the other side of double duty, the need not just to defend the revolution against its more obvious external enemies but to be aware of the dangers that threatened and weakened it from within, could not really be countenanced. For them, any discussion of errors made in the years before Stalin came to power were so many hostages to fortune, admissions that would sully the perfect image needed to defend the revolution now. Serge took the opposite view. He believed that the revolution could not be well defended like this, that only (moral issues again) a clear and honest account of the revolution as it had actually been could both attract new supporters and ensure future success. The debate over what actually happened at Kronstadt and why was thus only one of many disputes

that would flare up between them. Other issues were inevitably raised
and canvassed: the measures taken by the party to substitute itself for
the soviets; the erosion of political pluralism within that framework;
the ending of workers' control through too hasty an adoption of one-
man management and an infatuation with Western production relations
(especially Taylorism);[19] the lack of controls over the use of repression
(particularly the CHEKA); and, especially, the disastrous decision by
the Central Committee on that 'black day in 1918', to apply the death
penalty without hearing the accused.[20]

More generally, Serge could not accept what he took to be Trotsky's
determination to 'affirm the infallibility of a general line of 1917–23'.[21]
For Serge, both Trotsky and Lenin were capable of committing, and
indeed committed, mistakes, some of them serious if not (yet) fatal. 'Why
not say so? We have no need of the fraudulent need of an infallible
Lenin.'[22] Rather, these errors could all be analysed and recognised
within a wider, less narrow framework than that offered by Trotsky.
Here the distinct character of Serge's libertarian version of Leninism
was revealed. To Serge, Trotsky's attempt to carve out a pure idealised
version of the past in practice reopened the door to the very authoritarianism which had weakened the party before the Stalinist assault. The
defence of doctrinal orthodoxy was ultimately authoritarian itself,
leading to 'a version of Leninism clearly polluted with the vices of
Bolshevism in its decay'. Serge came to believe in the end that his own
opposition to Stalin, which was equally but differently Leninist, was of
a different order, was 'a resistance to totalitariansism in the name of the
democratic ideals expressed at the beginning of the Revolution'.[23]

Despite their differences and, on Trotsky's over-hasty part, a cessation
of relations in his very last years, Serge remained deeply loyal to Trotsky
until the end.[24] One of his finest writings was a deeply moving biography
(written in cooperation with Trotsky's widow Natalia) of the Old
Man.[25] In it he expressed again not just his admiration for Trotsky but
his unshakable support for the great and historic achievements of the
Bolsheviks of 1917, and reaffirmed the necessity of rescuing that legacy
from the wreckage and depredations of Stalinism. In particular, Serge
continued to reject any facile linkage between the great early period
and the Stalinist nightmare that followed. The gulf between them was
filled with the blood of his closest and dearest comrades in the two decades
that had followed his own most fundamental political commitment. To
those who then and since have tried to use the crimes of Stalinism to
bury the revolutionary Bolshevik tradition, Serge developed the perfect
final riposte:

It is often said that the germ of Stalinism was in Bolshevism. Well, I have no objection. Only, Bolshevism also contained many other germs – a mass of other germs – and those who lived through the enthusiasm of the first years of the Revolution ought not to forget it. To judge the living man by the death germs which the autopsy reveals in a corpse – and which he may have carried with him since his birth – is this very sensible?[26]

THE DOCUMENTS

Victor Serge. 'The Old Man and the Fourth International'[27]

There is no other explanation for the mad proscriptions which are destroying the structure of the regime, except hatred and fear. Fear for himself, for the system, for Socialism. The system is not workable (and the secret ballot, a measure evincing mistrust of the petty bureaucrats, will not improve it much). Socialism has been compromised. And he himself is at the mercy of a centurion's madness.

The substitute team has been shot as a precaution. Only the Old Man remains.

He is all the greater since not a drop of blood that has been shed lies at his door. And he alone remains.

Exiled to Alma Ata; banished to Prinkipo; interned in Norway; the butt of all conceivable insults and the systematic revision of history; his name expunged from the dictionaries and removed from the museums; all his political associates in prison – perhaps massacred tomorrow in one way or another – the Old Man remains as he was in 1903 with Lenin, in 1905 as the president of the first Soviet in the first Revolution. He remains as he was in 1917, with Lenin at the head of the masses, in 1918 at the battle of Svyazshsk, in 1920 at the battle of Petrograd; during the entire Civil War at the head of the Red Army, which he formed; at the head of a true party uncompromising despite persecution; at the head of an international party with neither masses or money, but preserving the tradition, preserving and renewing the doctrine – a party overflowing with devotion. The Old Man is only fifty-seven, not so old at that. Everyone thinks of him, since it is forbidden to think of him; and he has everything that the Leader has not: a revolutionary soul, a brilliant pen, and men willing to go through fire with him.

As long as the Old Man lives, there will be no security for the triumphant bureaucracy. One mind of the October Revolution remains, and that is the mind of the true leader. At the first shock, the masses

will turn towards him. In the third month of the war, when the difficulties begin, nothing will prevent the entire nation from turning to
the 'organiser of victory'. Everyone knows how trials are made, and
what the crown prosecutor's words are worth. A single gust of wind
will dispel all these stagnant vapours.

All his life the Old Man has served the Revolution with unflagging
firmness and devotion. His very mistakes were made with so much
honesty and passion that they do not diminish his stature. As early as
1920 he counselled the NEP, in 1922 he was for industrialisation; and
ever since 1923 for the renovation of the party through inner party
democracy and the struggle against bureaucracy. In 1927 he foresaw
the defeats of the Chinese Revolution. In 1931 he stood for the united
front of proletarian parties, which might have saved Germany from
Nazism; he condemned the economic adventure of forced collectivisation and the execution of the five year plan in four years; in 1930 he
foresaw that Stalin would decimate Lenin's party.

To permit his books in the Soviet Union would indeed suffice to
make the position of the brilliant leader untenable and re-awaken the
Bolshevism of the great years. Doubtless not a one enters. But where
is the Chinese wall that does not some day crumble in one spot or another?

The victorious reaction in the heart of the Socialist revolution, based
on a new privileged class, has brought about one more turn in the Third
International: the conversion to bourgeois democracy. In the midst of
a civil war in which the foundations of capitalist property are, by the
very logic of events, continuously undermined, the Communist party
of Spain declares: 'We are for the defence of Republican order and respect
for private property.' But President Azana, by no means a communist,
takes good care not to talk the same language; he signs decrees confiscating the property of the rebels and their accomplices. Changing its
base, the Third International passes from the class struggle to collaboration with the middle bourgeois; and at times this seems to be merely
a manoeuvre in a vaster complex of acts tending to the preparation of
war.

The Old Man, disposing of all the arsenal of revolutionary Marxism,
opposes this Third International with the idea of a Fourth. The new
International is still weak, still in the process of birth, and yet a ferment
to be feared.

Let certain journalists call it a plot of the Gestapo, just as their
colleagues used to call the Third International a Judeo-Masonic plot
cooked up by the Germans.

They will not prevent it, in any case of war or a sharpening of the class struggle, from becoming the germ or one of the germs, that of a new Bolshevism, in the greatest sense of the word.

In Russia most of all, Stalin's fear and hatred, mingled perhaps with a grain of remorse, are nothing more than prophetic.

And now everything is permissable against Trotsky. The only thing that startles us is the successful blows delivered at the right of asylum and international law in general. In menacing tones the USSR demands of Norway the internment and expulsion of the exile – and obtains its demand. Never did the Government of the old Russian autocrats, harassed by authentic terrorists, who lived unmolested in Geneva, London and Paris dare to dream of anything like this... Trotsky's archives, deposited in the Institute for Social History in Paris, were stolen last November by adroit specialists, equipped with acetylene blow torches, and having an automobile at their disposal. They carried out their orders to the letter, touching nothing else. Having no fear, they will never be caught. When Mexico consented to grant asylum to the man for whom 'the planet is without a visa', the Communist Party of that country announced that it would provoke disturbances to prevent his landing... When, in Paris, the International Bureau for the Right of Asylum is requested to express itself on the scandal of Trotsky's internment in Norway, it politically replies that it is interested solely in the victims of fascism. Does this Bureau not think that the socialists, the anarchists, and the communists banished from the USSR after having been persecuted there, are not entitled to the same rights as refugees from Germany and Italy? That is a strange point of view, the logic of the Stalinist 'liberal'.

Victor Serge. The Life of the Oppositionists [28]

Leon Davidovich Trotsky has not only been outrageously calumniated, vilified, excluded from the museums, from literature, from history – he who, more than anyone else, has entered into true history as the organiser of the revolutionary victory – deported, banished, deprived of Soviet nationality; he has also been systematically struck at through his family. His wife, Natalia Ivanovna Sedova, his son Leon Lvovich, his daughter Zinaida Lvovna, because of their attachment to husband and father, have been treated as public enemies and have forfeited their Soviet nationality. His daughter Zinaida was unable to withstand this atmosphere of persecution. She committed suicide in 1933 in Berlin. His older daughter had died of tuberculosis in Moscow a short time earlier, in a state of penury. I know where her tuberculosis came from, having seen her, still an adolescent, actively working in Petrograd – the imperilled city – in the difficult moments. His two sons-in-law, Man Nevelson and Platon Volkov, have lived only in prison and deportation since 1928. At the end of 1935 Volkov was in Semipalatinsk. His younger son, Sergei, who remained in Russia, was not interested in politics. An engineer and professor of technology in Moscow, he disappeared in 1935, as did his young wife. They are said to have been seen deported or imprisoned in Krasnoyarsk (Siberia).

Of his four secretaries, one, Glazman, committed suicide in 1923; we already know that another, Butov, died in prison of a hunger strike lasting fifty days; the two survivors, Poznansky and Sermux, have been in captivity since 1928. Finally, the first wife of Trotsky, divorced for some thirty years, but who remained his friend and comrade, Alexandra Lvovna Bronstein, a pedagogue esteemed in Leningrad, who has behind her more than forty years of devotion to the working-class, has been deported for years to the Tobolsk region. She had charge of Trotsky's grandchildren. What has become of them?

Victor Serge. 'Obituary. Leon Sedov'[29]

Leon Lvovich Sedov died on 16th February at eleven o'clock in the morning in a Paris hospital, as a result of two operations made necessary by a sudden attack of appendicitis. For several months Sedov had been complaining of various indispositions, in particular of a rather high temperature in the evenings. He wasn't able to stand up to such ill-health. He had been leading a hard life, every hour taken up by resistance to the most extensive and sinister intrigues of contemporary history – those of a regime of foul terror born out of the dictatorship of the proletariat. It was obvious that his physical strength was exhausted. His spirits were good, the indestructible spirits of a young revolutionary for whom socialist activity is not an optional extra but his very reason for living, and who has committed himself in an age of defeat and demoralisation, without illusions and like a man. Such epochs alternate, in our century, with other periods, of revival and strength, which they prepare the way for – which it is the job of all of us to prepare the way for.

Leon Lvovich seemed amazingly true to himself, in the middle of a daily life where there was no shortage of emotional strain, and of misfortunes. Our meetings were always hasty, anxious, tense for fear of wasting a minute. Five minutes after I shook his hand for the first time, we were working together to identify *agents provocateurs*, the Sobolevicus brothers (Senine); we combed our memories, unfortunately without success, for the name of a wretched man shot long ago, an enthusiastic little French comrade, who in Paris and then in Constantinople had been the collaborator of Jacob Blumkin, and who had been shot at the same time as he was (1929), probably without ever knowing why. Only once was some sort of human contact established between us, as we were roaming, after midnight, near the Place de Breteuil, between us the shadow of Ivan Nikitich Smirnov, one of the sixteen executed after the first Moscow trial. Sedov had known him well; he spoke to me sadly about his wife, Safonova, who had testified against him at the trial, and thereby ensured his ruin, and her own. Sedov spoke favourably of her: 'She was a true Communist, a person of fine character: they must have convinced her that she was saving him in order to get her to take that attitude; and she was shot herself afterwards...' It was the same time as the Rue Michelet affair. Then Trotsky was interned in Norway. Sedov was afraid that Stalin's political police would manage to kidnap his father in Oslo, or kill him later, on a cargo-boat... Sedov, with the eyes of experience, could see danger looming when it was still a long way off. A few months went by and Ignaz Reiss was murdered the day before the meeting that had been fixed with Leon Lvovich and some other friends... Amid all these circumstances Sedov kept the good humour of a practical man; he was so anxious that his face was permanently wrinkled into a frown, but he could still smile easily, and he was always wondering what had to be done next so that he could do it straight-away. He was by no means a pure theoretician or a dreamer: he had the temperament of a technician who could not be bothered with rest. A humble technician of the revolution in years of reaction: he would not have sought to be praised in any other terms.

What a passion-filled life he had led! As a child he had shared his father's internment in Canada, and experienced the first rejoicings at the Russian Revolution, that magnificent time of newly unfurled red flags, when everything seemed to be simple and within grasp; his father's fame, his father's victories, the dangers to his father, his travels, his portraits in all the public buildings, his speeches which galvanised the crowds; the agony of the Civil War... There was no place amid all this for childhood, he needed a grown man's courage – and what could be more simple? As an adolescent he had lived through the difficult years of the struggle against the bureaucracy – plots, suicides, theses, discussions, oppositions, Lenin's death... The young man stood alongside his father in 1927, when defeat was inevitable, with exile or execution into the bargain. He was there when they broke down the doors of a modest home in Moscow, in order to seize the Organiser of Victory and deport him to Central Aisa, near the Chinese border. He was at Alma Ata when unknown assailants tried to break into the exile's home; Sedov defended that home. Later he was at Prinkipo, where Trotsky's house was burned down by mysterious hands. He was in Berlin when the Trotskyist group there was disrupted by the activity of provocateurs, and when his sister Zinaida took her own life... He was torn in two in his private life; he has left a wife and child in Russia. He was a good mathematician, and skilled in military matters (which, in August 1937, made him consider going to Spain; his friends advised him strongly against it).

Stateless – yet more devoted than anyone to the workers' homeland of Russia! He obtained visas and residence permits only with the greatest difficulty; he had escaped from Germany before Hitler came to power, and lived in poverty in the XVth *arrondissement*. Such poverty, sometimes, that he explained to me that one meal a day was quite adequate, but that in the end you felt the effects of it. He was just coming to the end of a period of privation when there opened up for him, and for all of us, the hell of the Moscow trials. It must be admitted: if anything could have broken men with wills of iron, it was this flood of tangled lies, of baffling confessions, culminating in the murder in cellars of those who were once the great leaders. The highest moral values formed by the revolution had collapsed into the mud. For Moscow Sedov was one of the main targets of a nameless intrigue, which was even more inept than it was pernicious. I remember his sheer amazement at the clumsiness of falsifiers who accused him of meeting people in a town which he could easily prove he had never visited. He worked tirelessly to gather together documents and evidence to refute the lies. M. Malraux, author of *Days of Contempt*, refused to testify on his behalf... The League for the Rights of Man had to be asked repeatedly before they would give him a hearing, and then they refused to take a position on the question. None the less there were courageous people willing to accept his evidence and documentation, at a meeting chaired by old Modigliani, who was familiar with totalitarian swindles... Those who were present, in a small hall in the Mutualité, at the confrontation between this chairman and his witness, across a conference table, will never forget the occasion: they learned how much passion and intelligence can be put into the search for truth.

Leon Sedov had long lived under constant threat. Although he was well aware of this, and was prudent by nature, he took few precautions, for precautions have their price... Stalin probably did not expect the resounding failure of the Moscow trials which satisfied nobody but the most well-tried time-servers. As the principal witness for the prosecution in the counter-trial initiated by history, of which the work done by the committees in Paris and New York is only a tiny part, Sedov had to be silenced, but skilfully, so as not to make the responsibility for the crime too obvious. If possible they wanted to set up a plausible accident. In November 1936 a section of his father's archives, transferred by his efforts to the Institute of Social History in the Rue Michelet, were stolen during the night by GPU agents who cut through a door with an oxyhydric torch. A few days later Sedov realised he was being shadowed; the French police arrested a former Russian emigré, a member of the 'Society of the Friends of the Soviet Fatherland', who had recently returned from Moscow... The investigation into the murder of Ignaz Reiss had revealed, through their own confessions, that Reiss's murderers, under the direction of the top GPU officials, had for a long time been shadowing Leon Sedov, with alarming skill. In the summer of 1936 Sedov had gone to spend a few weeks by the sea in the south of France; Renata Steiner, who was arrested in Switzerland for having prepared the ground for Reiss's killers, took lodgings in the same boarding house; every day she reported on his movements to another of those charged in the Reiss affair, Semirensky, who was living in the neighbouring house. He lived in Paris, under a false name, right next door to Leon Sedov. A little later, when Sedov had planned to travel to Mulhouse, the same executioners prepared an ambush for him in the station of that town. It was only by chance that Sedov didn't make the journey.

Did he die a natural death? The medical evidence seems to confirm that he did. But in the atmosphere we live in, how can we dismiss terrible suspicions? Is it not possible to artificially provoke such ailments? Killers lived right alongside him. They may have missed their chance at a particular moment without letting him escape for good. If this is the case, medical tests will tell us nothing. For my part, I prefer to ignore this hypothesis: let us not add to what is already certain in this nightmare, which is great enough already... Thus in one way or another the cynical warning of Radek to the 'Trotskyists of France and Spain' has been fulfilled: they are 'paying dearly'. Andrès Nin, disappeared – murdered – in a prison of the Spanish Republic: Kurt Landau, who was, with Trotsky and Rosmer, a member of the First International Secretariat of the Communist Left Opposition, has disappeared likewise; Erwin Wolf, who was Trotsky's secretary in Oslo, has disappeared (and an agency report – admittedly unconfirmed – has announced that Erwin Wolf has been shot in Moscow, at the beginning of February, at the same time as Antonov-Ovseenko. Kidnapped in Barcelona, shot in Moscow?)... Sedov, finally, dead of natural causes... A year of horrors!

In him Trotsky may have lost his last child. His eldest daughter, Nina, died of tuberculosis in Leningrad during the period of his deportation. The Central Committee of the Party refused to give the exile permission to see her on her death-bed. His younger daughter, Zinaida, committed suicide in Berlin a few days after being stripped of her Soviet nationality, which meant she was cut off for ever from her husband and her homeland. His younger son, Sergei Sedov, a technician who was not involved in any kind of political activity, disappeared in Moscow about two and a half years ago, with his wife. We heard he was deported to Krasnoyarsk, and then agency despatches reported his arrest in this town where he was said to have 'attempted to cause the mass asphyxiation of workers in the factory where he was employed'. Since then, there has been no news of him. Has he been shot? Imprisoned in a northern concentration camp? Who is even trying to find out?

In Leon Lvovich, Trotsky has lost more than a son of his own blood – he has lost a son in spirit, an irreplaceable companion in struggle. Let him at least know that this dark hour we are all with him, unreservedly. Whatever may divide us, in doctrine and in history, is in human terms of infinitely less importance than what unites us in the service of the working class against dangers which demand from each of us the greatest steadfastness. I know that I am writing here for many friends and comrades, who differ in their ideas, in their language, in their forms of action: and who are sometimes sharply divided by controversy – but who are united in something essential which gives meaning to their lives. We have all lost in Sedov a comrade of rare quality.

Farewell, Leon Lvovich, you leave us a proud memory. Let us go forward.

Victor Serge

Victor Serge. 'In Memory: L.D Trotsky'[30]

He was hardly forty-five when we began calling him 'The Old Man', as we had Lenin at a similar age. All his life he gave one the feeling of a man in whom thought, action and his personal life formed a single solid block, one who would follow his road to the end, on whom one could always absolutely depend. He would not waver on essentials, he would not weaken in defeat, he would not avoid responsibility or lose his head under pressure. A man with so profound an inner pride that he became simple and modest. Proving his powers at an early age (he was President of the first Petersburg Soviet in 1905, at 28), he was from then on sure of himself, and was able to look at fame, government posts, the greatest power, in a purely utilitarian way, without either contempt or desire. He knew how to be harsh and pitiless, in the spirit of a surgeon performing a serious operation. During the Civil War and the terror, he could write a sentence like: 'There is nothing more human, in a time of revolution, than energy.'

If I had to define him in one word, I would say he was a doer. Yet he was also attracted by research, contemplation, by poetry and creation. Fleeing from Siberia, he could appreciate the beauty of the snowstorms; in the thick of the 1917 Revolution, he speculated on the role of the creative imagination in such events; during his Mexican exile, he admired the amazing forms of the cactus plant and made expeditions to dig up fine specimens for his garden. A religious unbeliever, he was sure of the value of human life, the greatness of man, and the duty of serving human ends.

I never knew him greater, and he was never dearer to me, than in the dingy rooms of the workers in Leningrad and Moscow, where I used to watch him, a few years earlier one of the two undisputed chieftains of the Revolution, talk for hours in order to convince a few factory workers. Still a member of the political Bureau, he was on the road to losing his power and probably also his life. (We all knew it, as did he, who spoke of it to me.) He had come to believe that it was once more on the order of the day to win over the workers one by one, as in the old days of illegality under the Czar, if revolutionary democracy was to be saved. And so thirty or forty poor workers listened to him, one or two of them perhaps sitting on the floor at his feet, asking questions and pondering his replies. We knew that we were more likely to fail than to conquer, but that too, we felt, would be useful. If we had not at least put up a fight, the Revolution would have been a hundred times more defeated.

The greatness of Trotsky's personality was a collective rather than an individual triumph. He was the highest expression of a human type produced in Russia between 1870 and 1920, the flower of a half century of the Russian intelligentsia. Tens of thousands of his revolutionary comrades shared his traits – and I by no means exclude many of his political opponents from this company. Like Lenin, like certain others whom the chances of the struggle left in obscurity, Trotsky simply carried to a high pitch of individual perfection the common characteristics of several generations of Russian revolutionary intellectuals. Glimpses of the type appear in Turgenev's novels, notably Bazarov, but it comes out much more clearly in the great revolutionary struggles. The militants of the Narodnya Volya[31] were men and women of this stamp; even purer examples were the Social-Revolutionary terrorists of the 1905 period, and Bolsheviks of 1917. For a man like Trotsky to arise, it was necessary that thousands and thousands of individuals should establish the type over a long historical period. It was a broad social phenomenon, not the sudden flashing of a comet, and those who speak of Trotsky as a 'unique' personality, conforming to the classic bourgeois idea of the 'Great Man', are much mistaken. The characteristics of the type were:

a personal disinterestedness based on a sense of history;

a complete absence of individualism in the bourgeois sense of the word;

a strong impulse to place one's individuality at the service of society, amounting to a kind of pride (but quite without vanity or desire to 'shine');

the capacity for personal sacrifice, without the least *desire* for such sacrifice;

the capacity for 'toughness', in the service of the cause, without the slightest sadistic overtones;

a sense of life integrated with both thought and action which is the antithesis of the after-dinner heroism of Western socialists.

The formation of this great social type – the highest reach of modern man, I think – ceased after 1917, and most of its surviving representatives were massacred at Stalin's orders in 1936–7. As I write these lines, as names and faces crowd in on me, it occurs to me that this kind of man had to be extirpated, his whole tradition and generation, before the level of our time could be sufficiently lowered. Men like Trotsky suggest much too uncomfortably the human possibilities of the future to be allowed to survive in a time of sloth and reaction.

And so his last years were lonely ones. I am told that he often paced up and down his study in Coyoacan, talking to himself. (Like Tchernichevsky,[32] the first great thinker of the Russian revolutionary intelligentsia, who, brought back from Siberia where he had spent twenty years in exile, 'talked to himself, looking at the stars', as his police guards wrote in their reports.) A Peruvian poet brought him a poem entitled 'The Solitude of Solitudes', and the Old Man set himself to translate it word for word, struck by its title. Alone, he continued his discussions with Kamenev – he was heard to pronounce this name several times. Although he was at the height of his intellectual powers, his last writings were not on the level of his earlier work. We forget too easily that intelligence is not merely an individual talent, that even a man of genius must have an intellectual atmosphere that permits him to breathe freely. Trotsky's intellectual greatness was a function of his generation, and he needed contact with men of the same temper, who talked his language and could oppose him on his own level. He needed Bukharin, Pyatakov, Preobrazhensky, Rakovsky, Ivan Smirnov, he needed Lenin in order to be completely himself. Already, years earlier, among our younger group – and yet among us there were minds and characters like Eltsin, Solnetsev, Ikovin, Dingelstedt, Pankratov (are they dead? are they alive?), he could no longer stride ahead freely; ten years of thought and experience were lacking in us.

He was killed at the very moment that the modern world entered, through war, a new phase of his 'permanent revolution'. He was killed just for that reason, for he might have played too great a historical role, had he ever been able to return to the land and the people of that Russia he understood so profoundly. It was the logic of his passionate convictions, as well as certain secondary errors stemming from this passion, which brought about his death; to win over to his views an obscure individual, some one who didn't exist, who was only a decoy painted by the GPU in revolutionary colours, he admitted him to his solitary study, and this nobody, carrying out orders, struck him down from behind as he bent over a commonplace manuscript. The pickaxe penetrated the head to a depth of three inches.

Victor Serge. 'On Trotskyism'[33]

The internal discords of Russian Communism produced a number of different repercussions in the working-class movement. Over the period when the Communist parties became dominated by a totalitarian mentality, various international Oppositions were formed. The most energetic of these was grouped around the last great survivor of Bolshevism's heroic epoch, Leon Trotsky, in his successive exiles at Istanbul, Oslo and Mexico.

With his incisive predictions of the coming world war, and of the social movements to which it would give birth, and with his simultaneous attachment to the doctrine of Bolshevism, Trotsky proclaimed from 1934 onwards the necessity of establishing a new revolutionary Marxist International. His mistake lay in believing that an international movement could be deliberately created in the period of the defeats of the European working class. An authoritarian mind despite his leading role in the CPSU's democratic Opposition, a schematic mind despite his wide-ranging Socialist culture, in a word a voluntarist, Trotsky managed to assemble in 1936 a few American, French, Dutch and other militants and proclaimed the foundation of the 'Fourth International'. It is not clear whether any real founding congress took place. The tiny groups and parties of the Fourth International have been divided even on this question, and the Fourth International, without having acquired any substantial influence anywhere, went on from expulsions to splits, mercilessly – and vilely – persecuted all this time by Stalinist-Communism which systematically used calumny and murder against its militants. (Erwin Wolf and Moulin in Spain, Rudolf Klement in France, Ignace Reiss in Switzerland and Trotsky himself in Mexico would all perish violently, murdered by Stalin's secret police.)

The Fourth International was constituted in an epoch when across the entire world Socialist Internationalism was disintegrating, when confusion reigned over defeated ideas and movements. It employed a 'Bolshevik-Leninist' language in countries where this form of theoretical expression was bound to be incomprehensible and constantly invoked a tradition which had been overlaid by the powerful forces of Russian totalitarianism. All that the Fourth International established were minute groups in various places which nowhere succeeded in playing any appreciable role. It had only one brain behind it, that of Trotsky, who gave it all its theoretical baggage. It attempted to apply mechanically to the Second World War the analysis and propaganda slogans which had been formulated for the situation of the war of 1914–18. Its methods of organisation, its polemical habits, the very language of its militants have been clearly polluted with the vices of Bolshevism in decay, in other words of the totalitarian mentality.

In the USSR itself, where the term 'Trotskyism' has been applied by the government to all the Oppositions, in order to justify their annihilation, the Fourth International seems to have no echo at all. The Left Opposition to which Trotsky belonged has been utterly exterminated with bullets. Any rare survivors, if there are any, will, like the whole of the Soviet younger generation, face the task of renewing the tradition of Socialist thought by assimilating the immense range of experiences which is demanded by a rigorous and unfettered critique of Bolshevism, by the rise of new ideas and of a new language.

The Fourth International has a few groups in the United States and some weak offshoots in other countries. Its doctrine remains that of Bolshevism from 1917 to 1927, grotesquely deformed by persecution, impoverished by a shortage of gifted figures, ossified and outdated. It can be considered only as a sectarian organisation whose possibilities for further development are severely limited.

As for the individual contribution of Trotsky, as fighter, historian and thinker: this has entered the heritage of Socialist culture.

Victor Serge. Entries from the Carnets, 1944[34]

January 15, 1944
A short warm letter from Natalia, in response to my New Year's greetings… It has been very bitter to feel how completely sectarianism was separating us, the only survivors of the Russian Revolution here and perhaps in the whole world. And this was not in the spirit of the real Bolsheviks. Great happiness for me in these few lines of shaky writing, in the same blue ink that the Old Man used, lines which seem to falter like Natalia's own footsteps in her garden which is a tomb. I reflect painfully how the book we have just published,[35] M[arceau] P[ivert], J[ulian] G[orkin] and I, with JG's uninspired pages on Bolshevism and Trotsky which he can never understand, is going to hurt Natalia: she will not perhaps realise my own solitude in these collaborations. There is nobody any more who knows what the Russian Revolution really was, and what the Bolsheviks were – and men judge without knowing, in elemental rancour and rigidity.

March 2, 1944
Have met young Siova,[36] Leon Trotsky's grandson, on the bus. He has an astonishing resemblance to his grandfather as shown in youthful photographs, only his Jewishness is less pronounced. Siova is in adolescence, must be seventeen or so. A bony, hardened, severe, sad face, and eyeglasses. 'Do you still speak Russian?' I ask him. 'No, I've completely forgotten it'. 'Then you'll have to learn it!' 'Why should I? For sentimental attachment, no thank you!' (This said violently.) I answer that Russia will be changed a great deal before long, that we must remain true to her – and keep great hopes. I'm aware that he doesn't think so, that my words are nonsense to him. He is living with Natalia, overlooking the tomb of Coyoacan, and sees only a few mediocre sectarians who have no way of understanding him. This is the second time his life has been uprooted. His mother, Zina Lvovna, committed suicide in Berlin; his father disappeared in the prisons; he himself received a wound during Siqueiros's[37] assassination attempt against Trotsky, in May 1940; he has seen his grandfather killed and knows the assassin as 'one of the comrades'.

We talk about David Alfaro Siqueiros, whose crime remains unpunished, who has just returned to Mexico and is enjoying material success... 'Yes, Natalia is going to get something done, the investigation is still on; but it's all quite useless', Siova says. His expression is hard and discouraged. But I was forgetting: he has seen his uncle, Liova, die in suspicious circumstances; and two tiny rival parties quarrelling despicably around the funeral. Liova's woman, Jeanne Martin des Pallières, politically attached to the adventurer Molinier, hysterical and ravaged by grief, wanted to keep this lad with her; a sort of abduction became necessary to take him from her and get him to Mexico, as Marguerite Rosmer did. I was on the council of family trustees sworn in before a notary in order to pass Siova's guardianship to the Rosmers.

Notes and References

Chapter 1: Victor Serge and Bolshevism

1. Marcel Liebman, *Le Leninisme sous Lenine* (Paris: Seuil, 1973), pp. 270–9, for a brilliant and cogent analysis of this.
2. On the pre-First World War anarchist–socialist divide see amongst others George Woodcock, *Anarchism* (Harmondsworth: Penguin Books, 1975); and Julius Braunthal, *History of the International: World Socialism 1943–60*, transl. Peter Ford and Kenneth Mitchek (London: Nelson, 1967), vol. 1.
3. Richard Parry, *The Bonnot Gang* (London: Rebel Press, 1987); see also the account of the trial and Serge's own views at that time in his *Memoirs of a Revolutionary*, transl. Peter Sedgwick (Oxford University Press, 1963), p. 42.
4. Serge, *Memoirs*, p. 4.
5. Serge, *Memoirs*, p. 4.
6. On the ignominious collapse of the European left in 1914, see Georges Haupt, *Socialism and the Great War – The Collapse of the Second International* (Oxford University Press, 1972).
7. Original opponents of the war in both France and Germany were to play key roles in the setting up of Communist parties, sections of the new Third Communist International, after the war. On France, see Robert Wohl, *French Communism in the Making* (Stanford University Press, 1966). On Germany, Ben Fowkes, *Communism in Weimar Germany* (London: Macmillan, 1984), chs 1 and 2. More generally on the line of filiation between opposition to the war and support for a new revolutionary International, see *The Communist International in Lenin's Time*, ed. John Riddell, (New York: Monad, 1984), vol. 1, covering 1907–16.
8. Serge, *Memoirs*, p. 48.
9. Serge, *Memoirs*, p. 53.
10. Serge, *Memoirs*, p. 54.
11. In his novel devoted to the Barcelona uprising, *Birth of our Power*, transl. Richard Greeman (London: Writers and Readers, 1977), and later in the *Memoirs*, Serge used the experience as an inspiration for the future:

> Tomorrow is great. We will not have prepared this conquest in vain. This city will be won, if not by our hands, at least by hands like

ours, only stronger; perhaps stronger by being better toughened through our very weakness. If we are beaten, other men, infinitely different from us, infinitely like us, will come down this Rambla on an evening like this, in ten years, twenty years, it matters not, planning this same conquest: perhaps they will think of the blood we have shed. Even now I think I can see them. I am thinking of their blood, which will also flow, But they will win the city. (p. 74)

12. Serge, *Memoirs*, p. 67.
13. Serge, *Memoirs*, p. 55.
14. See not just his *Memoirs* but also both his fictional and historical accounts of the first years of the Revolution: *Conquered City*, transl. Richard Greeman (London: Writers and Readers, 1978), and *Year One of the Russian Revolution*, transl. Peter Sedgwick (London: Allen Lane, 1972).
15. Serge, *Year One*, pp. 128–135. Serge's view of the mass radicalisation process of 1917 has been stikingly confirmed by recent historical scholarship. See for example Alexander Rabinowitch, *The Bolsheviks Come to Power* (London: Verso, 1979), or S. Smith, *Red Petrograd* (Cambridge University Press, 1983).
16. Serge, *Memoirs*, and his letter to Comrade Michel (copy in the Musée Sociale, Paris) and documents in this chapter.
17. Serge, letter to Comrade Michel.
18. Serge, 'Le Tragique d'une révolution', *La Vie ouvrière*, 4th year, no. 152 (21 March 1922).
19. Serge, *Year One*, p. 216.
20. Serge, *Year One*, p. 216. Also see the withering comments on anarchists in the letter to Michel.
21. See the debate sparked off by his April thesis more generally on the complex relations between Lenin, the more conservative old guard and the more radical rank and file throughout 1917, in the works of Alexander Rabinowitch and Marcel Liebman.
22. For the best discussion of this, see the essay by Norman Geras, 'Between the Russian Revolutions', in *The Legacy of Rosa Luxemburg* (London: Verso, 1976).
23. See the account of this debate in Serge, *Year One*, p. 100.
24. Excerpted from Victor Serge, 'La Ville en danger, Petrograd, l'an II de la révolution'; first published in *La Vie ouvrière*, nos 57, 58, 59, 60 and 61 (July 1920). This journal of the seige of Petrograd by the Whites was written over November–December 1919. It was printed as a pamphlet in 1924 (Paris: Librairie du Travail) and again in 1971 as an appendix to Serge's *L'An I de la révolution russe* (Paris: Maspero, 1971). Published here in English for the first time in translation by Peter Sedgwick.

25. General Mamontov was a White Russian general operating against the Bolsheviks in the South of Russia.

26. Serge here invokes the precedent of the Paris Commune whose employment of the tactic of hostage-taking from among counter-revolutionaries was drafted by Marx in *The Civil War in France, 1871* (London: M. Lawrence, 1933). The Commune, however, took and shot hostages only from active opponents, not from their families. The Bolshevik practice of taking reprisals against the relatives of opponents had been initiated in 1918, with Trotsky's vigorous participation.

27. Translation of Victor Serge's letter to Comrade Michel, copy in the Musée Sociale, Paris. Published here in English for the first time in translation by Peter Sedgwick.

28. The addressee is Michel Kneller, alias Relenque (or Relenk), alias Le Terrassier. Little is known about him, in particular about his knowledge of Russian or how Serge knew him so confidentially (apart from addressing him as 'tu' in comradely fashion, the letter is perilously frank). Kneller was one of the French syndicalist delegates to the founding congress of the Red International of Labour Unions in Moscow, 3–19 July, 1921. He became considerably mistrusted by other French delegates through his trying to win favour with the Russian controllers of the RILU and the Comintern by portraying himself as the key figure in the syndicalist movement of France. In the 1930s, he became close to Leon Jouhaux, the moderate and anti-Communist leader of the CGT.

29. Henri Sirolle, a Paris railway union secretary, was also a French delegate to the first RILU congress in 1921. There he defended the record of anarchism against Bukharin's attacks, and opposed Kneller's personal manoeuvrings in Moscow shortly after the congress. He and Kneller vigorously interceded with the Soviet authorities for the imprisoned Russian anarchists on hunger-strike, and along with the Spanish RILU delegates signed an agreement with the Bolsheviks whereby the anarchist prisoners were allowed to leave the country.

30. The split in the anarchist-universalists (a pro-Soviet anarchist group who published the journal *Universal)* remains mysterious, but the positions of Alexander Shapiro (a moderate and pro-Soviet libertarian who had been editor of the syndicalist *Golos Truda* but had then rallied to the Soviet government, working in its Foreign Affairs Commissariat) and Grigorii Maximov (founder of *Golos Truda* in 1918 after *Golos Truda*'s suppression by the *Volnyi* Bolsheviks; be continued as an open syndicalist activist despite repeated arrests) had some principled grounds for divergence. These differences between Russian anarchists were rendered obsolete shortly after this letter of Serge, when, following the Kronstadt events, the universalists were arrested on trumped-up charges of banditry, Maximov and Shapiro were jailed by the CHEKA and all

anarchist political activity was suppressed. Shapiro, Maximov and the leading anarchist-universalists left Russia for exile after 1922.

31. Apollon Karelin, who collaborated with the Bolsheviks to the extent of joining the All-Russian Soviet Executive, and whose Anarchist-Communist Federation justified the 'temporary dictatorship' of the Bolsheviks, was shortly to see the destruction of the organisation in the wake of the Kronstadt uprising and the elimination of anarchism.

32. Despite extensive research, it has proved impossible to find any other reference to this obscure group, one of many that proliferated in the early years of the revolution, or to the language Serge claims it invented. The editor would be most grateful for any information about the group's origin and activities for any future edition of this work.

33. V.M. Eikkenbaum (Voline) had been active in *Golos Truda* in 1917–18. Following its suppression by the Leninists, he went to the Ukraine, where he was active in the anarchist federation Nabat. This grouping was dissolved by the CHEKA in late 1920 and, along with others who had been involved in its direction, Voline was despatched to prison in Moscow, where he was involved in the anarchist hunger-strike during the RILU congress. He was allowed to leave for the West in 1922.

34. Boris Souvarine (Lifchitz) was at this time an animator of French Communism and apparently destined to be the principal leader of the French Section of the Comintern. He was expelled from the French party in 1924 after he supported Trotsky. His journal *Bulletin Communiste*, which he had edited as an official CP organ, became a Left-Opposition outlet until his rupture with Trotsky in 1929.

35. From Serge, 'La tragique d'une révolution', *La Vie ouvrière*, 4th year, no. 152 (21 March 1922). *La Vie ouvrière* had been relaunched by Pierre Monatte as a revolutionary-syndicalist organ in 1919 after its predecessor of the same name had been banned during the First World War. By 1922 it had passed out of his control and soon became the organ of the faction around Gaston Monmousseau, who wished to move the newly split left-wing trade union, the CGTU, to the side of the French Communist Party and Soviet Russia generally. The present translation of Serge's text has been shortened by omitting a discussion on the Soviet trade unions and of a postscript replying to anarchist criticism of his position. Published here in English for the first time in translation by Peter Sedgwick.

36. Serge's account of Kronstadt's demands is here very inaccurate, and indeed conflicts with the fair and just summary of the Kronstadt programme given in his 1937 writings on the revolt (see Chapter 4 below) and in his *Memoirs of a Revolutionary*, written in the 1940s. The Kronstadters never demanded 'freedom of small trading', only peasant control of their land and cattle (without employing hired labour). The report that they called for 'Soviets against the party' or, in another

Bolshevik version, 'Soviets without Communists', is also a myth: free soviet elections, with the participation of all parties of the left, was their actual platform. Since Serge was in Petrograd at the time of the Kronstadt rising, and in sympathetic contact with anarchist mediators of the dispute, his retelling of the Soviet regime's falsifications of the sailors' demands is particularly culpable.

37. French newspaper reports anticipated the rising by two weeks, and may have reflected rumours inspired by knowledge of tensions between Kronstadt and the Soviet authorities. Serge's speculation about the role of foreign intelligence (oddly ascribed to an influence on Communist Party members rather than to any other source of discontent) is partly supported by Paul Avrich's researches (published in his *Kronstadt 1921* [Princeton University Press, 1970]), disclosing a secret plan for a rising in Kronstadt drafted in early 1921 by the emigré 'National Centre' of the Kadet politicians. Avrich makes it clear that no evidence exists of the actual implementation of this plan, or of any contact between the 'Centre' and the Kronstadt leaders.

38. Extracted from Victor Serge, 'Le Problème de la dictature', *La Vie ouvrière*, 4th year, no. 159 (19 May 1922). The article is by-lined 'Kiev, April 24, 1922', although, as Serge makes clear in his *Memoirs*, he never visited that city at any point. Published here in English for the first time in translation by Peter Sedgwick.

Chapter 2: The Correspondence

1. Serge to Trotsky, 9 August 1939 (Letter 41 here).
2. Serge to Sedov, 21 April 1936 (Prefatory Letter here).
3. Trotsky to Serge, 24 April 1936 (Letter 2 here).
4. See Letter 35 here, 5 March 1937.
5. 'Victor Serge and Leon Trotsky: Relations 1936–1940', transl. Richard Greeman. Published in Spanish in *Vuelta*, vol. 6, no. 63 (19 February 1982).
6. See note 268 below.
7. Susan C. Weissman, 'Victor Serge: Political, Social & Literary Critic of the USSR, 1919–1947: The Reflections and Activities of a Belgo-Russian Revolutionary Caught in the Orbit of Soviet Political History' (PhD thesis, University of Glasgow, 1991), pp. 334–5.
8. From the moment of Serge's arrest in 1933 up until his release in 1936, the pages of *La Révolution prolétarienne* were full of a sustained campaign for his release, waged under the guidance of Magdeleine Paz who organised the Comité Victor Serge. Supported by Charles Plisnier and Jacques Mesnil, Leon Werth, Marcel Martinet, Georges Duhamel, Charles Vildrac, Maurice Parijanine and Boris Souvarine, it became something of a cause célèbre. See Weissman, 'Victor Serge', pp. 283–8,

and Bill Marshall, *Victor Serge—The Uses of Dissent* (New York and Oxford: Berg, 1992) pp. 14–15. Also see Herbert R. Lottman, *The Left Bank – Writers, Artists and Politics from the Popular Front to the Cold War* (London: Heinemann 1972). For Serge's own impressions see his *Memoirs of a Revolutionary*, transl. P. Sedgewick (Oxford University Press, 1963), pp. 317–19.

9. See Weissman, *'Victor Serge'*, pp. 334–5; also Elspeth K. Poretsky, *Our Own People* (Ann Arbor, University of Michigan, Mich.: 1969).

10. While it was ultimately Stalin who sanctioned this shift in policy, it was essentially a bowing to the inevitable and was as much the outcome of pressure within the Comintern after the elevation of the Bulgarian Commumist Georges Dimitrov to a leading role in the Communist International's executive. See E.H. Carr, *The Twilight of the Comintern, 1930–1935* (London: Macmillan, 1982), Ch. 3, pp. 123–46.

11. David Caute, *Communism and the French Intellectuals, 1914–1960* (London: Andre Deutsch, 1964), ch. 3, pp. 112–16.

12. Serge, *Memoirs*.

13. Greeman, 'Victor Serge and Leon Trotsky'.

14. Weissman, 'Victor Serge', p. 332.

15. Trotsky to Serge, 24 April 1936 (Letter 2).

16. Greeman, 'Victor Serge and Leon Trotsky' and Leon Trotsky, *Diary in Exile* (London, 1958), p. 54.

17. Trotsky to Serge, 3 June 1936 (Letter 13).

18. Isaac Deutscher, *The Prophet Outcast – Trotsky 1929–40* (Oxford University Press, 1970), p. 43.

19. Deutscher, *The Prophet Outcast*, p. 43.

20. Deutscher, *The Prophet Outcast*, pp. 43–4.

21. Deutscher, *The Prophet Outcast*, p. 44.

22. Baruch Knei-Paz, *The Social and Political Thought of Leon Trotsky* (Oxford University Press, 1979), p. 413.

23. Deutscher, *The Prophet Outcast*, p. 201.

24. Deutscher, *The Prophet Outcast*, p. 202.

25. Serge to Trotsky, 27 May 1936 (Letter 12)

26. Serge to Trotsky, 27 May 1936 (Letter 12).

27. Trotsky to Serge, 19 May 1936 (Letter 10).

28. Trotsky to Serge, 9 June 1936 (Letter 17).

29. David A.L. Levy, 'The French Popular Front, 1936–1937', in Helen Graham and Paul Preston (eds), *The Popular Front in Europe* (London: Macmillan, 1987) p. 62.

30. Levy, 'The French Popular Front, 1936–1937', pp. 67–8.

31. Trotsky to Serge, 9 June 1936 (Letter 17).

32. Leon Trotsky 'A Program for the French Revolution', in David Salner (ed.), *Leon Trotsky on France* (New York: Monad Press, 1979), part 2, pp. 78–9.

33. Trotsky, 'A Program', p. 78.
34. Trotsky, 'A Program', p. 129.
35. Trotsky, 'A Program', p. 134.
36. Serge to Trotsky, 16 June 1936 (Letter 18)
37. Trotsky to Serge, 3 July 1936 (Letter 21).
38. Trotsky to Serge, 3 July 1936 (Letter 21).
39. See Trotsky, 'The New Revolutionary Upsurge and the Tasks of the Fourth International' in Salner, *Leon Trotsky on France,* part 3.
40. Trotsky to Serge, 3 July 1936 (Letter 21).
41. Alexander Werth, *The Twilight of France 1933–1940, A Journalist's Chronicle,* ed. D.W. Brogan (London: Hamish Hamilton, 1942), p. 108.
42. Werth, *Twilight of France,* p. 110.
43. Arthur Mitzman, 'The French Working Class and the Blum Government (1936-37)', in *International Review of Social History,* vol. IX, 1964, part. 3, p. 368.
44. Mitzman, 'The French Working Class and the Blum Government', p. 375.
45. Jacques Danos and Marcel Gibelin, *June '36 – Class Struggle and the Popular Front in France,* transl. Peter Fysh and Christine Bourry, eds. Peter Fysh and Peter Marsden (London: Bookmarks, 1986), p. 162.
46. Serge to Trotsky, 24 June 1936 (Letter 19).
47. Greeman, 'Victor Serge and Leon Trotsky' and Serge to Trotsky, 24 June 1936.
48. Serge to Trotsky, 27 July 1936 (Letter 24).
49. See Victor Serge, 'Observations sur les thèses "Le Nouvel essor révolutionnaire"' (original in Serge papers, Musée Sociale, Paris), 19 July 1936, transl. Peter Sedgwick, 'A New Revolutionary Upturn?'.
50. Trotsky to Serge, 30 July 1936 (Letter 25).
51. See this volume, Chapter 3: introduction.
52. Trotsky to Serge, 22 August 1936 (Letter 30).
53. Deutscher, *The Prophet Outcast,* pp. 324–5.
54. Serge to Trotsky, 30 August 1936 (Letter 31).
55. See Deutscher, *The Prophet Outcast,* pp. 325–54 for a fuller account of this.
56. José Peirats, 'Prelude to the May Days' in Vernon Richards (ed.), *The May Days Barcelona 1937* (London: Freedom Press, 1987), p. 11.
57. Serge, *Carnets,* 'My Break with Trotsky'; see this volume, last document in Chapter 4.
58. Serge to Leon Sedov, 21 January 1937.
59. Serge to Trotsky, 10 January 1937 (Letter 34).
60. Serge, *Carnets,* 'My Break with Trotsky'; see this volume, Documents, chapter 4.
61. See Chapter 4 below for the Kronstadt debate which was raised by Trotsky in an interview with a German journalist who compared the

tactics adopted by the Communists in Spain to the tactics of the Bolsheviks during the Kronstadt rising of 1921.

62. See prefatory note to Letter 35 here.
63. Trotsky to Serge, 5 March 1937 (Letter 35).
64. Trotsky to Serge, 15 April 1938 (Letter 38).
65. Trotsky to Serge, 15 April 1938 (Letter 38).
66. Both these articles are included in the Documents in Chapter 4 below.
67. Serge to Trotsky, 18 March 1939 (Letter 39).
68. Serge to Trotsky, 18 March 1939 (Letter 39). See postscript to this letter and 'My Break with Trotsky' from the *Carnets*. Also Documents, Chapter 4 below.
69. Serge to Trotsky, 18 March 1939 (Letter 39). See the postscript to the letter.
70. An account of Zborowski's activities within the Fourth International can be gained in Deutscher, *The Prophet Outcast*, pp. 347–9, 390–6, 405–10. See also Weissman, 'Victor Serge', pp. 384–7.
71. Leon Trotsky, with John Dewey and George Novack, *Their Morals and Ours, Marxist vs. Liberal Views on Morality* (New York: Pathfinder Press, 1986), Appendix 1.
72. Leon Trotsky, 'The Moralists and Sycophants against Marxism', in *The New International*, August 1939.
73. Serge to Trotsky, 9 August 1939 (Letter 41).
74. Trotsky to Serge, 6 May 1939 (Letter 40).
75. Richard Greeman, private communication on forthcoming biography of Serge, section 'Victor Serge on France'.
76. See this volume, Chapter 1, introduction by Philip Spencer.
77. Deutscher, *The Prophet Outcast*, p. 435.
78. Deutscher, *The Prophet Outcast*, p. 435.
79. Serge to Trotsky, 18 March 1939 (Letter 39).
80. Serge to Trotsky, 18 March 1939 (Letter 39).
81. Serge, 'Thirty Years after the Russian Revolution', unpublished manuscript, Mexico City, July – August 1947. Serge Archive, Mexico.
82. Serge to Sedov, 21 April 1936, from the Trotsky Archive, Harvard.
83. Boris Mikhailovich Eltsin, a comrade of Serge's in internal exile at Orenburg, had been a Bolshevik since 1903, President of the Ekaterinberg Soviet in 1917, and an unrepentant follower of Trotsky in the disputes of the 1920s. Sick and old, he came to Orenburg from the prison at Suzdal. He appears as the character 'Elkin' in Serge's novel *S'il est minuit dans le siècle* (Paris: Grasset, 1939), transl. Richard Greeman as, *Midnight in the Century* (London: Writers and Readers, 1982).
84. Eleazar Solntsev, a historian and economist, had been linked with Trotsky as a young Opposition leader since 1923. He continued Trotskyist activities in 1927–28 while on official missions to Germany and the

United States, and was recalled and jailed for five years, a sentence doubled at its expiry by administrative decree.

85. Adolf Senin, alias Abraham Sobolevicius, later alias Jack Soble, was along with his brother Ruvelius Sobolevicius (alias Roman Well, later alias Robert Soblen) a Lithuanian who became leader of the German section of the International Left Opposition in 1931. The following year the Sobolevicius brothers led a split from the Trotskyists into the German Communist Party. Both were unmasked in 1957 as Soviet secret agents working in the US. Robert Soblen committed suicide after his conviction for espionage. The brothers admitted to having been Stalinist spies since 1931.

86. The deletions in the text here were, one must assume, made by Sedov or by Trotsky's Secretariat before the Harvard Archive acquired the collection of Trotsky documents.

87. Vexhall was the village about 30 miles north of Oslo where Trotsky and his wife lived as guests of the Norwegian Social Democrat editor Konrad Knudsen, during his period (June 1935 to December 1936) of political asylum in Norway.

88. Dumbadze was a former member of the Central Committee of the Georgian Communist Party. His sufferings as a Left Oppositionist with a physical disability, in atrocious deportation conditions, is described by Serge in Letter 4 below.

89. Victor Eltsin, a former secretary of Trotsky's in the mid-1920s, had known Serge from the early years of the Left Opposition. His deportation to the inhospitable north (Archangel) followed a five-year prison sentence.

90. Plisnier, a Belgian novelist and poet, had been a Communist in the wake of the Russian Revolution and then joined the Trotskyist Opposition in Belgium (1928). He became primarily devoted to literature, winning the 1937 Prix Goncourt for his novel *False Passports*. He was active in the campaign to have Serge liberated which was built around the Paris International writers' congress in 1935.

91. Natalia Ivanovna Sedova: Trotsky's wife since their meeting in Paris in 1902, and mother of their two sons Leon Sedov and Sergei Sedov.

92. Mikhail Glazman, a secretary to Trotsky during the civil war and an Oppositionist, committed suicide in 1924 after being expelled from the party. Georgi V. Butov, also a one-time secretary to Trotsky, joined the Opposition and was sent in 1928 to a Moscow prison, where he died on hunger-strike, reportedly after refusing to make a false confession implicating his chief. Yakov Blyumkin, a former Left Social Revolutionary who turned Bolshevik in 1918, was a member of the GPU's foreign intelligence division, entrusted with missions abroad even though a known Opposition sympathiser. Returning home from one such mission, he made contact with Trotsky during the latter's exile

in Prinkipo (Turkey) in 1929, and took a message back for the Oppositionists in Russia. Once back in Moscow he was arrested and shot.

93. The Russian-language *Bulletin of the Opposition* was published from various successive cities outside Russia (Paris at the time Trotsky wrote to Serge) from July 1929 to August 1941.

94. Leon Trotsky, *The Revolution Betrayed*, to be published later in 1936 (Paris: Grasset).

95. 'Printed sheet' is a Russian measure of book length; 200 printed sheets were about 7,000 words.

96. Leon Lesoil was a founder of the Belgian Communist Party, expelled in 1927 for Trotskyism. In line with Trotsky's policy of 'entryism' he and his group joined the Parti Ouvrier Belge, the main labour party of that country. The group was expelled from the POB and formed the Parti Socialiste Révolutionnaire, the Belgian Section of the Fourth International movement, in October 1936. Lesoil died in a concentration camp in 1941 after being arrested by the Nazis.

97. Walter Dauge had come into the Belgian Left Opposition recently from Action Socialiste, a left reform tendency in the POB. He edited the Belgian section's paper *L'Action socialiste révolutionnaire* when the section was still 'entryist' in the POB and was then active in the PSR from 1936 to 1939. He ceased to be in the Trotskyist movement when the Second World War broke out, became a collaborator under the Occupation and was killed by partisans in 1944.

98. Fernand Godefroid was secretary of the POB's national youth movement, the Jeunes Gardes Socialistes, and was suspected of hostility to the Trotskyists who had entered the party and its youth wing.

99. Gosizdat was the Soviet state publishing agency responsible for foreign authors.

100. Sergei Sedov, the Trotskys' second son, who although a dedicated engineer without political affiliation was arrested by the GPU in 1936 and disappeared forever.

101. A prison and deportation complex in the Moscow region, near Vladimir.

102. A Moscow prison.

103. Serge's acute sensitivity over the repercussions on his residence permit of any public identification of himself as a Trotskyist continues in the correspondence, and forms a topic of reproach in a letter he sent to Pierre Naville and Gerard Rosenthal of the French section on 26 April 1939 (Serge Archive, Vlady and Jean Rière), claiming that the Fourth International's open polemics against him were endangering his visa conditions of politicial non-activity.

104. A. Tarov was the pseudonym of the Armenian Left Oppositionist Arven Davtian, a mechanic and Soviet citizen who after a militant career (Bolshevik in 1917, Left Oppositionist in 1927) had been arrested in 1928 and 1931. Transported to Siberia and the isolator at Verkhne-

Uralsk, he was then banished to Central Asia, from where he escaped to Iran in 1933. He wrote an account of his experiences for the *Bulletin of the Opposition* in 1935, as well as other exposés of Soviet conditions. His fate after this is obscure, and he is rumoured to have been executed by the Nazis in or after 1942.

105. Dr. Anton Ciliga was a leading Yugoslav Communist (of Politburo status in 1925) who joined the Left Opposition and was arrested and deported in March 1930. After three years in the Verkhne-Uralsk isolator and two in exile, he was compelled to leave Russia in 1935. In 1938 he published his reminiscences *Au pays du grand mensonge* (translated into English as *The Russian Enigma* [London: Routledge and Kegan Paul, 1940]). He returned to Yugoslavia in 1940, was arrested the following year and subsequently wrote for the Ustasi press of the Fascist state of Croatia.

106. Boris Souvarine (Lifchitz) was an early and brilliant leader of the French CP, but was expelled in July 1924 after supporting Trotsky at the Thirteenth CPSU Congress. He used his old CP journal *Bulletin communiste* to propagate Trotsky's ideas, but in 1929 rejected the Left Opposition. His small Cercle Marx-Lenine became the Cercle Communiste-Democratique, expressing his disillusion with Leninism. He subsequently devoted himself to high-quality Sovietological work.

107. Maurice Paz was a former French CP member who founded an Oppositional current in 1925. He founded the Trotsky organ *Contre le courant* in 1927 and broke with Trotsky two years later following a visit to him at Prinkipo. His wife Magdeleine Marx Paz followed the same course; she distinguished herself in the campaign for Victor Serge's release in 1933–5. Both the Pazes had joined the SFIO by the time of Trotsky's reference to them here.

108. Boris Souvarine's *Stalin: A Critical Study of Bolshevism*, the first serious biography, was published in France in 1935; the English translation of Secker and Warburg appeared in 1939.

109. 'Sacred union' of the Socialist supporters of the First World War.

110. That is, the parties of the Second International (which accepted an exiled Menshevik affiliate) were now expelling its Trotskyists.

111. Feodor Dan, a leading Menshevik leader in Russia before and after 1917. Expelled from the USSR in 1921, he published the Menshevik exile organ *Socialistichesky Vestnik*.

112. Emile Vandervelde was a major figure in the POB and the Second International between the two world wars. He was a coalition cabinet minister several times, including a spell in office in the First World War.

113. Léon Blum was an outstanding figure in the French Socialist Party over many decades. He had pressed for the expulsion of the Trotskyists from the party at its congress in July 1935, and was soon (June 1936) to become Prime Minister of the Popular Front government.

114. The reference is to Karl Liebknecht, the German internationalist revolutionary murdered along with Rosa Luxemburg in Berlin in 1919, with the connivance of the Social Democratic government.

115. Alfred Rosmer had been an old collaborator of Trotsky from First World War days and was active in the early French and international Communist movements. Expelled from the French CP in 1924, he was active in the revolutionary-syndicalist *La Révolution prolétarienne*, and then helped to found the French Section of the International Left Opposition around the journal *La Verité* (1929). He distanced himself from Trotsky after 1930.

116. The main point of disagreement between Trotsky and Rosmer had been over the former's support for the brothers Raymond and Henri Molinier, who conducted a high-handed and adventuristic style of politics around the French Section. By the time Trotsky corresponded with Serge, he had himself broken with the Moliniers.

117. Marguerite Rosmer, Alfred's companion and political comrade.

118. Alfred Rosmer, *Le Mouvement ouvrier pendant la Première Guerre mondiale*, whose first volume was published in Paris in 1936 (to be followed by a second in 1959).

119. Georges Vereeken, a Trotskyist active in the Belgian taxi-drivers' union, was opposed to entryism into the POB. He had led the dissident Trotskyist group Spartacus after 1935, which fused with the main section when the entryists were expelled from the POB later in 1936. The three 'currents' identified by Trotsky were thus those of two long-standing Trotskyists (Lesoil and Vereeken), one for and one opposed to entryism, and a recent recruit (Dauge), not entryist in the sense of having previously been Trotskyist but won from the left of the entered party.

120. Paul-Henri Spaak had stimulated a left current in the POB against its moderate leadership in 1933, and was sufficiently attracted to Trotsky to visit him in France in the summer of 1934; in March 1935 he joined a government formed with the left of the Catholic Party, inaugurating a long and respectable career which would climax in his becoming Secretary-General of NATO.

121. Marceau Pivert inspired the Gauche Révolutionnaire of the French Socialist Party. He joined the Blum administration after 1936 but remained a vocal opponent of its temporising with the bourgeoisie, quitting the SFIO to found a new (and unsuccessful) party, the Parti Socialiste Ouvrier et Paysan (PSOP) in 1938.

122. Alexandra Lvovna Sokolovskaya (Bronstein), Trotsky's first wife and an Oppositionist; she had been arrested in 1935 and deported.

123. Maria Lvovna Sokolovskaya, sister of the above, also deported and unheard of since.

124. The Associated Press. The statement, using information, provided by Serge, of the persecutions of prisoners and deportees, was drawn up on 22 May 1936; a French translation, 'La Nouvelle constitution et la repression en URSS' was published in no. 2 of the *Service d'information et de presse* of the Ligue Communiste Internationaliste, Paris, June 1936.

125. Trotsky's letter was actually dated the 24th.

126. Anita Russakova was the younger sister of Serge's wife, whose 'technical help to the Trotskyites' consisted of typing some of her brother-in-law's translations. She spent years in the camps after her arrest and was released after Stalin's death.

127. The International Secretariat (or IS) of the International Left Opposition was the guiding body of the Trotskyist movement, usually based in Paris. It was in constant communication with Trotsky himself.

128. Further details about these victims and their political backgrounds are given in Serge's article on the deportees of Orenburg which is in the Trotsky papers (Harvard Archive document no. 17399). It was published in Russian with a few deletions in *Bulletin of the Opposition* no. 51, July–August 1936, and in full in French in *Cahiers Leon Trotsky* (Grenoble), no. 7/8, 1981, pp. 221–8. Serge's *Memoirs* have some moving human portraits of this group of deportees (pp. 307–12).

129. This was the frame-up whereby the Left Opposition's distribution press was said by the GPU, in September 1927, to be linked with a White ex-officer from Wrangel's forces, who was of course a police stool-pigeon.

130. G.Y. Yakovin was a particularly important figure: a Bolshevik since 1914, an Oppositionist since 1923 who never capitulated, he performed useful analysis on international questions, including Weimar Germany. His first arrest had been in 1928/9 after organising an illegal strike, and his life after that was a succession of arrests and deportations.

131. Liuba Russakova, the daughter of Russian revolutionary exiles active in France, had returned to Russia at much the same time (1919) that Serge first arrived there. She married Serge soon afterwards. Between the time of Serge's first imprisonment (1928) and his later long arrest and deportation (1933) her mental state underwent progressive deterioration and she was treated frequently by Soviet psychiatrists. It cannot be said what was the nature of her disorder: the Soviet use of the term 'schizophrenia' was probably not in conformity with the restricted definitions of modern Anglo-American medicine. Her condition fluctuated, but in a deteriorating direction, and Serge left her in a mental hospital near Aix in the south of France in 1940 when he was about to leave for Mexico to flee from the Nazis.

132. Vladimir Kibalchich (Vlady) was almost 16 at the time Serge wrote here. Serge's daughter Jeannine was 18 months old.

133. This appears to be a mistake on Serge's part: his letter was dated the 25th.
134. In fact, accusations that Serge was terroristically inclined were directed against him by the French CP journalist Jacques Sadoul in 1937. Sadoul used Serge's 1910–11 links with the anarchist 'Bonnot Gang' in order to smear him. See Trotsky's open letter in support of Serge during this campaign of slander, no. 35 below.
135. The 'amalgam' was one of Trotsky's words for the Stalinists use of guilt-by-association slanders.
136. Serge is obviously referring to Trotsky's letter of 8 May, which may have been postmarked the following day.
137. This is Serge's report on the Orenburg deportees referred to in Letter 6 (note 128 above).
138. Ida Shumskaya was an Old Bolshevik who was to die as the result of her isolator and camp experiences at the end of the 1930s.
139. Alfred Rosmer.
140. *L'Action socialiste révolutionnaire* was the journal of the Trotskyists until late 1936, when it was replaced by *La Lutte ouvrière*, the organ of the new open party outside the POB.
141. Trotsky's relations with the syndicalist grouping around the 'RP' had long been stormy. Soon after the journal was founded in 1925, he sent an appeal to it as a spokesperson for the Communist International, asking its editors to close it down and take their differences with the French Communist Party to a Comintern appeal (*La Révolution prolétarienne*, no. 10, October 1925). Once in exile, Trotsky worked with the 'RP' collective as a left anti-Stalinist tendency, but broke with their main animator, Pierre Monatte (an old associate of his from both the First World War and Communist International activity – see note 169 below), when in 1929–30 the latter preached revolutionary-syndical-ism, in opposition to party-building, and trade-union unity and autonomy, in contrast to Trotsky's vision of a separate, party-led unionisation. See 'Monatte a franchi le Rubicon', 5 December 1930, in *Leon Trotsky: Le Mouvement communiste en France (1919–39)*, ed. Pierre Broue (Paris, 1967) pp. 362–8. Trotsky was to change his position on trade-union unification, becoming in August 1934 a keen proponent of fusion between the CGT (then Socialist-led) and the CGTU (Communist-led), in view of the Fascist danger. He pressed this fusion policy at a personal meeting during his stay in France, with the hesitant leadership of the teachers' union (Fédération de l'Enseignement), which was close to the Trotskyists. See Pierre Broué, 'L'Action clandestin de Trotsky en Dauphine (1934–35)', *Cahiers d'histoire* (Lyons), vol. 13, 1968, pp. 327–41. But his movement towards the position he had condemned in the 'RP' group in no way muted his suspicion of its syndicalism.

142. Henri Barbusse had been a celebrated anti-war novelist and founder of revolutionary and pacifist movements among writers: the review *Clarté* in 1919 and the Amsterdam-Pleyel peace movement (a forerunner of the Popular Front) over 1932–5. A loyal Communist Party member since 1923, he had died, in the year before Serge and Trotsky began this correspondence, at a Comintern congress in Moscow.

143. Romain Rolland, novelist, historian of the arts, pacifist and Nobel prizewinner (1915), moved in the 1930s to participate in Communist-backed literary fronts as well as the Amsterdam-Pleyel anti-war movement. He defended the Moscow trials and supported the Munich Agreements of 1938 and was otherwise kept in line by his very pro-Soviet wife.

144. This took place in March–April 1936, when Bukharin, then in very low standing in the Soviet hierarchy, was part of a delegation seeking to purchase the archives (including Marx manuscripts) of the German Social Democratic Party.

145. Again, it seems this is a mistake on Serge's part; Trotsky's letter was dated the 19th (with a postscript added on the 20th).

146. Jacques Mesnil was a Socialist writer and journalist who had been active in resisting the 'Union Sacrée' during the First World War. Although he attended the Third Congress of the Comintern in 1921 (where he met Serge), he was to form part of the nucleus of the revolutionary-syndicalist *La Révolution prolétarienne*.

147. The weekly paper of the French Trotskyist Section, founded in 1929. It was replaced in 1936 by *La Lutte ouvrière*.

148. N.I. Karpov, formerly an army commissar and professor of agricultural science, had been part of the Leningrad centre of the Opposition in the 1920s. Evgeny Preobrazhensky, a Bolshevik since 1904, had been a Central Committee member from 1917 to 1920 (and in the latter year part of its Secretariat). An Oppositionist since 1923, he specialised in economics, advocating industrialisation against Bukharin's policy of appeasing the peasants. Expelled from the party in 1927, he capitulated to Stalin two years later, was arrested during the purges and disappeared, never having been put on trial. Marenko remains obscure.

149. The novelist André Gide became close to Communism at the beginning of the 1930s, but in 1936, following a journey to the Soviet Union, distanced himself from the various CP fronts in France, writing a disillusioned book about his Russian visit, *Retouches à mon retour de l'URSS* (Paris: Gallimard, 1937). He met Serge for political discussion following his break with the CP and the consequent Stalinist attacks on his book and his homosexual personal life. Serge's open letter to Gide, when the latter was still favouring the Soviet and CP line, was published in both the *Bulletin of the Opposition* (no. 51, July–August 1936) and in

the Catholic-left monthly *Esprit* (no. 45, June 1936). (The open letter to Magdeleine Paz was also contained in the latter publication.)

150. This is of course Serge's error for 1936.

151. Maurice Parijanine (Donzel) had lived in Russia from 1907 to 1920 and translated many of Trotsky's works into French. As a writer he had been a regular contributor to *Clarté* and *L'Humanité* in the mid-1920s but by 1936 he was a collaborator with the independent left journal *Les Humbles*.

152. It was actually called *Destin d'une révolution: URSS 1917–1937* and was published in 1937 (Paris: Grasset); American edition *Russia Twenty Years After*, transl. Max Shachtman (New York: Pioneer, 1937; Connecticut: Hyperion Press, 1973); English edition *Destiny of a Revolution*, (London: National Book Association, Hutchinson, 1937).

153. This is Serge's first outline of the idea for his novel *Midnight in the Century* (published as *S'il est minuit dans le siècle*, Paris: Grasset, 1939). It actually covers only the post-1934 period of the Oppositionists' deportations.

154. Trotsky's *Revolution Betrayed* (1937, pp. 265–70) does envisage a kind of Socialist pluralism in a reformed Soviet Union, with free competition in elections among 'Soviet parties'. Serge claims (*Memoirs*, p. 348) that he had encouraged Trotsky to include 'a declaration of freedom for all parties accepting the Soviet system'. No trace of this specific demand is found in Serge's extant letters to Trotsky, but it is possible that this passage represents the core of it.

155. The project for a new constitution in the USSR was being elaborated through a steered public debate. The Constitution that was adopted in December 1936 incorporated many formal provisions for the civil rights of citizens.

156. The article on 'The New Constitution of the USSR' had appeared in *Bulletin of the Opposition*, 1936.

157. The anarchist 'Black Guard' of armed militants had occupied a number of buildings in Moscow in April 1918 and was disbanded, with some bloodshed, by 5,000 Soviet troops led by Dzerzhinsky as head of the CHEKA. Serge justifies this action in *Year One*, p. 215.

158. This letter has been lost from both the Serge and Trotsky archives.

159. At the time of Lenin's first formulation of the centralised vanguard party in the 1900s, both Luxemburg and Trotsky had denounced the conception as an autocratic one, in separate writings of 1904. Trotsky subsequently, as a convert to orthodox 'Leninism', stated that his criticisms of Lenin's organisational ideas at that time were immature.

160. This particular version of the 'state capitalist' thesis is only one of several within the Trotskyist, let alone the Marxist tradition of theories about the USSR. The question as to whether the Soviet state bureaucracy constitutes a new 'ruling class' (a sort of collective capitalist) has been answered affirmatively even by those who regarded Hitler's Germany

and Mussolini's Italy as predominantly regimes of private capitalism. And the view that such Fascist regimes were evolving towards a form of oligarchical collectivism also displayed by the USSR can be expressed in a way which denies that this new, exploitative social order is in any sense capitalist. The debate reported by Serge represents an early stage of the argument as to the 'class character' of the Soviet state, conducted of course by a group of deportees deprived of access to theoretical literature. However, even the summary given here by Serge does strikingly anticipate some themes in discussion among anti-Stalinists on the left outside Russia in later decades.

161. Khristu Rakovsky, an Old Bolshevik of Bulgarian and Romanian antecedents, a man of great ability and highly cultured, had been a collaborator of Lenin and his then rival Trotsky among the Russian emigrants and in the international movement against the First World War. After the revolution, Rakovsky was President of the Soviet government in the Ukraine (1919–23) and a Central Committee member (1919–25). A close personal friend of Trotsky, he joined all the struggles of the Opposition, was expelled, arrested and deported in 1927, and continued oppositional writing on tactics and theory. In 1934 he sent a telegram to the Central Committee announcing his recantation of Opposition because of the war danger, and followed this up with a loyal article in *Pravda*. He appeared as a defendant in the third great Moscow trial (1938), where he was condemned to 25 years' imprisonment, dying three years later in unknown circumstances.

162. Leon Sosnovsky, principal speaker for the Bolshevik fraction of the All-Russian Soviet Executive at the outset of the revolution, then a distinguished journalist and publicist, was also an early Oppositionist (expelled and deported in 1927) and a late capitulator (1934). He disappeared and died in the Great Purge (1937).

163. Varsenika Kasparova, of Armenian origin and a Bolshevik since 1904, fulfilled political and administrative functions in the Red Army during the civil war, and later was a leading figure both in the Comintern and the Communist-sponsored international women's movement. She moved progressively over to the Left Opposition between 1927 and 1929.

164. Ivan Byk, a former Bolshevik fighter in the Ukraine, campaigned for the Workers Opposition and suffered many years of imprisionment as a result. He eventually shared Serge's exile at Orenberg, but his fate after Serge's release is uncertain.

165. Feodor Dingelstedt, a Bolshevik since 1910 and an active organising figure for Petrograd and the Baltic fleet in 1917, was a Soviet expert on India and a theoretical contributor within the Opposition (joined in 1923). He disappeared in the purges without trial.

166. Sergei Kirov, Politburo member and head of the Leningrad party, was assassinated on 1 December, 1934 by an assailant whose motives remain mysterious.
167. I.P. Pavlov, the conditioned-reflex psychologist who became a dominant figure in official Soviet science. Note that Trotsky accepts the diagnosis of 'schizophrenia' in Liube even though Serge (in Letter 12) says he personally thinks her condition is not as serious as this.
168. Max Eastman, *Artists in Uniform: A Study of Literature and Bureaucraticism* (New York: Octagon Books, 1972).
169. Pierre Monatte, a proofreader and revolutionary-syndicalist, had founded *La Vie ouvrière* in 1909 and ran an anti-war group of the same name (to which Trotsky was a visitor), in Paris in opposition to the 'Union Sacrée'. He joined the French CP in 1923 but was expelled the following year, and in 1925 founded the 'RP' journal. See note 141 above.
170. Robert Louzon, an engineer, worked for *La Vie ouvrière* before the First World War and then joined the CP, working on *L'Humanité* before he left it with Monatte and Rosmer to create *La Révolution prolétarienne*, in which he remained active following the Second World War.
171. Leon Jouhaux was a General Secretary of the CGT when it was divided from the Communist-led CGTU (1921–36) and when it was the name of the unified union federation including the Communist syndicates (1936–40). He then led the moderate trade union (Force Ouvrière) which split from the (now Communist-dominated) CGT in 1947.
172. There is no trace in the archives of Serge's letter to Trotsky from Paris raising the issue of Nin.
173. Andreu (Andrès in Castilian) Nin Perez was an old acquaintance of both Trotsky and Serge, though personally closer to the latter. National Secretary of the CNT, he crossed over to the Communist International in 1921 and stayed in Moscow to work as Secretary of the Red International of Trade Unions (RILU or Profintern). He joined the international commission of the Left Opposition and was expelled from the CPSU in 1927, managing to leave the Soviet Union in 1930. Returning to Spain, he was imprisoned on several occasions: his correspondence of argument with Trotsky (1930–32) has not been published in full. An important writer on nationality questions, comparative political regimes and Spanish questions, Nin was martyred by GPU torturers and assassins in 1937 as a leader of the more revolutionary wing of the anti-Franco resistance. For the nature of the political evaluations separating Nin (and his party the POUM) from Trotsky and the Trotskyists, see Chapter 3 below.
174. Joaquin Maurin Julia was, like Nin, a CNT militant who embraced Communist affiliations in the early 1920s. Founder of the newspaper

La Batalla as a Communist organ in Spain, he was active in the Spanish CP until 1931, when his Catalan-Balearic Federation broke away from it to merge with other groupings in the Bloque Obrero y Campesino (BOC). Trotsky regarded the BOC as a nationalistic and Bukharinist splinter group, and strongly opposed the unification between it and Nin's Left Oppositional caucus to form the POUM in 1935. Maurin spent the years 1936 to 1946 in the prisons of the Franco authorities.

175. The BOC.

176. Vereeken did indeed become reconciled to the official grouping of Belgian Trotskyists, when his tendency and theirs fused to establish the PSR later in the year. But he abandoned the PSR in October 1937.

177. Andrew Smith, *I Was a Soviet Worker* (London: Robert Hale, 1937).

178. David Ryazanov was an ex-Menshevik converted to Bolshevism in 1917, who directed the Marx-Engels Institute in Moscow from 1921 and engaged in scholarly historical work. He vanished during the Great Purge.

179. Jakob Walcher, a founder of the Communist Party of Germany, was expelled from it in 1928 along with the faction of Brandler and Thalheimer, which was anti-Stalin but not particularly Trotskyist. This grouping fused with left dissidents from the Social Democrats to form, in 1931, the Sozialistischer Arbeiter Partei (SAP), which after Hitler's rise became a strong influence among the radical anti-Nazi emigrants. James Maxton was a member of Parliament and major figure in the Independent Labour Party of Britain. Trotsky's attack on Walcher and Maxton refers to their parties' membership of a 'centrist' international rival to Trotskyism, the International Bureau of Revolutionary Socialist Unity (the 'London Bureau').

180. Jean Longuet of the French SFIO and Georg Lebedour of the German SPD were 'soft' internationalists during the First World War, of the type denounced by Lenin for refusing to break with Social-Democracy and go over to an insurrectionary position.

181. The 'secure address' is not in the surviving text.

182. Trotsky's host at Vexhall, Norway.

183. A reference to Lenin's *'Left-Wing' Communism – An Infantile Disorder* (London: Communism Party of Great Britain, 1920): the phrase 'infantile disorder' is quite friendly in this context, and alludes to the 'growing pains' of a new movement.

184. The journal of Vereeken's Belgian anti-entryist group.

185. Roger Salengro, the Socialist Minister of the Interior, now in office in Blum's Popular Front government: he was opposed to the factory occupations and had the French Trotskyist paper *La Lutte ouvrière* seized. As the result of a slander campaign in the far-right press (which

accused him of having been a deserter in 1915), he committed suicide in November 1936.

186. Marcel Cachin, a conformist member of the French CP's leadership who had been a patriotic Socialist deputy in the First World War and a member of a French mission in 1917 designed to keep Russia in the war. He converted to Communism after a visit to Moscow in 1920 and remained a CP ornament until his decease in 1958.

187. Alexander Kerensky, the Prime Minister of the Russian provisional government from August 1917 until its overthrow by the October Revolution.

188. Irakli Tseretelli, the prominent Georgian Menshivik who, as a Minister and moderate leader during the course of 1917, was a particular target for Trotsky's scorn in *The History of the Russian Revolution*, transl. Max Eastman (London: Pluto Press, 1977), originally published in 3 volumes (New York: Simon and Schuster, 1932; London: Gollancz, 1932–3).

189. Mining area of Belgium.

190. Leon Emery was a literary critic and professor at Lyons, who at this time was active in the Frontiste movement built around Gaston Bergery's newspaper *La Flèche*. A militant trade unionist and a member of the Comité de Vigilance des Intellectuels Antifascistes, during the Occupation Emery moved to a friendly position towards the collaborators.

191. The translator was Parijanine.

192. Reproduced here after this letter; the author is unknown.

193. The publishing house Rieder in Paris, which in 1930 had put out Trotsky's *My Life* and was also the publisher of Serge's three novels sent out from France in 1930–32.

194. Published in May 1935 in the Paris literary review *Les Feuillets bleus*. The reference to Serge's poems in a cheap edition is unclear: it was not until 1938 that his collection of poetry (some dating from Orenburg) was published by the magazine *Les Humbles* under the title *Resistance*.

195. The Belgian Fascist movement Rex (with Leon Degrelle as its charismatic leader) reached its peak in 1935 and 1936, with 271,000 votes and 21 seats (out of 202) in the parliamentary elections of 24 May in the latter year. Having started as a development of the Catholic youth movement, it lost influence after this when it was condemned openly by the Church. Despite its intervention on the side of the Belgian strikers, it never gained working-class support and its presence intensified anti-Fascist consciousness in the workers' organisations. During the Nazi occupation of Belgium, Degrelle became a Waffen-SS commander and leader of a contingent on the Russian front, but his movement remained small.

196. Ademard Hennaut had split from the main Belgian Left Opposition in 1929–30 over Trotsky's support for the Soviet claim to the Far Eastern

railway (across China), having been one of the founders of the first Left Opposition group inside the Belgian CP. His own group, the Liga der Internationele Kommunisten, remained outside the official Trotskyist movement until its demise in 1940.

197. Ersilio Ambroggi, a leading Italian Communist, had remained in the USSR after 1922, when a Fascist court in his homeland sentenced him in absentia to a long imprisonment. He was expelled from his party in 1929 and left the USSR in 1933. Settling eventually in Belgium (where Serge met him) he was arrested in 1940 and delivered to the Italian authorities, who passed him on to a Nazi concentration camp. When he returned to Italy in 1945 he tried to rejoin the CP but was refused readmission until 1958. Serge's reference to his old 'Bordigist' loyalties is a reference to his identification for a period with Amadeo Bordiga, a founder of the Italian Communist Party who broke with the Third International because he refused to recognise the tactic of the united front promulgated by Lenin: the Bordigists worked for some years with the Left Opposition.

198. The magazine with Serge's short story 'Mer blanche' (see no. 194).

199. Trotsky, *The Revolution Betrayed*.

200. This was a draft for the thesis 'The New Revolutionary Upsurge and the Tasks of the Fourth International', drafted for consideration at the first international conference of the (still formally unfounded) Fourth International. This was announced for Geneva, but actually took place in Paris in July 1936.

201. A.J. Muste, a former Calvinist pastor who had become an active participant in the US Trotskyist movement in this period.

202. This particular draft appeal never seems to have reached the press; it does not appear in the record of Trotsky's published writings. Possibly the advent of the Moscow trial in August overtook plans for the circulation of this document.

203. The literary censorship department of the Soviet authorities.

204. The All-Russian Soviet Executive.

205. Trotsky, *The Revolution Betrayed*, which was published in Serge's translation by the Paris firm of Grasset later in the year.

206. Marcel Hasfield, a veteran anarchist opponent of the First World War, who joined *La Vie ouvrière* in 1922 and *Contre le courant* (the Trotskyist organ of the Pazes) in 1928. From the 1920s onwards, he was the founder and editor of the Librairie du Travail, a publishing medium for dissident-Communist and left-wing works, including seven of Serge's own works.

207. Muste was in Paris for the international conference of Fourth International groupings that took place in July. He was to fall out with the movement over the tactic of 'entryism', with the American Trotskyists conducting their own entry, into the small Socialist Party of the

United States, in December 1936. Muste in due course returned to being a pastor, and was active as a radical Christian in the US peace and civil rights campaigns down to the 1960s.

208. N. is Pierre Naville, a former Surrealist whom Serge had previously met in Russia in 1927 and introduced to Zinoviev and Trotsky. Expelled from the French CP in the following year, Naville animated a succession of Trotskyist groups in France and joined the Secretariat of the Movement for the Fourth International. He entered the French Socialist Party, despite his reservations about the tactic, and was expelled first from the SP (1935) and then from the Fourth International (1939) because, along with others of the French Section, he refused to enter the Parti Socialiste Ouvrier et Paysan, an eclectic left-wing grouping which did not survive the war's outbreak. Later he was active in the New Left formation the PSU (Parti Socialiste Unifié). He was author of a large number of works on sociological and political questions, as well as of a study of Trotsky, *Trotsky vivant* (1962).

209. R. is Jean Rous, a lawyer who progressed in the French Trotskyist ranks from the Ligue Communiste (1932) to the Groupe Bolshevik-Leninists of 'entryists' within the Socialist Party who were expelled from it in 1935. He then led the Parti Ouvrier Internationaliste (POI), an ephemeral fusion of three Trotskyist groupings founded in June 1936, and as a member of the International Secretariat (IS) of the budding Fourth International was emissary to Spain during the civil war and revolution. After the Second World War, he joined the SFIO and became active in anti-colonial campaigns. Rous gravitated towards the New Left PSU, and served as adviser to the government of Senegal after it won independence from France.

210. The 'Molinier case' revolved around Raymond Molinier, whose personal financial power and political factionalism embroiled a succession of organisations of the French Section (of Trotskyism), from the Ligue Communiste through the GBL to the newly-fused POI which expelled him in July 1936 shortly after it was founded. He and his following then reconstituted their former Parti Communiste Internationaliste (PCI) and the split continued.

211. Maurice Dommanget was an old internationalist from the First World War, an activist in *La Vie ouvrière*, and a Communist Party dissident, resigning from the CP in 1930 following his opposition to the sectarian tactics of the 'third period.' A teacher of history who wrote prolifically on French revolutionary and labour traditions, Dommanget was a leading light of the journal *L'Ecole emancipée* and the trade union Fédération Unitaire de l'Enseignement. He campaigned vigorously against the Moscow trials, but was never in the Left Opposition movement itself.

212. Maurice Wullens, the founder of the literary anti-war review *Les Humbles* (1914), which in the 1930s took up the questions of Serge's confinement in Russia and the Moscow trials. An anarchist and pacifist sympathiser, Wullens lost his friendship with Serge at the time of Munich when *Les Humbles* printed an apologia for the Third Reich in the name of free debate.

213. Simone Weil had been close to syndicalist and Trotskyist groups in the early 1930s, but became disenchanted with revolutionary violence following her stay in Spain after the outbreak of the civil war there. She remained deeply concerned with questions of social oppression, including the condition of the working class, from a Catholic-humanist standpoint. An exile in London after the Occupation, she starved herself as a means of solidarity with her undernourished people in France, and as a consequence died in 1943.

214. Albert Treint had risen in the French Communist Party to become its General Secretary in 1924 during the campaign of 'Bolshevising' the CPs, then supported by the Comintern under Zinoviev. Having in this capacity organised the expulsion of a number of CP members who were to form early elements of the French Left Opposition, he was himself expelled from the party in 1928 when he declared in favour of the Zinoviev–Trotsky Joint Opposition. His small Opposition grouping in France never successfully integrated with the organisations of the French Section, and in 1934 he joined the SFIO.

215. Lasterade was the leader of the Communist Union group, stemming from a split of the Communist League in November 1933. It published a bulletin, *L'Internationale*.

216. When Serge wrote, the Spanish Civil War had just broken out, with Franco's rising and the massive counter-mobilisation of the Spanish workers and peasants.

217. The international conference of Fourth International supporters held in July in Paris.

218. Gustave Noske (1886–1946), War Minister in the right-wing Social Democrat government of Germany between 1918 and 1920, was responsible for the suppression of the uprising led by Rosa Luxemburg and Karl Liebknecht. Friedrich Ebert (1871–1925), Secretary of the SPD, aided the generals in crushing the revolutionary movement in Germany between 1918 and 1919.

219. A nineteenth-century French Socialist and thinker.

220. Manuel Azaña y Diaz was a liberal politician who was Prime Minister of the Spanish Republic in 1931–3, and in 1936 became successively Prime Minister and President in the wake of the Popular Front's victory. His party, the Republican Left, was party to the electoral accords of the Popular Front in January 1936, which Nin's POUM had also signed.

221. Vassili Federovich Pankratov, formerly a sailor in the Russian navy, had helped lead the revolutionary movement in Kronstadt. Following the revolution, he worked for the GPU until his arrest in 1928; thereafter he spent years in prison and shared Serge's exile at Orenburg. His fate after Serge's release is uncertain, although family survivors still live in Moscow.

222. *La Lutte ouvrière*, newspaper of the French Trotskyists.

223. Michel Collinet, a former Ligue Communiste member who broke with Trotskyism over trade-union tactics around 1930 and joined the SFIO, where he became active in Marceu Pivert's Gauche Révolutionnaire. He later joined the PSOP.

224. Jesus Hernández, Politburo member of the Spanish CP and soon to become Minister of Public Education in the Caballero and Negrin governments of the Spanish Republic. After his break with Stalinism in 1943 following a traumatic residence in the Soviet Union, he published a book of memoirs, *Yo fui un ministro de Stalin* (Madrid: G. del Toro, 1974), denouncing CP intrigue in the Spanish Civil War and exposing the murder and torture of Andreu Nin by the GPU.

225. Desiderio Trillas, leader of the UGT (combined Socialist and CP union) dockworkers' section, and a Communist rather than a Socialist.

226. Francisco Largo Caballero, a veteran Socialist who, having functioned as Minister of State to the Primo de Rivera dictatorship of the 1920s, moved left and, during the period when he was nicknamed the 'Spanish Lenin', headed the Popular Front government of 1936. He was eliminated from it the following year, through pressure from Moscow and the CP after he had refused to take repressive measures against the POUM and the anarchist left.

227. Francisco Ascaso, a leading anarchist who, after exile and deportation abroad as an initiator of bank robberies, assassinations and other acts of political violence, returned to Spain at the outbreak of the civil war. He was killed as the leader of an anarchist column which stormed the Atarazanas Barracks in Barcelona, held by Franco's troops.

228. Federación Anarquista Ibérica, a secret organisation founded by anarchists in 1927 in order to keep the libertarian trade union the CNT (Confederación Nacional del Trabajo) away from both reformist and Communist influences.

229. This is Serge's confusion over dates. The letter he ascribes to 8 August was actually written on the 10th; while the one on the forfeiture of Soviet citizenship was in fact *two* letters before that.

230. Grigori Zinoviev, the once-powerful colleague of Lenin, head of the Communist International, controller of the Leningrad Bolsheviks and member of the 'triumvirate' with Stalin and Kamenev in 1924–26, formed a Joint Opposition with Trotsky in 1928 but capitulated the following year. Expelled from the party and then readmitted in

subsequent years, he had been held indirectly responsible for the murder of Kirov in 1934, and at the time Serge wrote was serving a ten-year prison sentence passed in 1935. The preliminary communiqué on the 1936 Moscow trial, in which he, Kamenev and 14 others were condemned to be shot, had been issued by the Soviet news agency TASS on 14 August.

231. The break-in at the rooms in Knudsen's house at Vexhall where the Trotskys were staying was conducted by members of Quisling's Nasjonal Samling Fascist organisation. They removed papers which they claimed to be proof of Trotsky's revolutionary international activities directed at governments friendly to Norway. At the trial of the Fascist burglars, Trotsky was cross-examined by their lawyer, and the Norwegian government used the publicity surrounding his insistence on free commentary about foreign affairs to impose onerous conditions on his residence in the country (transfer to a remote area, censorship of his every communication, a ban on visitors and a day-and-night police guard) which prevented him publicly responding to the accusations of the Moscow trial of 1936.

232. The statement on the 'Trotskyist-Zinovievist-terrorist plot' with the Gestapo, the agenda for the impending Moscow trial: Trotsky heard the TASS statement over the radio at Knudsen's house.

233. The 'J. Fabre' who wrote the article on Spain in the recent issue of *L'Action socialiste révolutionnaire* referred to here does not appear in other Trotskyist sources of the time, and is possibly a pseudonym for some other Belgian militant.

234. In 1930 Valentin Oldberg, a Russian of Menshevik background, had posed as a Trotskyist and tried to become Trotsky's secretary at Prinkipo. He aroused suspicion in the German Opposition and was sent packing. He turned up in the Moscow trial of 1936 as a defendant, 'confessing' his role as an intermediary between Trotsky and the Nazis in organising terrorist acts, and was condemned to death.

235. Trotsky's *Revolution Betrayed* was sent to the publishers before the announcement of the show trials in Moscow. It therefore contains only a few lines noting the trial, in an addendum to its introduction.

236. The letter is written in French (slightly incorrect) by Trotsky because each communication from him outside the Norwegian government's internment at Hurum had to be read by a censor.

237. Punterwald was the only visitor Trotsky was allowed to have, and his signature was placed on all outgoing correspondence (as in this case).

238. Owing to the Norwegian government's restrictions on Trotsky's contact with the media, with the censor confiscating his writings, the burden of conducting a propaganda defence against the trial accusations fell upon his son Lev Lvovich Sedov (who produced the *Livre rouge sur le procès de Moscou*, 1936; first published in part in Russian in

Bulletin of the Opposition, no. 52/53, October 1936; published in English as *The Red Book on the Moscow Trials*: documents collected and edited by Leon Sedov [London: New Park Publications, 1980]), upon Serge himself, and upon other sympathisers abroad.

239. The long interval between this letter and its predecessor of September 1936 is due to Trotsky's continuing internment at Hurum and his migration with Natalia in December to a new political asylum in Mexico. The voyage there, on a petrol tanker, took over three weeks and the Trotskys entered Mexico on 9 January 1937.

240. *De Lenine à Staline* (from Lenin to Stalin) was brought out in January 1937 as a special number of the Paris magazine *Le Crapouillot*. Serge wrote it in a month, sending 30 pages of copy every two days to the publisher. The editor, Jean Galtier-Boissière, pointing out that Serge was also working on *Destin d'une révolution* on alternate days, remarks that 'Never had I had dealings with a collaborator so punctual and so masterly with the pen. He kept his promises exactly and the number appeared at the prescribed time [...] I have never known a writer so well organised. *De Lenine à Staline* exploded in Paris like a bomb' (*Memoires d'un Parisien*, Paris, 1961, p. 327).

241. The revised title for the book previously referred to as *Défense de l'URSS*, and published by Grasset in Paris.

242. In the actual title of the committee, the task of 'Investigation into the Moscow Trial' came before 'the Defence of Freedom of Opinion in the Revolution'. Its members included André Breton, Dommanget, Emery, Galtier-Boissière, Daniel Guerin, Martinet, Monatte, Magdeleine Paz, the journalist Georges Pioch, the writer Henry Poulaille, Rosmer, Wullens and Serge himself.

243. The supporters of Serge on Spanish and POUM questions were Vereeken of the Belgian PSR and Henryk Sneevliet of the Revolutionary Socialist Workers' Party of Holland (RSAP). The 'many other comrades' who opposed them were the other parties and groupings of the Fourth International movement, including the International Secretariat. Trotsky had a brief period of conciliation towards the POUM in August 1936, expressed in his letter of 19 August to Serge (no. 29) and in a letter to Jean Rous in Barcelona two days previously, hoping for 'a sincere and lasting rapprochement' with Nin and other POUM leaders and a move 'to improve relations with the syndicalists: Leon Trotsky *The Spanish Revolution (1931–39)* (New York; Pathfinder Press, 1973), p. 240. This letter to Rous remained without influence as it was intercepted by the Italian Fascist secret service (and was only published from their archives in 1970). From 1937 onwards Trotsky encouraged the anti-POUM majority of his followers. The issues of disagreement in the International were (1) POUM's acceptance of the Popular Front electoral programme with the 'bourgeois' Republicans

in January 1936; (2) the entry of the party into the Catalan government (Generalitat) in September 1936, along with the CNT, the united Socialist-Communist Catalan Party (the PSUC), and the petty-bourgeois Esquerre Republicaña and Unio de Rabassaires; (3) later, the conduct of the POUM in the Barcelona 'May Days' rising of 1937, when the Trotskyists accused it of failing to take power and capitulating to the passive CNT.

244. N.I. Yezhov, People's Commissar of the Interior: he disappeared in the purge of 1938.

245. Sadoul had been sent to Russia during the First World War as a military attaché reporting to the French government, and continued to inform it regularly on Russian matters till January 1919. Having crossed over to the Bolsheviks, he was condemned to death (in November 1919) in absentia by a French tribunal. His final letter to the French Minister who was his overseer was in defence of the Russian Bolsheviks, and he became part of the French Communist group in Moscow.

246. Sadoul returned to France in 1924 and was acquitted after a new trial.

247. Jacques Duclos, a leading Communist deputy and Politburo member who became Thorez's adjutant (See no. 249) in the leadership after 1931. Regarded by some observers as being specially in the confidence of Moscow, he continued his career as a prominent CP parliamentary leader after the Second World War.

248. Paul Vaillant-Couturier, a founding CP member in 1920, soon became a member of the Central Committee and the editor of *L'Humanité*. He was one of the party's most prominent orators and journalists.

249. Maurice Thorez, a faithful follower of the Comintern line who had been a Politburo member of the CP since 1925 and became its General Secretary from 1930 to 1963. The party built up a legend around Thorez as the faithful *fils du peuple* from solid working-class stock. At the end of the Second World War he returned from the USSR, where he had spent the war years, and became a minister in the first De Gaulle government.

250. Rivera was Trotsky's host in Mexico and at that time sympathetic to his politics, having broken with the Mexican CP in 1927 over the expulsion of the Left Opposition in Russia. He was to have a bitter political split with Trotsky and the Fourth International in 1939.

251. Pamphlet on the Moscow trial, published by Cahiers Spartacus in Paris.

252. Trotsky's *Les Crimes de Staline*, dealing with the Moscow trial and published by Grasset in Paris during 1937.

253. Serge's belief that there was a serious tendency in the Fourth International towards splitting the POUM and founding a new party was exaggerated. The IS's main reporter on Spanish affairs, Rous, was opposed to a split, and both his report and the resolution officially carried

at the extended Bureau of the Centre of the FI (attended by Serge in Amsterdam on 11 and 12 January 1937) refrained from suggesting any policy of rupture with the POUM.

254. Gorky's widow, who ran a Political Red Cross in Moscow as a relief centre for political prisoners of whatever persuasion.

255. In central Siberia, just below the Arctic Circle.

256. M.M. (Adolf) Yoffe, an Old Bolshevik and sometime Ambassador to Paris, who during the Opposition struggle of the 1920s was part of a close circle around Trotsky. He commited suicide in November 1926, leaving a long letter to Trotsky justifying his act. See Deutscher, *The Prophet Unarmed*, pp. 380–4.

257. V.V. Kossior, a Trotskyist of long standing, is referred to here in the context of his leadership of the Trotskyist groups in exile in the Soviet Union, particularly those at the Vorkuta camp.

258. In the considerable interval between this letter and its predecessor, public disagreements had taken place between Trotsky and Serge both on Spain and on the responsibilities of the Bolsheviks in the Kronstadt rising of 1921. Trotsky publicly adopted a position opposed to Serge (as well as to his political supporters in Spain, Vereeken and Sneevliet) in the article 'The Insurrection in Barcelona (Some Preliminary Remarks)' dealing with the POUM's allegedly passive role in the 'May events' of 1937 in that city (in his *The Spanish Revolution (1931–39)*, p. 266; the article had first been published in the Paris *La Lutte ouvrière* on 10 June 1937). Internal discussion material in the Trotskyist movement was also aligning Trotsky and the FI majority against Serge and other pro-POUM militants. On Kronstadt, see Chapter 4 below, for Serge's criticisms of Trotsky's observations expressed in September and October 1937. Trotsky's reply to his critics on Kronstadt (including Serge) would be published later in 1938, so that at the time Serge sent these condolences he would have been unaware that polemic was about to intensify.

259. The death of Sedov two days previously in a Paris hospital, following a mysterious illness with an unexplained turn towards fatality. The inquest revealed no definite proof of foul play, but the GPU was certainly informed of Sedov's transfer to the hospital (via their informer in the Opposition, 'Etienne') and was in a position to assassinate him by some chemical means. Serge had worked closely with Sedov in the defence of Trotsky during the Moscow trial, and had a warm and positive appreciation of him.

260. Serge's obituary of Sedov appeared in *La Révolution prolétarienne*, no. 265, 25 February 1938.

261. Martov was the leader of the left tendency of the Mensheviks, who opposed both the White counter-revolution and the revolutionary seizure of power by the Bolsheviks. Trotsky uses his name frequently

in his attacks on the POUM as a synonym for passivity and incapacity for revolutionary deeds.

262. In December 1936 Serge had accepted an invitation from the POUM party organ *La Batalla* to become its collaborator and correspondent, and had, in replying, announced himself to be a member of the POUM thenceforth.

263. In the year between Trotsky's last letter to him and this communication from Serge, there had been a further exchange of polemics on Kronstadt: see Serge's articles in *The New International* quoted in Chapter 4 below, with the reference to Trotsky's 'More on the Repression of Kronstadt', October 1938. Trotsky's repudiation of Serge's support for the pro-POUM minority in the International had moved from purely internal comment to a public show of disdain (see the next note). And, as will be evident from Serge's postscript to this letter, accusations and suspicions about a GPU agent in the Trotskyist ranks, sometimes voiced by Serge and sometimes directed against him by others, were by now threatening any possibility of a balanced and calm discussion of differences.

264. 'Victor Serge and the Fourth International', *Bulletin of the Opposition*, no. 70, October 1938, reprinted in *Writings of Leon Trotsky (1938–39)* (New York: Merit Publishers, 1969), p. 138. Here Trotsky describes Serge's relationship with the FI as that 'of an opponent' whose political position could be defined only as one of 'changeability'. His actions of support for alleged opponents of the International like the POUM and the Spanish anarcho-syndicalists had 'deprived his own 'politics' of any consistency whatsoever and turned it into a series of personal combinations, if not intrigues'. The article concludes: 'neither the Russian section nor the International as a whole takes any responsibility for the politics of Victor Serge'. See Documents, Chapter 4 below.

265. Ignace Reiss (or Poretsky: cover-name 'Ludwig') was a former member of the Polish Communist Party who had moved over to the intelligence service of the Red Army and the foreign service of the GPU. A revolutionary idealist who was shocked by the 1936 Moscow trial, on 17 July 1937 he wrote a letter of resignation from the service of the GPU, sending it (along with the Order of the Red Banner he had been awarded) to the CPSU Central Committee. He then tried to come out of hiding and cross over to the Opposition, using Sneevliet and Serge as intermediaries, but was murdered on 4 September before a rendezvous with them could be kept.

266. Trotsky's 'Intellectual ex-Radicals and World Reaction' appeared in the Belgian Section's *La Lutte ouvrière* for 11 March (given in *Writings of Leon Trotsky (1938–39)*, p. 194). In it Serge is classed among the 'temporary fellow-travellers of Bolshevism' who have broken with revolutionary or radical perspectives. Obviously basing himself on a

misleading account of Serge's article 'Marxism in Our Time' in *Partisan Review,* September 1938 (see Chapter 4 below), Trotsky attributes to Serge the view that 'Bolshevism is passing through a crisis which presages in turn "the crisis of Marxism"'. But, in Trotsky's view, it was rather 'Victor Serge himself [who] is passing through a "crisis", i.e., has become hopelessly confused like thousands of other intellectuals'. See Documents, Chapter 4 below.

267. Serge did not yet know that the Belgian Trotskyist paper would refuse to print his reply to Trotsky. In the end he sent it to the PSOP organ *Juin 36,* which published it on 21 April 1939. Since its contents overlap with Serge's other writings on Trotsky translated for the present collection, it is not printed here. It was republished as an appendix to Rudolf Rocker (ed.), *Les Soviets trahis par les bolcheviks* (Paris, 1973), and was also in the Dreyfus selection of Serge–Trotsky exchanges, *La Lutte contre le Stalinisme,* ed. Michel Dreyfus (Paris: Maspero, 1977) pp. 230–4.

268. Lilia (Eliana) Ginsberg was a Russian political exile in Paris, whose first married name was Estrine and whose second was soon Dallin. In Trotskyist circles, where (after an earlier Menshevik loyalty) she had become a member of Sedov's inner cabinet, she was known personally as Lola; her political pseudonyms were Paulsen and Yakovlev. The Russian group of the Left Opposition in Paris was full of mutual suspicion regarding the identity of a probable Stalinist agent in their midst. Lola Ginsberg was entirely innocent, but she unwittingly protected and lent credibility to the real agent, Etienne, who remained undiscovered until he moved to the United States. Ginsberg (now Dallin) continued a supportive relationship with both the Trotskys after their move to Mexico, but ceased any connection with the Fourth International and militant politics.

269. Elsa (Elisabeth) Reiss or Peretsky was the widow of the murdered Ignace Reiss. She was among those in this small circle who cast suspicion on Serge himself as being a tool of the Stalinist secret police.

270. The party name of Mark Zborowski, who had infiltrated Sedov's entourage on behalf of the GPU since the early 1930s. 'Etienne' remained trusted by the others in the Russian section who suspected one another, and by Trotsky himself. His allegation, made to Serge, that the Russian section had refused to investigate suspicions about Ginsberg, may or may not have been true. Zborowski, a student of anthropology, made an academic career in this discipline which continued even after his unmasking by the United States authorities in 1955.

271. The bitterness of the accusations from the anti-Serge members of the Russian group was already known to Trotsky when he received this letter, including the charge that Serge himself was a GPU dupe or

instrument. According to Pierre Broué, who has worked on the correspondence between Lola Ginsberg and Trotsky, and has also discussed
the matter with both her and Trotsky's old secretary Van Heijenoort,
Trotsky's attitude was that these allegations against Serge were too ill
founded to be voiced openly, but they should not be lost sight of.

272. Boris Nicolaevsky was a much-respected figure among the Russian
emigrants. He had been a leading Menshevik politician but now ran
the Paris branch of the Amsterdam Institute of Social History. He was
a one-time an associate of the Marx-Engels Institute in Moscow, and
the co-author of a scholarly biography of Karl Marx.

273. Trotsky's diagnosis of 'crisis' in Serge is taken from his belief (see note
266) that Serge had written of the 'crisis of Marxism'.

274. The relevant issue of the *Bulletin* was actually no. 77/78 for May–June
1939.

275. Serge had translated Trotsky's pamphlet *Their Morals and Ours* (Paris:
Editions du Sagittaire, 1939), an ethical defence of the practices of civil
war Bolshevism, for the Paris publisher which produced it in March
1939. The *prière d'insérer*, or promotional prospectus, put out by these
publishers for their edition gave a highly misleading summary of
Trotsky's case; for example: 'For Trotsky, deceit and violence, if they
are placed in the service of a justified end, should be employed without
hesitation.' The text of the prospectus is translated as Appendix C to
Leon Trotsky, with John Dewey and George Novack, *Their Morals
and Ours: Marxist vs. Liberal Views on Morality* (New York: Merit
Publishers, 1969; Pathfinder Press, 1973).

276. The accusing article by Trotsky, 'The Moralists and Sycophants against
Marxism', insinuated that either Serge or 'one of his disciples who
imitates both his master's ideas and his style' had written the prospectus,
which was described as 'a little egg' deposited in 'a strange nest', that
is, the pamphlet *Their Morals and Ours* itself. Aside from the prospectus's
alleged authorship, much of 'The Moralists and Sycophants' is devoted
to an attack on Serge both for his criticisms of the Bolshevik record
and for his sympathy with non-Trotskyist Socialists like Pivert (or with
dissident Trotskyists such as Sneevliet).

277. Gerard Rosenthal, a long-time member of the French Left Opposition,
like Pierre Naville a former Surrealist who met Trotsky in Moscow
in 1927; at this time he was Trotsky's lawyer in Paris.

278. While the *Bulletin of the Opposition* did not publish this letter from Serge,
its issue no. 79/80 (August–September 1939) carried a note from
Trotsky ('Another Refutation by Victor Serge', Appendix B, p. 76 in
Their Morals and Ours) accepting Serge's denial of having anything to
do with drafting the prospectus. But Trotsky refused to accept that the
outline of Serge's argument sketched in 'The Moralists and Sycophants'
was at great variance with Serge's own published opinions. Serge's views

as 'developed at the present time [...] tend to subordinate the class struggle of the proletariat to the norms of petty-bourgeois morality'. Indeed there were in Serge no 'definite views, but rather a confused mood of uncertainty, disillusionment, dissatisfaction, and repulsion from Marxism and proletarian revolution', in which Serge had fallen 'under the influence of petty-bourgeois scepticism'. His 'unending refutations' were 'devoid of any political content whatever'. See also this volume pp. 158–9.

Chapter 3: Serge, Trotsky and the Spanish Revolution

1. Richard Greeman, unpublished typescript 'War in Spain', in the possession of the editor of this volume.
2. Literature on the Spanish Civil War is extensive and politically wide-ranging. This overview draws on the best known and the most accessible works: E.H. Carr, *The Comintern and the Spanish Civil War*, ed. Tamara Deutscher (London: Macmillan, 1984), Antony Beevor, *The Spanish Civil War* (London: Orbis, 1982), Franz Borkenau, *The Spanish Cockpit* (London: Pluto Press, 1986), Gerald Brenan, *The Spanish Labyrinth* (CUP, 1990), José Peirats, *Anarchists in the Spanish Revolution* (London: Freedom Press, 1990), Hugh Thomas, *The Spanish Civil War* (London: Eyre and Spottiswoode, 1961). Specific reference to these books is only made where a direct quote is used.
3. Carr, *The Comintern*, p. 1.
4. Carr, *The Comintern*, p. 3.
5. Carr, *The Comintern*, p. 17.
6. David Caute, *The Fellow-Travellers– A Postscript to the Enlightenment* (London: Weidenfeld and Nicolson, 1973), pp. 169–70.
7. Carr, *The Comintern*, p. 25.
8. Isaac Deutscher, *Stalin – A Political Biography* (revised edn., Harmondsworth: Penguin, 1990), p. 415.
9. Deutscher, *Stalin*, p. 416.
10. See Documents in this chapter.
11. See Documents in this chapter.
12. Most liberal histories pay scant attention to the May 1937 events in Barcelona; it has been left to the anarchists and former POUM members such as George Orwell to flesh out the details. But see more particularly Victor Alba's work on the POUM *Spanish Marxism v. Soviet Communism – A History of the POUM*, published in English with Stephen Schwartz, (New Brunswick, NJ: Transaction Books, 1988) and the work of Augustin Souchy *et al.*, *The May Days, Barcelona 1937*, ed. V. Richards (London: Freedom Press, 1987)
13. See Nin-Trotsky correspondence in Trotsky, *The Spanish Revolution 1931–1939* (New York: Pathfinder 1973), Appendix, pp. 367–400.

14. Greeman, 'War in Spain'.
15. Greeman, 'War in Spain'.
16. Trotsky to Serge, 5 June 1936 (Letter 14 in Chapter 2).
17. Serge to Trotsky, 27 July 1936 (Letter 24 in Chapter 2).
18. Serge to Trotsky, 10 August 1936 (Letter 26 in Chapter 2).
19. Trotsky to Serge, 19 August 1936 (Letter 29 in Chapter 2).
20. Further evidence of the direction of Trotsky's thoughts at this time can be gained from the letter sent to his representative in Barcelona, Jean Rous, dated 16 August 1936, suggesting that 'As for Nin, Andrade and the others [of the POUM], it would be criminal to let ourselves be guided now in this great struggle by memories of the preceding period.' This letter, however, appears never to have arrived at its destination. It was seemingly intercepted by the Italian secret service and only came to light in 1970, when its text was published in the French paper *Le Monde*. The full text is available in Trotsky, *The Spanish Revolution*. See also Greeman, 'War in Spain'.
21. Serge to Trotsky, 10 January 1937 (Letter 34 in Chapter 2).
22. George Vereeken, *The GPU in the Trotskyist Movement* (London: New Park Publications, 1976); first published as *La Guepou dans le mouvement trotskyiste* [Paris, La Pensées Universelle]), p. 175.
23. See Documents in Chapter 4 below.
24. See Documents in this chapter.
25. Serge to Trotsky, 20 March 1937 (Letter 36 in Chapter 2).
26. See prefatory note and Letter 35, Trotsky to Serge, 5 March 1937 in Chapter 2 above.
27. Interview with Havas, from Trotsky, *The Spanish Revolution*, pp. 242–3.
28. 'A Strategy for Victory', from Trotsky, *The Spanish Revolution*, p. 245.
29. Letter to the editorial board of *La Lutte ouvrière*, from Trotsky, *The Spanish Revolution*, p. 250.
30. Burnett Bolloten, 'Barcelona: the May Events', in Souchy *et al.*, *The May Days, Barcelona 1937*; first published in B. Bolloten, *The Spanish Revolution* (University of North Carolina Press, 1979), p. 67.
31. Greeman, 'War in Spain'.
32. Greeman, 'War in Spain'.
33. Carr, *The Comintern and the Spanish Civil War*, p. 43.
34. Greeman, 'War in Spain'.
35. See Leon Trotsky on Makhno and Kronstadt in the Documents, Chapter 4 below.
36. See Documents, Chapter 4 below.
37. Serge to Trotsky, 18 February 1938 (Letter 37 in Chapter 2).
38. Trotsky to Serge, 15 April 1938 (Letter 38 in Chapter 2).
39. See Weissman, Introduction to Chapter 4 and Documents, Chapter 4.
40. Trotsky to Serge, 19 August 1936 (Letter 29 in Chapter 2).

41. First published as 'Una Carta del Gran Revolucionario Ruso Victor Serge', in *La Batalla*, Madrid, 30 August 1936; later as 'Adhesion Cordial y Solidaridad Total: un Hermoso Mesaje de Victor Serge al proletariado espanol' in *POUM*, Barcelona, 9 October 1936. Translated from Serge's French copy held by his son Vlady. The final paragraph appears in the French but not in the Spanish text. Published here in English for the first time in translation by Peter Sedgwick.

42. The town in Spanish North Africa which the rebels used as their base and from which the rebellion was signalled in July 1936.

43. Alcala Zomora, leader of the Progressive Party, who became Prime Minister of the first Spanish Republic in 1931, and President of the Republic from June 1931 to May 1936.

44. This is Serge's pamphlet *Lenine 1917: La Pensée et l'Action de Lenine depuis son Départ de Suisse jusqu'a la Prise du Pouvoir* (Paris: Librairie du Travail, 1925).

45. The system of workers' control put into place following the almost total collapse of the Republican government on the rebellion of July 1936.

46. Juan Andrade was a Left Oppositionist member of the Spanish Communist Party who joined the POUM when it was formed by Nin. Julian Gorkin was one of the leaders of the POUM, along with Nin. He survived the debacle at the end of the civil war and went into exile in Mexico. He collaborated with Serge on various writing projects when Serge himself found refuge in Mexico City in the 1940s.

47. First published as 'Una Carta de Victor Serge. Muchas Combatientes de Octobre Estacion Rapidamente entre Nosotros', in *La Batalla*, 5 October 1936. Published here in English for the first time in translation by Peter Sedgwick.

48. From *La Révolution prolétarienne*, no. 236, 10 December 1936. Published here in English for the first time in translation by Peter Sedgwick.

49. Edgar André, an anarchist militant killed in the early days of the civil war.

50. G.K. Ordjionikidze (1886–1937), a Bolshevik of long standing who accommodated himself to the Stalinist faction during the political struggles of the 1920s, was placed in charge of industry by Stalin. His death in 1937 was shrouded in mystery; it is likely he was poisoned, possibly on the orders of Stalin.

51. Nikolai Muralov (1877–1937) was a Red Army General, shot in 1937.

52. G.L. Piatakov was a follower of Trotsky who capitulated to Stalin following the defeat of the Opposition in 1927. He was eventually arrested and disappeared.

53. Letter to POUM Executive Committee, in *La Batalla*, January 1937. Published here in English for the first time in translation by Peter Sedgwick.

54. Ivan Smirnov (1881–1936), a civil war veteran, became a member of the Left Opposition and was expelled from the party in 1927. He capitulated and was reinstated, but was arrested again in 1933 and was shot following the first Moscow trial in 1936.
55. From *Les Humbles*, Cahiers no. 4-5, 2nd series, April-May 1937. Published here in English for the first time in translation by Peter Sedgwick.
56. Quiepo de Lleano, Spanish General who, along with Franco and Mola, engineered the anti-Republican coup of July 1936.
57. This refers to Pablo Yague, a Spanish CP member responsible for food supply in the Madrid Defence Junta. He was badly wounded in December 1936 by CNT militants who stopped his car at a checkpoint.
58. Juan Comorera, the PSUC's Secretary-General and a member of the Generalitat, the Catalan government.
59. Buenaventura Durruti, the most revered Spanish anarchist of the time; a syndicatist veteran and political terrorist, with a heroic record as the organiser of working-class resistance in Barcelona against the Franco coup and then as a militia leader. Whether or not his death was due to a bullet fired by undisciplined anarchists is open to discussion, but Serge's hint that Stalinists may have been responsible is just vague accusation.
60. Berneri was a philosophy professor and a long-standing anarchist who after Mussolini's victory left his native Italy for exile in Germany and France. He went to Spain to fight in the Ascaso column, carrying on propaganda against collaboration with the Popular Front government in his jounal *Guerra di Classe*, published in Barcelona.
61. From Trotsky, *The Spanish Revolution,* pp. 267–8.
62. From *La Révolution prolétarienne*, no. 253, 25 August. 1937. Published here in English for the first time in translation by Peter Sedgwick.
63. From Trotsky, *The Spanish Revolution*, pp. 302–3.
64. From Trotsky, *The Spanish Revolution*, pp. 317–18.

Chapter 4: Kronstadt and the Fourth International

1. The phrase is Vlady's (Serge's son).
2. Private conversation with Vlady outside Trotsky's compound in Coyoacan, 20 August 1990, on the fiftieth anniversary of the death of Trotsky.
3. Victor Serge, 'Intransigence, Intolerance, Conflicts', 2 October 1944, *Carnets*, transl. John Manson (Arles: Actes Sud, 1985), p. 145.
4. Serge, 'Intransigence, Intolerance, Conflicts', *Carnets*, p. 146.
5. Serge, 'Intransigence, Intolerance, Conflicts', *Carnets*, p. 146.
6. A comrade with whom Serge shared his final exile in Mexico.
7. Serge to Kostiuk, 22 June 1947.

8. Serge, 'Intransigence, Intolerance, Conflicts', *Carnets*, p. 146.

9. Serge, 'My Break with Trotsky,' *Carnets*, pp. 44–7.

10. Serge, 'My Break with Trotsky,' *Carnets*, pp. 44–7.

11. Serge, 'My Break with Trotsky,' *Carnets*, pp. 44–7.

12. Serge, *Memoirs of a Revolutionary,* transl. Peter Sedgwick (Oxford University Press, 1963), p. 348.

13. But Serge's enthusiasm was less than Trotsky's in 1936, when Trotsky wrote to Serge in envy that Serge would be off to Paris where the 'birth-pangs of the French Revolution' had begun with a massive strike. Trotsky to Serge (in Russian), 9 June 1936. Serge replied with a cautionary note: 'The wonderful strikes in France and here show clearly that the working class is recovering after its phase of depression and extreme fatigue, and is entering a new period of struggle. In such a situation one may hope for anything, so long as one does not expect an immediate all-round upsurge.' Serge to Trotsky (in Russian), Brussels, 16 June 1936. (Chapter 2 above, Letters 17 and 18).

14. Serge to Lev Lyovich Sedov (in Russian), 21 January 1937: Boris Nicolaevsky Collection, Hoover Archive, Stanford University.

15. Leon Trotsky, 'The Hue and Cry over Kronstadt', 15 January 1938, *The New International*, April 1938.

16. Victor Serge, 'A Letter and Some Notes', *The New International*, February 1939, p. 53.

17. Victor Serge, 'Reply to Ciliga', *The New International*, February 1939.

18. *Bulletin of the Opposition,* no. 73, January 1939, p. 16.

19. Victor Serge, 'Marxism in Our Time', *Partisan Review*, vol. V, no. 3, August–September 1939, pp. 26–32.

20. Leon Trotsky, 'Intellectual ex-Radicals and World Reaction', 17 February 1939, published in *Writings (1938–1939)* (New York: Merit Publishers, 1969), pp. 194–6.

21. Serge to Trotsky (in Russian), Paris, 18 March 1939 (Chapter 2 above, Letter 39).

22. For more on the suspicions planted within the Left Opposition as to who was the NKVD agent, see S.C. Weissman, 'Victor Serge: Political, Social & Literary Critic of the USSR, 1919–1947', PhD thesis, University of Glasgow 1991 (UMI Dissertation Information Service, Michigan: Ann Arbor, 1991) pp. 76–9.

23. Trotsky, *Writings, Supplement (1934–1940)* (New York: Pathfinder, 1979) p. 872.

24. Lev Lyovich Sedov to his mother, Natalia Sedova, 16 April 1936. Having vented his own frustration at his father's inconsistent meddling with the French Trotskyists, Sedov never sent this letter, and remained publicly his father's most ardent supporter. The letter was found in the Boris Nicolaevsky Collection, Hoover Archive, Stanford University, series 231. It was also cited by Dale Reed and Michael Jakobson in 'Trotsky

Papers at the Hoover Institution: One Chapter of an Archival Mystery Story,' *American Historical Review*, vol. 92, no 2, April 1987, p. 366.

25. Leon Trotsky, *Their Morals and Ours: Marxist vs. Liberal Views on Morality*, with John Dewey and George Novack (New York: Merit Publishers, 1969) p. 37.

26. *Prière d'insérer*, Trotsky, *Their Morals and Ours* (Paris: Editions du Sagittaire, 1939); published in English in Trotsky *et al.*, *Their Morals and Ours*, Appendix C.

27. Trotsky, 'The Moralists and Sycophants against Marxism' in Trotsky *et al.*, *Their Morals and Ours*, p. 41.

28. In a particularly vicious attack on Serge, Trotsky replied to Serge's letter criticising the creation of the Fourth International: 'When the Fourth International becomes "worthy of the name" in the eyes of Messrs. Litératteurs (sic), dilettantes, and Sceptics, then it will not be difficult to adhere to it. A Victor Serge (this one, or another) will then write a book in which he will prove (with lyricism and with tears!) that the best, the most heroic period of the Fourth International was the time, when bereft of forces, it waged a struggle against innumerable enemies, including petty-bourgeois sceptics.': Leon Trotsky, '"Trotskyism" and the PSOP', *Writings (1938–39)* p. 134.

29. Trotsky, *Writings (1938–39)*, p. 45.

30. Trotsky, *Writings (1938–39)*, p. 50.

31. Serge, *Memoirs*, p. 349.

32. American radical journalist and critic, formerly close to Trotsky but later a pacifist, then an independent liberal. In his role as editor of *Partisan Review*, and together with his wife Nancy, he supported Serge by offering him material help. The MacDonalds were instrumental in obtaining Serge's visa for Mexico in 1941.

33. Serge to Dwight MacDonald, 22 October 1939: MacDonald Papers, Yale University archive.

34. Angelica Balabanova had been the first Secretary of the Comintern Executive. After her expulsion from the Third International, she lived in various European countries. By the time Serge wrote here, she was resident in the US, where she lived until her death in 1965.

35. Serge to Angelica Balabanova, 23 October 1941: Serge Archive, Mexico.

36. Trotsky, *Bulletin of the Opposition* no. 79–80, August–September 1939, p. 31. The English translation is published as Appendix B in Trotsky *et al.*, *Their Morals and Ours*

37. Trotsky, *Bulletin of the Opposition,* no. 79–80, August–September,1939, p. 31, 'esli ne on lichno, to kto-libo iz ego uchenikov ili edino-muishlennikov. Predpolozhenie o tom, chto prospekt napisan Viktorem Serzhem, vozniklo u raznuikh tovarishchei, nezavisimo drug ot druga.

I ne mudreno: prospekt predstavlyaet prostoe rezyume noveishikh propovedei Viktora Serzha!'

38. Pierre Frank, Trotskyist and founder of the French Section; a member of the Interational Secretariat. During the period 1922–3, he acted as Trotsky's secretary.

39. Published as 'Victor Serge's Crisis' in *Writings, Supplement (1934–1940)*, p. 836 (Chapter 2 above, Letter 40).

40. Victor Serge, 'Secrecy and Revolution – A Reply to Trotsky', published posthumously by Peter Sedgwick to set the record straight in *Peace News*, London, 27 December 1963, p. 5.

41. Private conversation, Mexico City, January 1986.

42. Private conversation, Los Angeles, October 1989.

43. Serge, 'My Break with Trotsky', *Carnets*, pp. 44–7.

44. Victor Serge, 'The Old Man', 1 August 1942, written in Mexico, 'to the memory of Leon Davidovich Trotsky' and published in Victor Serge and Natalia Sedova, *The Life and Death of Leon Trotsky*, transl. Arnold J. Pomerans (New York: Basic Books, 1975), p. 4.

45. Serge, 'Secrecy and Revolution — A Reply to Trotsky'.

46. Serge and Sedova, *The Life and Death of Leon Trotsky*, pp. 2–5.

47. Serge, *Memoirs*, pp. 348, 350.

48. From *Socialist Appeal*, 24 August 1937.

49. Nestor Makhno, anarchist schoolmaster and ex-convict, who formed the 'Ukrainian Army of Insurgent Peasants' and fought alternately against the Whites and the Reds during the civil war.

50. White Russian general during the civil war, operating largely from a base in the Caucasus.

51. From *La Révolution prolétarienne*, Paris, no. 254, 10 September 1937, pp. 702–3. Published here in English for the first time in translation by Peter Sedgwick.

52. Serge is here referring to Wendelin Thomas. See previous document.

53. The extract quoted here is the same as in the previous document from *Socialist Appeal* and would have been picked up by Serge from the Russian-language *Bulletin of the Opposition*.

54. Ida Mett, anarchist journalist who added her own comments to the discussion on Kronstadt.

55. Kalinin, President of the Soviet Republic, whose ill-judged attempts at negotiation with the Kronstadt sailors during the crisis of 1921 more than likely exacerbated the situation.

56. Emma Goldman (1869–1940), an anarchist of Russian birth who lived in the US from the age of 17 until her deportation to Russia in 1919. She was in Petrograd during the period of the Kronstadt revolt and had supported the Bolsheviks up until the time of the Kronstadt affair. Alexander Berkman (1870–1936), an anarchist who was also resident in the US, had spent 14 years in prison following an attempt on the

life of Henry Clay Frick during the homestead strike of 1892. Imprisoned again in 1917 for his anti-war stance, Berkman was deported with Goldman in 1919 and was in Petrograd with her at the time of the Kronstadt rising.

57. Klimert Voroshilov (1881–1969), Red Army general and military tactician. Member of the Politburo, the CPSU, and later the People's Commissar for Defence, he survived Stalin's purges. Pavel Dibenko (1889–1939), an old Bolshevik and Red Army leader, was purged by Stalin in 1938, along with Mikhail Tukhachevsky (1893–1937)

58. From *La Révolution prolétarienne*, Paris, no. 257, 25 October 1937, pp. 749–50. Published here in English for the first time in translation by Peter Sedgewick.

59. *La Lutte ouvrière* was the newspaper of the POI, the French Section of the Fourth International.

60. Leonid Serebryakov, a long-standing revolutionary organiser of the Soviet railway union, became a prominent figure in the Opposition. He was purged and shot in 1937.

61. From *The New International*, April 1938, pp. 105–6.

62. From *The New International*, July 1938, pp. 211–12.

63. John G. Wright, a Trotskyist who entered the discussion on Kronstadt with an article in *The New International* in April 1938.

64. A Marxist historian who had some contact with Lenin.

65. From *The New International*, July 1938, pp. 238–9

66. First published in France as *Au Pays du grand mensonge*, in 1938, then in England as *The Russian Enigma* (London: Routledge and Kegan Paul, 1940).

67. From 'A Letter and Some Notes' in *The New International*, February 1939, pp. 53–4.

68. From *Partisan Review*, vol. 5, no. 3, 1938, pp. 26–32.

69. Herman Gorter (1864–1927), a member of the Dutch Socialist Party, opposed the war in 1914. He helped found the Dutch CP in 1918 and the German CP in 1920.

70. From *Writings (1938–39)*, p. 142.

71. From *Socialist Appeal*, 17 March 1939, p. 145.

72. It is evident from the tone of Trotsky's attack here that it is unlikely he ever read or even saw Serge's article 'Marxism in Our Time' in *Partisan Review*. It is probable that he was informed of its content by the same corrupted channels of information that would later create the controversy over the publicity insertion in the original French edition of *Their Morals and Ours* (1939).

73. From 'The Moralists and Sycophants against Marxism' in *The New International*, August 1939, p. 231. Republished in Trotsky *et al.*, *Their Morals and Ours*.

74. Unpublished letter in the Serge Archive, Mexico. Published here in English for the first time in translation by Peter Sedgwick.

75. Published in Paris by Georges Valois, 1932.

76. Serge is here referring to his book *Portrait de Staline* (Paris: Grasset, 1940).

77. From *Carnets* (Paris: Juillard, 1961; and Arles: Actes Sud, 1985). Published here in English for the first time in translation by Peter Sedgwick.

Chapter 5: Victor Serge and the Left Opposition

1. Victor Serge, *Memoirs of a Revolutionary*, transl. Peter Sedgwick (Oxford University Press, 1963), p. 190.

2. A good history of this still needs to be written. The best work so far is Fernando Claudin, *La Crisis del movimiento comunista* (Paris: Ruedo Iberico, 1970) transl. Brian Pearce as *The Communist Movement: From Comintern to Cominform* (Harmondsworth: Penguin, 1975), part 1.

3. Serge, *Memoirs*, p. 191.

4. The classic account of these Oppositions is the second volume of Isaac Deutscher's biography of Trotsky: *The Prophet Unarmed, Trotsky: 1921–1929* (Oxford University Press, 1959).

5. Serge, *Memoirs*, p. 220.

6. For the best recent analysis of how that path was actually taken and why, see Michal Reiman, *The Birth of Stalinism*, transl. George Saunders (Indiana University Press, 1987). Reiman's account of the paranoid improvisation that hurtled the Stalinists towards civil war strikingly confirms the accuracy of much of the Opposition's contentions at the time.

7. On the different waves of capitulation by Oppositionists to Stalin see Deutscher, *The Prophet Unarmed*.

8. Victor Serge, *From Lenin to Stalin*, transl. R. Manheim (New York: Anchor Foundation, 1973) pp. 57–8.

9. Serge, *From Lenin to Stalin*, pp. 115–6.

10. Serge, *From Lenin to Stalin*, p. 58.

11. Letter sent by Serge on 1 February 1933 to friends in Paris (Magdeleine and Maurice Paz, Clara and Jacques Menail, and Marcel Martinet) shortly before his arrest by the GPU in Leningrad. The letter arrived in Paris through intermediaries. The translation given here is from the text Serge had published as part of his pamphlet *Seize Fusillés à Moscou* (Paris: Cahiers Spartacus, no 1, new series 1936; reprinted as no. 51, series 8, 1972; both ed. René Lefeuvre).

12. See Claudin, *The Communist Movement*, on the twin reformisms of Social Democratic and Communist parties in the Popular Front.

13. Serge described his difficulties in publishing anything in the major left-wing press at the time in his *Memoirs*, p. 328. The collusion between Socialists and Communists at the time of maximal Stalinist repression

makes for ironic reading today when there is such smugness among the former at the demise of their rivals.

14. Trotsky telegraphed Serge almost immediately he heard of his release and initiated a lengthy correspondence, some of which is published in Chapter 2. See also the collection of letters edited by Michel Dreyfus: *Victor Serge, Leon Trotsky – La Lutte contre le Stalinisme, correspondance inédits, articles* (Paris: Maspero, 1977).

15. Victor Serge, *Conquered City* transl. R. Greeman (London: Writers and Readers, 1978), *Year One of the Russian Revolution,* transl. and ed. Peter Sedgwick (London: Allen Lane, 1972), and many shorter pieces.

16. Serge, *Memoirs*, pp. 190–1.

17. See, for example, the brilliant portrait of Stalin as a prisoner of fear and rancour in Serge, *From Lenin to Stalin*, pp. 100–8; there is a parallel fictional version in *L'Affaire Toulaev* (Paris: Seuil, 1948; transl. Willard Trask *The Case of Comrade Tulayev* [Harmondsworth: Penguin, 1968]).

18. Compare, for example, the depth and insight of *The Case of Comrade Tulayev* with Arthur Koestler's much more superficial and grossly overrated *Darkness at Noon*, transl. Daphne Hardy (Harmondsworth: Penguin, 1964).

19. Taylorism: A system of industrial shop-floor management that in this context tied wages to piece-rates, so-called after its originator, an American engineer, F.W. Taylor (1865–1915). For a discussion of this principle in relation to the Soviet economy at the time referred to here, see Samuel Farber, *Before Stalinism – The Rise and Fall of Soviet Democracy* (Polity Press, 1990, pp. 75, 76 and 79) and E.H. Carter, *Bolshevik Review,* vol. II, no. xvi (1952) p. 111.

20. *The New International,* July 1938 (see Chapter 4 above, Documents). All of these issues have recently been the object of a lucid and sympathetic analysis by Samuel Farber in his *Before Stalinism: The Rise and Fall of Soviet Democracy* (Cambridge: Polity Press, 1990). Farber's views are very much in line with those of Serge on all of these issues. See also the work of Carmen Sirianni, *Worker's Control and Socialist Democracy – The Soviet Experience* (London: Verso, 1982).

21. *The New International,* July 1938, p. 211.

22. *The New International,* July 1938.

23. Serge, *Memoirs*, p. 350.

24. The dispute over the *prière d'insérer* to *Their Morals and Ours* is discussed in earlier chapters, together with Trotsky's addendum to *Their Morals and Ours*, 'The Moralists and Sycophants against Marxism'. Serge had most ironically just written an eloquent article restating its absolute centrality. 'Marxism in Our Time', a brilliant piece, still worth reading today, unfortunately lies beyond the scope of this section. It was published in the American journal, *Partisan Review*, in 1938. See also this volume, Chapter 2, Letter 41, and Chapter 4.

25. Victor Serge and Natalia Sedova, *The Life and Death of Leon Trotsky*, transl. Arnold J. Pomerans (New York: Basic Books, 1975); first published as *Vie et Mort de Leon Trotsky* (Paris: Maspero, 1973) in 2 volumes.

26. *The New International*, February 1939, p. 54.

27. From *From Lenin to Stalin*, pp. 108–110.

28. From *Destiny of a Revolution*, ch. 5.

29. From *La Révolution prolétarienne*, no. 265, 21 February 1938. Translated here by Ian Birchall.

30. From 'In Memory: LD Trotsky', in *Partisan Review*, vol. 9, no. 5, 1940, pp. 388–91.

31. 'Narodnya Volya' or 'People's Will Party' was formed from a split in the Land and Liberty secret society and advocated terrorism as a means of bringing about social change in Russia. This organisation was effectively smashed in 1881 following its assassination of Tsar Alexander II.

32. This is Serge's spelling of the name Chernichevsky. His book *What Is To Be Done* inspired Lenin in his youth to such an extent that he used the same title for his own book on pre-revolutionary Russia.

33. Unpublished manuscript by Serge from the Serge Archive, Mexico. Undated. Published here in English for the first time in translation by Peter Sedgwick.

34. From the *Carnets*. Published here in English for the first time in translation by Peter Sedgwick.

35. Serge is here referring to P. Chevalier, J. Gorkin, M. Pivert and V. Serge, *Los Problemas del socialismo en nuestro tiempo* (Mexico City: Ediciones Ibero-Americans, 1944), pp. 9–45.

36. This is Vsevolod Volkov (Seva), Trotsky's grandson and the son of Platon Volkov and Trotsky's daughter, Zinadia. Platon Volkov disappeared in the Soviet Union and Zinadia was allowed abroad with her son but committed suicide in Berlin in 1933. Thereafter Seva was brought up by Trotsky's son Lyova and his companion Jeannine. After Lyova's death Trotsky invited Seva and Jeannine to Mexico. Jeannine's reluctance to countenance the move resulted in legal moves by the Trotskys to gain custody of the boy. See Deutscher, *The Prophet Outcast*, pp. 403–5. Volkov still lives in Mexico.

37. David Alfaro Siqueiros, one of Mexico's great painters, who attempted an attack on Trotsky's life in May 1940. He went into hiding and eventually returned to Mexico after Trotsky's death (hence the later reference to Natalia's futile efforts to bring him to justice).

Select Bibliography

Primary Sources

Note: Works by Serge and Trotsky used for this volume are too numerous to list here – separate volumes only are included, in chronological order of edition used.

Archives
Serge Papers, Musée Sociale, Paris.
Jean Rière Papers, Paris.
Serge Archive, Mexico City.
Trotsky Archive, Houghton Library, Harvard University.
Boris Nicolaevsky Collection, Hoover Archive, Stanford University.

Theses
Greeman, R., 'Victor Serge: The Making of a Novelist 1890–1928' (PhD, Columbia University, 1968).
Marshall, W., 'Ideology and Literary Expression in the Works of Victor Serge' (DPhil, Oxford, 1984).
Weissman, S.C., 'Victor Serge: Political, Social & Literary Critic of the USSR, 1919–1947; The Reflections and Activities of a Belgo-Russian Revolutionary Caught in the Orbit of Soviet Political History' (PhD, University of Glasgow, 1991).

Works by Serge
(1937) *Destiny of a Revolution*, transl. M. Shachtman (London: National Book Association, Hutchinson).
(1940) *Portrait de Staline* (Paris: Grasset).
(1944) *Los Problemas del socialismo en nuestro tiempo*, written with P. Chevalier, J. Gorkin. M. Pivert (Mexico City: Ediciones Ibero-Americanas).
(1961) *Carnets* (Paris: Juillard; and Arles: Actes Sud, 1985).
(1963) *Memoirs of a Revolutionary*, transl. P. Sedgwick (Oxford University Press).
(1968) *The Case of Comrade Tulayev*, transl. W. Trask (Harmondsworth: Penguin).
(1972) *Year One of the Russian Revolution*, transl. and ed. P. Sedgwick (London: Allen Lane).
(1973) *From Lenin to Stalin*, transl. R. Manheim (New York: Anchor Foundation).

(1975) *The Life and Death of Leon Trotsky*, written with Natalia Sedova, transl. A.J. Pomerans (New York: Basic Books).
(1977) *Birth of Our Power*, transl. R. Greeman (London: Writers and Readers).
(1978) *Conquered City*, transl. R. Greeman (London: Writers and Readers).
(1982) *Midnight in the Century*, transl. R. Greeman (London: Writers and Readers).
(1985) *Carnets* (Arles: Actes Sud).

Works by Trotsky:
(1930) *My Life* (Paris: Rieder).
(1936) 'La Nouvelle constitution et la repression en URSS', in *Service d'information et de presse* (Paris: Ligue communiste internationaliste).
(1937 *Les Crimes de Staline* (Paris: Grasset).
(1937) *The Revolution Betrayed* (Paris: Grasset).
(1958) *Diary in Exile* (Cambridge Mass.: Harvard University Press, 1976)
(1967) *Leon Trotsky: Le Mouvement communiste en France (1919–39)*, ed. P. Broue, (Paris).
(1969) *Their Morals and Ours: Marxist vs. Liberal Views on Morality*, with J. Dewey and G. Novack (New York: Merit Publishers, and Pathfinder Press, 1973 and 1986).
(1969) *Writings of Leon Trotsky (1938–1939)* (New York: Merit, and Pathfinder, 1974).
(1973) *The Spanish Revolution (1931–1939)* (New York: Pathfinder)
(1977) *The History of the Russian Revolution* (London: Pluto Press).
(1979) *Leon Trotsky on France*, ed. D. Salner (New York: Monad).
(1979) *Writings of Leon Trotsky: Supplement (1934–1940)*
(New York: Pathfinder).
(1981) *Cahiers Leon Trotsky* (Grenoble).

Journals, newspapers, with contributions by Serge or Trotsky or referred to in the text and notes
L'Action socialiste révolutionnaire
Ahora
La Batalla
Bulletin communiste
Bulletin of the Opposition (Byulleten' Oppozitsii)
Clarté
Clé
Contre le courant
Le Crapouillot
L'Ecole emancipée
Esprit
Les Feuillets bleus
La Flêche

Golos Truda
La Humanidad
L'Humanité
Les Humbles
L'Internationale
Journal de Barcelone
Juin 36
La Lutte ouvrière
Mundo Obrero
The New International
Partisan Review
Peace News
POUM
Pravda
La Révolution prolétarienne
Socialist Appeal
Socialistichesky Vestnik
Solidaridad Obrera
Treball
Universal
La Verité
La Vie ouvrière
Voix du peuple

Secondary Sources

Note: Not an exhaustive list but those works used extensively or directly
referred to in the text and notes.

Alba, V. and Schwartz, S. (1988) *Spanish Marxism v. Soviet
Communism – A History of the POUM* (New Brunswick, NJ: Transaction
Books).
Avrich, P. (1970) *Kronstadt 1921* (Princeton University Press).
Beevor, A. (1982) *The Spanish Civil War* (London: Orbis).
F. Borkenau (1962) *World Communism – A History of the Communist Interna-
tional* (Ann Arbor: University of Michigan Press).
—— (1986) *The Spanish Cockpit* (London: Pluto Press).
Braunthal, J. (1967) *History of the International* (London: Nelson).
Brenan, G. (1990) *The Spanish Labyrinth* (Cambridge University Press).
Broue, P. (1968) 'L'Action clandestin de Trotsky en Dauphine (1934–35)'
in *Cahiers d'histoire* (Lyons).
Carr, E.H. (1982) *The Twilight of the Comintern, 1930–1935* (London:
Macmillan).
—— (1984) *The Comintern and the Spanish Civil* War, ed. T. Deutscher
(London: Macmillan).

Caute, D. (1964) *Communism and the French Intellectuals, 1914–1960* (London: Andre Deutsch).

—— (1973) *The Fellow-Travellers – A Postscript to the Enlightenment* (London: Weidenfeld and Nicolson).

Ciliga, A. (1938) *Au pays du grand mensonge*, transl. (1940) as *The Russian Enigma* (London: Routledge and Kegan Paul)

Claudin, F. (1970) *La Crisis del movimiento comunista* (Paris: Ruedo Iberico); transl. (1975) B. Pearce, *The Communist Movement: From Comintern to Cominform* (Harmondsworth: Penguin).

Danos, J. and Gibelin, M. (1986) *June '36 – Class Struggle and the Popular Front in France*, transl. Peter Fysh and Christine Bourry, eds. Peter Fysh and Peter Marsden (London: Bookmarks).

Deutscher, I. (1959) *The Prophet Unarmed – Trotsky 1921–29* (Oxford University Press).

—— (1970) *The Prophet Outcast – Trotsky 1929–40* (Oxford University Press).

—— (1990) *Stalin – A Political Biography* (Harmondsworth: Penguin).

Dreyfus, M. (1977) *La Lutte contre le Stalinisme* (Paris: Maspero).

Eastman, M. (1972) *Artists in Uniform: A Study of Literature and Bureaucratism* (New York: Octagon Books).

Farber, S. (1990) *Before Stalinism* (Cambridge: Polity Press).

Fowkes, B. (1984) *Communism in Weimar Germany* (London: Macmillan).

Galtier-Boissière, J. (1961) *Memoirs d'un Parisien* (Paris).

Geras, N. (1976) 'Between the Russian Revolutions', *The Legacy of Rosa Luxemburg* (London: Verso).

Gide, A. (1937) *Retouches à mon rétour de l'URSS* (Paris: Gallimard).

Graham, H. and Preston, P. (eds.) (1987) *The Popular Front in Europe* (London: Macmillan).

Greeman, R. (1982) 'Victor Serge and Leon Trotsky: Relations 1936–1940', in *Vuelta*, vol. 6, no. 63 (in Spanish).

Haupt, G. (1972) *Socialism and the Great War* (Oxford University Press).

Hernández, J. (1974) *Yo fui un ministro de Stalin* (Madrid: G. del Toro).

Hore, C. (1986) *Spain 1936* (London: Socialist Workers Party).

Knei-Paz, B. (1979) *The Social and Political Thought of Leon Trotsky* (Oxford University Press).

Koestler, A. (1964) *Darkness at Noon*, transl. D. Hardy (Harmondsworth: Penguin).

Lenin, I.V. (1920) *'Left-Wing' Communism – an Infantile Disorder* (London: Communist Party of Great Britain).

—— (1964) *State and Revolution*, in *Collected Works*, vol. 25: June–September 1917 (Moscow: Progess Publishers).

Liebman, M. (1973) *Le Leninisme sous Lenine* (Paris: Seuil)

Lottman, H.R. (1972) *The Left -Bank Writers, Artists and Politics from the Popular Front to the Cold War* (London: Heinemann).

Marshall, B. (1992) *Victor Serge – The Uses of Dissent* (New York and Oxford: Berg).

Marx, K. (1933) *The Civil War in France, 1871* (London: M. Lawrence).

Mitzman, A. (1964) 'The French Working Class and the Blum Government (1936–37)', in *International Review of Social History*, vol. IX, part. 3.

Naville, P. (1962) *Trotsky vivant*.

Parry, R. (1987) *The Bonnot Gang* (London: Rebel Press).

Peirats, José (1990) *Anarchists in the Spanish Revolution* (London: Freedom Press).

Poretsky, E. (1969) *Our Own People* (Ann Arbor: University of Michigan Press).

Rabinowitch, A. (1979) *The Bolsheviks Come to Power* (London: Verso).

Reed, D. and Jakobson, M. 'Trotsky Papers at the Hoover Institution: One Chapter of an Archival Mystery Story', in *American Historical Review*, vol. 92, no. 2, April 1987.

Reiman, M. (1987) *The Birth of Stalin*, transl. G. Saunders (Indiana University Press).

Riddell, J. (1984) *The Communist International in Lenin's Time* (New York: Monad).

Rocker, R. (1973) *Les Soviets trahis par les bolcheviks* (Paris).

Rosmer, A. (1936, 1959) *Le Mouvement ouvrier pendant la Première Guerre mondiale* (Paris) 2 volumes.

Sedov, L.L. (1936) 'Livre rouge sur le procès de Moscou', first publ. in Russian in *Bulletin of the Opposition*, transl. 1980 as *The Red Book on the Moscow Trials* (London: New Park Publications).

Sirianni, C. (1982) *Worker's Control and Socialist Democracy* (London: Verso).

Smith, A. (1937) *I Was a Soviet Worker* (London: Robert Hale).

Smith, S. (1983) *Red Petrograd* (Cambridge University Press).

Souchy, A., Peirats, J., Bolloten, B., and Goldman, E. (1987) *The May Days, Barcelona 1937*, ed. V. Richards (London: Freedom Press).

Souvarine, B. (1935) *Stalin: A Critical Study of Bolshevism* (transl. [1939] London: Secker and Warburg).

Thomas, H. (1961) *The Spanish Civil War* (London: Eyre and Spottiswoode).

Vereeken, G. (1976) *The GPU in the Trotskyist Movement* (London: New Park Publications).

Werth, A. (1942) *The Twilight of France 1933–1940*, ed. D.W. Brogan (London: Hamish Hamilton).

Wohl, R. (1966) *French Communism in the Making* (Stanford University Press).

Woodcock, G. (1975) *Anarchism* (Harmondsworth: Penguin).

Index

Published by Pluto Press

Year One of the Russian Revolution

Victor Serge (translated and edited by Peter Sedgwick)

New Preface by Paul Foot

'Vital reading' *Tribune*

ISBNs hardback: 0 7453 0658 6   softback: 0 7453 0659 4

Socialism: Past and Future

Michael Harrington

'Harrington ... is a scholar of extraordinary diligence and depth.' J.K. Galbraith

ISBNs hardback: 0 7453 0774 4   softback: 0 7453 0775 2

Socialism: What Went Wrong?

An Inquiry into the Theoretical and Historical
Roots of the Socialist Crisis

Irwin Silber

'A provocative, well written volume.' Paul Buhle (author of
Marxism in the United States)

ISBNs hardback 0 7453 0715 9   softback: 0 7453 0716 7

Order from your local bookseller or contact the publisher on
081 348 2724.

Pluto Press 345 Archway Road, London N6 5AA